The **Fairytale** *in* **New York**

THE STORY OF CAVAN'S FINEST HOUR

PAUL FITZPATRICK

Ballpoint Press

Published in 2013 by Ballpoint Press
4 Wyndham Park, Bray, Co Wicklow, Republic of Ireland.
Telephone: 00353 86 821 7631
Email: ballpointpress1@gmail.com
Web: www.ballpointpress.ie

ISBN 978-0-9572072-6-4

Book design and production by Elly Design

Cover photograph: The Cavan and Kerry teams parade around the Polo Grounds
pitch before the All-Ireland final in New York on September 14th, 1947

Printed and bound by GraphyCems

Contents

For my mother, Susan,
for support and good humour all the time

Foreword

BY EUGENE McGEE

*Mystique An air or attitude of mystery and
reverence developing around something or someone*

I can think of no better description of this book 'The Fairytale In
New York' than the word mystique as outlined above. It deals in
essence with possibly the most famous football game in GAA
history, the All-Ireland final between Cavan and Kerry played in the
Polo Grounds in New York on September 14, 1947. In the near-130-
year history of the GAA it remains the only senior final in either
football or hurling to have been played outside Ireland and there
is only the remotest chance that this record will be broken.

Mystique and mystery were the dominant themes in everything
concerning this extraordinary sporting event and as the years have
gone by that mystique deepened rather than faded which is
astonishing. All the participants, footballers, officials, mentors,
media people and just plain hangers-on of the time have now
passed away but in county Cavan itself, and wherever Cavan
people are located around the globe, the wonderment has never
waned. And this book brings all those people to life in astonishingly
graphic detail.

The most important background to this whole affair was the high
profile the Cavan football team had acquired in the years preceding
and immediately after that Polo Grounds match when over a
period of 24 years they played in ten All-Ireland finals, drawing two
and winning five. Only Kerry had bettered that with nine titles in
the same period. So in terms of Irish sport at the time Kerry and
Cavan were regarded as major national sporting icons.

But there has always been more to the build-up and the
implementation of the Polo Grounds venture than a mere game of
football. There was colossal political manouevring within the GAA
to get this game in New York, instigated by a legendary Kerryman
in the Big Apple, John Kerry O'Donnell, and implemented with
enormous cunning and guile by a Canon Hamilton from Clare. The

whole idea seemed preposterous from start to finish not just in GAA circles but in the nation at large and even today the idea of moving the All-Ireland final from Croke Park to a run-down baseball stadium in New York seemed what it eventually turned out to be – a fairytale.

This is a brilliantly constructed book by Paul Fitzpatrick from Redhills in Cavan and considering he is just 29, his understanding of the background that existed in the late 1940s in his own county and further afield is proof of enormous research in Ireland and New York. This book is written in a Cavan context mainly and maybe a similar effort will be forthcoming from a Kerry author in the future.

I was born and reared right on the Cavan border and close to heroes like Phil 'The Gunner' Brady and other Cavan stars. It was Cavan who influenced my young GAA life and everywhere we went we were meeting heroes, Mick Higgins, John Wilson, Tony Tighe, John Joe O'Reilly, the legendary 'Gallant John Joe' and on and on. When I managed the Cavan senior team in the 1980s, even then I could feel the impact of the Polo Grounds game in everyday life.

Even to this day you will see many of the Twitterati and internet posters brandishing their Cavan allegiances with the phrase: Unbeaten in the Polo Grounds! That's one GAA record that is secure in Cavan history. Finding real and diverse characters in this book was scarcely a difficult task for the author because their memory has never faded in their native place.

The author has also adeptly encapsulated Irish life in those Spartan economic days when emigration was the norm by referring in this book to life as it was actually lived in the period of the Polo Grounds.

You don't have to be from Cavan to really enjoy this book because it is a microcosm of how Ireland lived, sported and played in very far off days. But this book will bring it all vividly to life like it has never been done before in relation to that historic Irish sporting event – complete, of course, with the mystique.

Acknowledgements

As I write, more than 12,000 Cavan supporters have just made their way home from Croke Park after watching their team die with their boots on against the might of Kerry in the All-Ireland quarter-final. For weeks, the county has hummed with football chat as a young team restored pride in Cavan football, and more.

When the dawn broke on the morning of a sixth championship match for the first time since Mick Higgins was captain of the team back in 1952, supporters sat up and took notice.

Something is stirring here among the drumlins; the Breffni boys are back. The Class of 2013 was young and exciting and the weary support has responded.

Because buried in the race memory of Cavan people are the stories of the big wins and bigger hits of the '30s and '40s and '50s, when the county sent out groups of young men to go to war, carrying their colours.

The echoes of those lost leaders still resonate.

In 1925, when Cavan lost to Kerry in an All-Ireland semi-final in Tralee, the first word back from the game came late on the Sunday night, via carrier pigeon. It was only 22 years later that the best 21 footballers in the county boarded a ship and an airplane and journeyed across the Atlantic to defend the honour of their tribe again.

Those amazing men blazed a trail and will live forever in story and song. It's only fitting that they are remembered in print, too. The past is a foreign country. In visiting it, it seemed like a fantasy.

The top sportswriter Kieran Shannon told me when I started this book that it would take me to different places, that I'd find myself sitting up late at night trying to get into the heads of footballers from another lifetime. He was right.

From sharing a beer or six with Jerry and Brian McGovern, sons of Owen Roe, in Cranford, New Jersey to sitting with Joe McManus, a man with almost a century of Cavan football history stored in his brain, in his home in Enniscrone, over-looking the Atlantic, this has been an adventure from start to finish.

The first person I met was Peter Brady and we sat in Kilnaleck, over-looking the Polo Grounds pub, where the Babe Ruth of Gaelic football was born. It was awe inspiring.

Because none of the Cavan men of '47 will read this, I hope I do justice to their achievements in the eyes of their families, friends and colleagues who so graciously shared their time to help me write this book, without whom it would have been impossible.

They are an unerring tribute to the gentlemen I think of as heroes and live on in them today, carrying memories like values. I thank the players first for the story, and the families for allowing me to tell it.

I got help from an army of people. My thanks to PJ Cunningham of Ballpoint Press, who got behind this from the start and kept badgering me until it was a *fait accompli*. Riding shotgun was Joe Coyle, who designed the book and provided welcome ideas from the throw-in. Thanks, men.

Huge thanks also to Eugene McGee for his words of advice, it's humbling to have the assistance of someone steeped in GAA and journalism lore.

The families and contemporaries of the 1947 team itself were the source of much of the anecdotes and background information on these pages.

When I mooted this idea, one colleague threw his weight behind it more than any other. Paul Neilan isn't a dyed-in-the-wool GAA man but he's a mighty confidant. Thanks, buddy, for the ideas and the enormous help every single step of the way.

Thanks to all the staff in The Anglo-Celt, especially Damian McCarney, for their help, and to my colleagues Kieran Shannon, Declan Bogue and also Shane Corrigan, who swapped exotic Milltown for San Fran but was always at the end of the line.

The amazingly-talented scribe Enda McEvoy shared his experience and wisdom along the way too, and I am extremely grateful to him. To Michael Foley, thanks.

I leaned on old newspapers, programmes and magazines for material and also an excellent book, The Star Spangled Final, by the late Mick Dunne.

Acknowledgements

Thanks to all of those who provided photos. In no order, we are grateful to Ray McManus in Sportsfile, Garret O'Reilly, Cavan County Museum, Raymond Dunne, Gaelic Art (www.gaelicart.ie), Brian O'Reilly, Jim McDonnell, Mark Gillick, Eamonn Gaffney, Tony Morris and Martin Brady. To the people who assisted me and welcomed me into their homes for interviews, to share memories, photographs, to provide feedback and give direction, or helped with checking facts, there would be no book without you all.

In no order, I would like to gratefully acknowledge Peter Brady in Kilnaleck; Brian O'Reilly, Naas; Paddy Donohoe, Cavan town; Martin Brady, Castleblayney; Johnny Cusack, Lavey; Hugh O'Brien, Cootehill; Ita, John and Noreen Wilson, Ashbourne; Barney Cully in Arva; Jim McDonnell in Bunnoe; Ray Carolan, Cavan Town; Tony Morris, Navan; Cathal Young Snr and Cathal Young Jnr, Dublin; Garrett O'Reilly, Dublin; Declan Woods, Killeshandra; Ollie Brady, Redhills; Joe McManus, Enniscrone; Steve Duggan, New York; Finbar O'Neill, Wexford; Mickey Walsh and Dermie Walsh, Cavan town; Ian O'Riordan, Dublin; Savina Donohoe and all the staff at Cavan County Museum, Ballyjamesduff; Maureen Fox and her mother Annie Fox, New York; Jerry and Brian McGovern, New Jersey; George Cartwright, Cornafean; Mark Gillick, Virginia; Raymond Dunne, Cavan town.

Overdue thanks, also, to Frank Mulrennan and Johnny O'Hanlon for their faith in giving a 24-year-old a job, and to Linda O'Reilly for her support always.

Thanks to my family, especially my mother Susan and brother Emmett, my grandparents and to Donal and Carmel Brady in Lacken, where there is always a welcome on the mat.

And deepest thanks to Valerie, for putting up with late nights, early mornings and ridiculous soliloquies. I might be reconstructed after all!

Paul Fitzpatrick
August 2013
Redhills, Co Cavan

Waiting Game

PATRICK McGOVERN had waved goodbye to the haunting hills and furrows of west Cavan as a teenager in the late 1920s. Times were tough and the family farm wasn't big enough for a houseful of hungry children. Needs must; Pat took the boat and wound up in New York, in the depth of a depression felt around the world.

For over two decades, he hung tough in the five boroughs, dabbling in work where he could get it and finding time to marry and raise a family of his own before he landed a job in General Motors out in Tarrytown.

He'd keep in touch with home, his nine brothers and two sisters, through letters. One, carrying a postmark from An Muileann Iarainn – Swanlinbar – had arrived in late August of 1947, which is why he found himself on a Monday morning the following month, pacing the docks, brow dripping under the Manhattan sun.

The heat was in the 80s and his shirt button was dancing a jig – Pat was excited, and nervous, too. This was a big day. Maybe the biggest he'd had in over 20 years; Owen Roe was coming.

Owen Roe was his brother, but he was a stranger. He knew the kid kicked football for 'Swad' and lately for Cavan. Now the game was bringing him to the Big Apple and Pat would meet him for the first time since his brother was a small boy, waving him off in Drumbar. His brain buzzed at the thought.

Suddenly, there was a murmur in the crowd and it came into view, brooding and majestic and growing larger on the horizon. The Mauretania. Within minutes the boat had docked but it felt like an eternity on the harbour waiting for the passengers to make their way off.

Eventually, Patrick couldn't wait any longer and he wangled his way on. Soon, he located the Irish footballers, nine Kerrymen, nine Cavanmen, seven officials from around the country, their accents blending, like turning the dial on a radio.

The thought struck him then that he wouldn't know Owen Roe. He stopped a man and asked him where Owen was. He wasn't sure. He asked a couple more and kept looking.

Eventually, he spotted a stocky man, biceps bulging, 20-something with a wide grin and wave of black, hair falling down over his forehead.

"Where's Owen Roe McGovern?" he asked him, looking around.

"You're talking to him," smiled Owen.

The brothers embraced.

You've gotta love New York.

The Wanderer

IT'S August, 1942 and Cavan are preparing to play Dublin in the All-Ireland semi-final in Croke Park. Studs rattle against the concrete, players pull ragged jerseys over their heads. Some are chatting, some are quiet. Big Tom, the Cavan captain, is doing much of the talking.

He was interrupted by a knock on the door of the dressing-room, which immediately opens. Outside stand two Military Police – 'Red Caps', as they are known – and they're here on a mission: bring the Cavan corner-forward into custody.

The player is Willie Doonan of Cavan Harps, a 22-year-old machine gunner in the British Army who is home on leave from the war and has joined up with the Cavan panel. The role of a private in the neutral Irish Army was no place for a fearless kid keen for some action and Willie had gone AWOL, heading north to enrol in another army which might see some action, give him a chance to make a few shillings, break some heads, maybe, and see some sights.

But here in the bowels of the big house, with 40,000 voices bleeding into one on the terraces, it is catching up with him. The Red Caps wanted their man. Willie is in a pickle...

* * *

If ever a man summed up the great ecumenism of sport, it was Doonan.

Swarthy and handsome, he was a wild man, they said. In a Cavan team which included teachers, vets, dentists, gardai, army officers and even a future Tánaiste, Doonan took the road less travelled. He was a townie, for one, and was seen to come from the wrong side of the tracks.

His ancestors originally came from Armagh and somewhere along the line settled in the deprived social housing of 'The Half Acre' in Cavan town; it was commonly held, at a time when it was a grievous insult, that Doonan came from Travelling stock. He didn't; it didn't matter.

Rural Ireland at the time was like a crowded room – a tangled necklace of claustrophobic communities, mostly isolated, largely uneducated. Men like 'Bill', as the newspapers called him, were regarded almost with a wry suspicion.

And he played the part. In time, he would even proffer a new word for the English language. When Cavan played Roscommon in the 1947 semi-final, he drew a line in the muck with the heel of his boot and told his direct marker that if he crossed it again, he'd be 'fuckalised'.

In 1949, he would be dropped from the team for the All-Ireland final against Meath after a run-in with a priest. Doonan, never one to stand on ceremony, didn't and, refusing to apologise for using foul language towards a man of the cloth, his place was taken by Jim McCabe. The story goes that Meath's Peter McDermott, who would have been his direct opponent, jumped for joy when he heard the news. Cavan would lose as 'the man in the cap' – who had never scored on Doonan – played hell.

In ways, Doonan was the pulse of the Cavan team. His fearlessness was infectious, so much so that Mick Higgins, the ingenious leader of the attack, made sure always to sit beside him before a big match.

Previewing the 1948 semi-final against Louth, The Anglo-Celt would use three words to describe Doonan: "Knows no fear".

A few weeks later, he played in the All-Ireland final against Mayo with a heavily bandaged hand, having been cut and burned while rescuing two people who were trapped when a house caught fire in Mitchell Street, Cavan, a few hundred yards from Doonan's home on 'the terraces' overlooking Breffni Park.

Willie had been mooching around, waiting for a pal to buy some cigarettes, when he spotted the fire in the nearby house-cum-shop. He sprinted across the street, broke through the shopfront window and carried the woman out in his arms.

One person lost their life and at the inquest, Doonan was hailed a hero.

"Willie Doonan played a man's part on the night," noted the deputy coroner, "but what else would we expect from a member of the Cavan All-Ireland team?"

But he was bred to be a rogue. "I only mitched one day from school in my school days, and that was with Willie Doonan," commented a former classmate, reminiscing, in the late 1980s, on the old days.

He was a born leader, and a man – as Shane MacGowan would say of himself – who would not be reconstructed.

As a 14-year-old in 1934, he 'jumped the train' to Tuam with his father, Johnty, uncle and brothers to watch Cavan take on Galway in the All-Ireland semi-final. All made it home safely, barring uncle Jack 'The Ga' Donohoe, who was forcibly ejected from the train.

It was Friday before he made it home on foot, where he was met by a raucous welcoming committee. Moore's Pub on the corner of Bridge St, they say, never did such business...

Four years later, Doonan was winning an All-Ireland minor medal with the county but, just as a swift call-up to the senior team beckoned, Willie went rambling, taking off with the Brits to Italy and North Africa.

In 1943, in Montecassino, he went missing. Breandán Ó hEithir chose the story as a conclusion to his magnificent 'Over The Bar' in 1984.

"One Sunday afternoon in September, Bill was no longer to be seen. He vanished as if the ground had swallowed him. It was considered unlikely that he had been shot as there was a lull in the hostilities at the time. It was a mystery," wrote Ó hEithir.

"A search was mounted and they found him at last. Even when they did, they found it difficult to attract this attention. He was up a tree on the side of a steep hill and seemed to be in a trance. And in a way he was. Private Doonan had eventually homed in on the commentary of the second half of the All-Ireland Football Final between Roscommon and Cavan from Croke Park."

That was Doonan – indispensible to his unit, and his team but a law unto himself.

Ó hEithir's book, as an aside, perpetuated the inaccurate 'Traveller' story. Over the years it would be reported as fact on several occasions. In 1995, 19 years after Doonan's death at the age of 56, a contributor to The Anglo-Celt, long-standing official Andy O'Brien, was so moved that he went to the trouble of researching Doonan's family history as far back as the marriage of his great-grandparents, James Dempsey and Mary Burns, in October, 1849. His parents, John Doonan and Mary Dempsey, he discovered, were married in 1911. "This proves," wrote the letter-writer, "that Willie Doonan was NOT a member of the Travelling community."

The story Ó hEithir chose may have grown legs – Doonan's version of the tale had an English radio operator calling out: "Hey Paddy, that stupid game of yours is on the radio" and flinging him the set, telling him to climb the tree to get reception – but it matters little. He fought in the bloodiest battle of World War II, getting raked by machine gun fire in the leg and ankle, an innocent, loveable rogue, a long, long way from home.

He liked a drink, too. If Doonan got paid on a Friday, it could be gone by Sunday, when he'd have to borrow a pound from someone. The following Friday, he'd scour Cavan town until he found the benefactor and paid him back. "But if he didn't find you that Friday evening, well, you were banjanxed because the following week someone else was at the top of the queue!" laughed one old teammate.

Doonan's status among the rank and file was paradoxical. On the one hand, he was a member of the most vaunted football team in history; on the other, he came from the 'Half Acre'. In that era, the perceived bad almost out-weighed the good.

There'd be sniping and gossip. When Doonan came before a county board committee for allegedly assaulting a referee in a league match against Ballinagh: (The ref: "He told me that if I awarded them a free, he would kill me") his own clubman found it hard to summon a stirring defence.

"Everyone knows this man, Willie Doonan, is very hard to control," sighed the Cavan Harps representative.

In time, though, Doonan would come to be regarded as one of the greatest No 2s in the history of the sport. Beneath the rough exterior was a gem of a player, and a man. His soccer experience – he played on army representatives teams in Italy, for Dundalk FC and guested for St Mirren while stationed in Scotland — taught him to volley the ball, for which he became renowned and his bravery and the esteem in which his teammates held him won over the naysayers.

And he truly was fearless.

After his football career finished, and ever the restless wanderer, he returned to England for 15 years. Once, while working on a building site (others say it was while walking home from a night out), he collapsed clutching his heart. The following morning, he was awoken by the shriek of a startled keeper of a local morgue. Willie laughed it off as the man trembled backwards and out the door...

His experience in the theatre of war – he was honourably discharged after being shot in the ankle at the gates of Rome in 1944, an injury he carried throughout his career – taught him never to be nervous going out on a football field.

"It's not if we'll win," his teammates would recall him crying as he left the dressing-room, "but how much we'll beat these hoors by!"

*   *   *

Here in Croker, though, with throw-in time approaching, it looks like he won't get the chance. But when he needs a hand he gets it; John Joe O'Reilly rises and accosts the men at the door. John Joe is Cavan's centre half-back and a captain in the army, based in The Curragh, and out-ranks them.

"Private Doonan," he announces, "will be handed over in Barry's Hotel after the match. He'll play for us first."

The men leave, Doonan plays, Cavan lose. After the game, the players converge in the hotel and get to talking. He was good enough to tog out for us even though he was only home on leave, says one. We can't see him getting lifted, agrees another, he's part of the team. Go, quick, Willie!

And Doonan is gone, scurrying out the back window, football boots over his shoulder, and across Mountjoy Square, where he sees a car headed for Cavan town and clambers in. That night, he drinks on home turf and, next morning, heads out the road and crosses the border, joining up with the forces again at Enniskillen, ready to be deployed in Europe again.

CHAPTER TWO

The Promoter

"Out of evil, cometh good... Cavan will rise again"
The Anglo-Celt on Cavan's controversial All-Ireland final defeat to Cork in 1945

THE first few months of '47 were cold. The snow started in January, heavy at first but then heavier until, all over the country, it was hard to know where the sunless sky ended and the earth began. In the 50 days between January 24 and St Patrick's Day, it would snow on 30.

It was like nothing ever seen before. The wind came unsparing from the east and 20-feet high drifts were common across the country. It started on the last Tuesday in February and fell for 50 hours continuously, the worst blizzard of the 20th century.

Roads were impassable, canals solid ice. Schools just closed their doors – even if the children could make it, the ink had frozen solid in the inkwells. And, a century after Black '47, death stalked the land again.

Farmers spent their days trawling the land, bent crooked against the blizzards, looking for little ripples in the banks of snow, indicating an animal breathing.

Coffins were laid in the snow, the ground too hard to dig. In Arva, neighbours cut a pass half a mile long to allow a donkey and cart through to collect a coffin, which had been shouldered across nine fields.

In Gowna, where the lake froze for the first time in three decades, the old people reckoned they hadn't felt such cold in 50 years. In February, the average temperature went as low as -16.8C in some parts of the country.

Cavan was hit hard, then, and west Cavan worst of all. In Owen Roe McGovern's Swanlinbar alone, it was reported early in the storm that 1,000 sheep were lost.

Three Killeshandra men got stuck in a 12-foot drift in Glan Gap on Tuesday, March 4. When they hadn't returned by Friday, a search party headed west, and they, too, were forced to abandon their vehicle. The second group braved 20-feet high drifts and walked through the night to Bawnboy, 12 miles away.

Country people dug themselves out of their homes and, at night, when the snowfall would stop and a hard frost rose up out of the ground, they went *ceilidhing* to their near-neighbours as usual, climbing across the mounds above the level of the roof and kicking the top of the door before climbing down and into the heat.

Men would spend days shovelling the snow until the banks on each side of the road were so high that they could hang their coats on the telegraph wires. The next morning, they'd start from scratch.

All around was tragedy. A national school teacher in Bailieborough brought three friends, armed with spades, as he headed to his father's funeral in Drumahair, to cut through the deepest snow but the men were forced to turn back at Ballinamore; it is not recorded if the man reached home to pay his last respects.

And then, on Paddy's Day, all of a sudden, came the thaw, and the country turned to sludge. Snow lay on high ground until May but elsewhere, when it receded, the countryside was a dirty brown, the mangled remains of broken poles, dead animals and bicycles strewn like wreckage in fields and ditches.

In Britain, the Minister for Fuel and Power, Emanuel Shinwell, received death threats and was placed under police guard. His Labour Party would be turfed out at the next election, as would De Valera's Fianna Fáil, as the people looked for someone to blame. It was a natural, if irrational, reaction – deprived of hope, the country looked for some vengeance at the ballot box.

Eventually, weeks of torrential rain gave way to sunshine. The clouds disappeared and the summer that followed was blissfully warm. The spring's frost, the old people reckoned, had killed off the badness in the ground and when it came to harvest time, the crops broke records all over the country. It was needed, too. The harvest of 1946 had been a disaster.

*   *   *

The All-Ireland senior football final of that year between Kerry and Roscommon on October 6 had been a draw, 2-4 to 1-7, the first since the Kingdom drew with Cavan in '37. Harvest time crept up days afterwards and panic ensued. Crops lay soaking in the fields and a catastrophic wash-out seemed inevitable.

Thousands of city-dwellers were roped in, unpaid, to limit the damage. Garda cars with loudspeakers mounted on their roofs toured the streets of Dublin and officials described the response as "magnificent". For many, it was a chance to slip the surly bonds of the Big Smoke for a few days, to get out of their national schools and offices and try something new. That and the 24,000 sandwiches prepared by the Red Cross helped entice a sufficient *meitheal* of workers to effectively save the harvest, helped by over 2,000 Irish troops.

For one man, it couldn't have been less convenient. The holiday plans of John O'Donnell, a colourful 47-year-old New York-based bar magnate, were knocked out of sync by the bad weather, and he wasn't happy.

O'Donnell came from Gleann na nGealt in the Dingle peninsula in west Kerry, a place known, presciently, maybe, as The Valley of the Mad. He had emigrated to Montreal as a teenager, where he became a lumberjack, and worked his way down to Detroit, picking up work in the Dodge plant like so many more hungry young Motor City emigrants.

By the time he was 40, he'd lived enough for three lifetimes – he'd been broke for three years after the Depression, had been a bricklayer and hit the jackpot when he opened his first tavern in 1935, not long after the end of the Prohibition era, at the corner of Eighth Avenue and 42nd St, off Broadway.

A decade later, he was buying his fifth.

*   *   *

In the wilds of Gleann na nGealt, tales abound of the 'raving mad' entering the valley and leaving sane. Those who know the valley best say that people find their way there by instinct.

Maybe that beautiful madness, and that instinct, stayed with O'Donnell, known to all as John 'Kerry' O'Donnell, or just 'John Kerry'. In Detroit, he'd played baseball but, during a short trip home, he'd taken up football, and he became obsessed, so much so that when the GAA began to struggle in New York, they turned to O'Donnell, who had by then made his base there, to steady the ship.

Inisfail Park, on the corner of 240th St and Broadway, was the home of GAA in the city since it was opened by a Cavanman, Willie Snow, and an Offaly native, Paddy Grimes, in the late 1920s but the falling stock of New York GAA meant that the association was in danger of losing their grounds.

Then-president in the city Jim Cotter turned to O'Donnell – a man with the resources and the impetus – to dig them out and take over the long-term lease, which he did, re-opening the grounds as Gaelic Park in May of 1945.

It was a disastrous time to invest in Gaelic games in New York. The Depression had had a devastating effect on the Irish community in America, most of whom were employed as unskilled labourers. The flood of young Irish coming off the boat slowed down to a trickle, too, and, naturally, putting food on the table took precedence over playing, or administering, football or hurling. The net result was that, by the end of World War II, Gaelic games had virtually disappeared in America.

"I was only in Gaelic Park, or whatever we called it then – Croke Park? – a short time when I was down to one saloon, one bar. It was so bad I thought by '46 I'd be on the Bowery. Gaelic Park was dragging me down," O'Donnell later recalled.

By '46, of course, he wasn't anywhere near that infamous, sordid, gang-infested Manhattan neighbourhood of flophouses, brothels and dive bars; O'Donnell would go on to become fabulously wealthy and extremely influential in the association at home and abroad.

While the GAA was at an all-time low when O'Donnell took over Gaelic Park, the country and city soon picked up and prospered and, with it, the Irish-American community. A rising tide after the war lifted all boats and John Kerry surfed the wave.

At one point, publicans bought cans of beer for 7c and sold them for 35c. O'Donnell purchased truckloads of the stuff. When Gaelic Park was in its pomp in the 1950s, there were five matches on Sundays and 35 taps were needed to quench the thirst of regular crowds of 5-6,000. Mothers and children attended dancing competitions. The Park was, it has been written, "an Irish oasis" in the bustling metropolis. In time, the Irish in New York prospered, with Mayor Bill O'Dwyer (a native of Bohola, Co Mayo) helping improve working conditions and pay, and John Kerry grew rich off them.

His GAA career, though, was a collision course with the authorities at home. He wanted to bring the best players to New York, but he wanted it done his way, and, for decades, he fought running battles with Croke Park. His power came from the fact that he ruled New York with an iron fist and had the resources to bring travelling parties over, a rare treat at the time for the top teams and officials. Thus, the tail of the GAA often seemed to be wagging the dog.

After one quarrel in the '50s, they made him change the name of his own private Croke Park, which he then titled Gaelic Park, the name that still holds today.

His philosophy in 'industrial relations' was revealing. Questioned once about a short-lived outbreak of peace that seemed to develop between New York and Croke Park in the '70s, he said: "There is nothing more dangerous than harmony."

And yet he was extremely generous and earned a reputation for taking young Irishmen and women under his wing and giving them a start in New York. When the Artane Boys Band's uniforms and instruments were destroyed in a fire in 1971, O'Donnell stepped in with a donation of £12,000.

O'Donnell had a way of ensuring his name stayed in the

newspapers at home. The celebrated Irish Independent GAA journalist John D Hickey described him once as "a very difficult man to converse with because of his penchant for talking in metaphors" but that didn't stop him quoting the Kerryman on a routine basis.

O'Donnell ran New York GAA affairs on an autocratic basis and absurdly put that body up as equal, if not superior, to Central Council. If Croke Park got a big game, he reasoned, why shouldn't Gaelic Park, New York have one as big, or even bigger?

Nothing ever seemed to run smoothly – there was always, it seemed, friction. O'Donnell didn't pick his fights – he just fought, and fought, and, often, got what he wanted for New York in the end.

There were times when it didn't work out. Dublin referee Clem Foley ended up with a broken jaw in 1970 after a New York v Cork National Hurling League final, with a New York player banned for a year from the city's board and for life back in Ireland.

O'Donnell and his board, unhappy with the referee's performance, took the ill-advised position that Foley only had himself to blame, and the former vowed that the ref would never set foot in Gaelic Park again, which resulted in an embarrassing stand-off in the mid-1980s, when Foley returned on an All-Star trip.

Cups, including Sam Maguire, went missing, bans were handed out, matches and tours cancelled, dignitaries snubbed. It was the banana republic of the GAA with the ubiquitous benevolent dictator holding the reins.

Kerry's Central Council delegate Micheál Ó Ruairc maybe summed the man up in January 1969. Around that time, O'Donnell had formed an unlikely alliance with an Australian PR guru called Harry Beitzel, who had bank-rolled Australian Rules trips to Ireland.

That month, O'Donnell generously offered to finance one-third of Kerry's expenses should they travel to Australia and New York for a tour. At the same time, he threatened to freeze the $16,000 coming from the proceeds of an upcoming series of Down games in New York and told the members of the Central Council they were "only a bunch of incompetents warming the seats of Croke Park".

"That tore it," Ó Ruairc reported to the Kerry county board, "because, unfortunately, he was making a request with the one hand and tossing a bomb with the second hand."

That was him.

Back in the mid-40s, however, all of that was ahead of them. In situ at Gaelic Park and losing money on it, O'Donnell needed a plan to invigorate the games in the city. He set about restoring the GAA to its rightful place, and he knew just the way to do it.

"It became patently clear," Maurice O'Hare has written, "to those with aspirations to rebuild the GAA in post-war America that its revival would have to be organised around an event of considerable import."

John Kerry was one such man, maybe, *the* man, and he knew exactly the event that was needed – a rumble in the Bronx to rival any sporting event the city had seen. But, to make it happen, he needed a friend.

Fairytale in New York

CHAPTER THREE

The Plan

WITH the 1946 harvest yet to be saved, the All-Ireland replay would have to be postponed. Word, however, hadn't reached New York in time. John Kerry was home for the game and couldn't believe his ears when he heard that he wouldn't see it.

"It was the first [draw] after a period of 10 or whatever number of years and I went over to see it. And on the bus at Gleann na nGealt I got on to go to Tralee and who was on the bus but Paddy Kennedy, Lord have mercy on Paddy," recalled John Kerry years later.

"He said: 'Where are you going' and I said: 'Where the hell do you think I'm going, the All-Ireland'. 'Oh', he said, 'it's called off'. I thought he was putting me on, as the Yank says, but he was telling the truth.

"He says 'the bad harvest', pointing to the lowlands and wangs of hay and the water up halfway on the wangs of hay. And I had to come back without seeing the All-Ireland.

"The All-Ireland was a draw and I immediately got in touch with Canon Hamilton for the replay. We didn't want the All-Ireland, just the replay. Canon got in touch with me and said: 'Sorry, they arranged that evening after the match that the replay would be in two weeks or whatever it was'. I only asked for the replay of the game."

And that was how it started.

*   *   *

Canon Michael Hamilton, a native of Clonlara in Co Clare, was known in GAA circles simply as 'The Canon'. Then chairman of the Munster Council, the priest was a man used to getting his own way.

"He was a very articulate man, highly-respected and with a great record of service in the Association," remembered former GAA President Paddy McFlynn.

Hamilton's association with Cavan and All-Ireland finals got off on an infamous note. The 1937 final, between Cavan and Kerry ended in stalemate – the last draw before the '46 decider which prompted John Kerry and The Canon to come together in the first place – but the Clareman played an important role.

When the legendary GAA journalist PD Mehigan, better-known by his pen-names Carbery and Pato, fell ill, the priest commentated on the game on Radio Éireann. However, it was his one and only broadcast, as The Canon made a fatal mistake. The match ended in a draw but the fledgling commentator announced that Cavan won by a point, prompting bonfires in Breffni, as thousands awaited the return of the champions.

They were to be disappointed later that night when the first supporters began to arrive home from Dublin, bemused at the reception and explaining that the match had ended in a draw. The turnstiles had been broken, the story goes, and up to 10,000 extra supporters, late because of a delay on the train, had gate-crashed the party. They sat everywhere, including on top of the scoreboard, with the result that no scores were recorded on it. Cavan raised a white flag in the final minute but ref Martin Hennessy disallowed the score for a throw by Paddy Boylan, prompting bitter conspiracy theories that the association, then in the process of a costly refurbishment of the Cusack Stand, had 'fixed' the draw with the referee.

(Times were simpler. After Jim Smith, an almost mythical figure in Cavan, went off injured in the replay, 72-year-old Patrick McCarren, listening in Cootehill, dropped to the floor, dead. His last words were, the Anglo-Celt reported, "that finishes Cavan".)

Canon Hamilton made light of his grievous error on the radio, and the loss was the GAA's gain, as Michael O'Hehir stepped into the breach for the replay. The Canon ploughed on and gained huge renown in the association, both in Clare and across the country. Like John Kerry, he was a man who dreamed big, and had the clout to make things happen. When the Clare county board re-opened Cusack Park in Ennis, he threw in the ball in to start the match – from a light aircraft.

He was remarkably intelligent, an arch-conservative and a

staunch defender of The Ban. He was a skilled linguist, who won the prestigious Solus scholarship to Maynooth University – not just in English but in Irish and French, as well – and a close confidante of Secretary General Pádraig Ó Caoimh, who had contacted him the day before the '37 final, when he was looking for that stand-in radio announcer.

And The Canon was a republican and never missed an opportunity to promote the cause, Irish language and games and, maybe a combination of all three – the GAA.

In his chairman's address at the Munster convention in Waterford in March 1946, he stated that: "Freedom can be maintained only as it has been won – by rigid and exclusive adherence to those traditional qualities which are characteristic of separate nationhood, their games and language".

Like John Kerry O'Donnell, he was a champion of the little man, too, as he proved at a meeting in Sixmilebridge once, when a recruiting officer, desperate to drum up enthusiasm for jobs in the expanding Bord na Móna, spent half an hour extolling the virtues of a life working as a turf-cutter.

Taking to the stage, The Canon stated that: "Col Stapleton's lecture seemed so good" that he and his colleague at the top table, a Fr Barry, wouldn't "bother to go to Lisdoonvarna" that year.

"I think we'll go to the bogs for our holidays instead," he said.

Then came the killer line.

"From the national point of view, a man working with Bord na Móna is working for his country. Every ton of turf produced here is a ton of coal less from England. The happiest man in the world today is an Irishman at home, provided he is prepared to work hard."

That was the creed of the time – church, country, GAA. Hamilton, mired in all three, was a man who could make things happen.

Later, in 1956, he would set about taking over a Gaelic games magazine called Gaelic Sportsman and re-titling it 'Nuacht Gaelach — Gaelic Weekly'.

"It will be our specific objective [in the magazine] to outline the GAA as a movement which has its roots in the resurgence of the national spirit towards the end of the last century, and which must continue its policy and its work until the last traces of conquest are obliterated," ran a call-to-arms disguised as an advertisement in the Irish Independent, worded, clearly, by the man himself.

By 1946, The Canon had just turned 50 and was at the peak of his considerable powers. It is impossible to overstate the influence he held in the GAA at the time. Congress waited with bated breath for his addresses every year. If he couldn't make it, it didn't matter – someone read it out.

Like another great cleric, the first patron Archbishop Croke, whose famous letter is included in the Official Guide to this day, Hamilton became a by-word for all the principles the Association held dear.

Chairman of the Clare county board for a quarter of a century from 1920 on, during which time he oversaw a rare Munster SHC final win in 1932, he also chaired the Munster Council and would, in time, become a member of Central Council, where he looked after the interests of New York.

Over the winter of 1946-47, Hamilton and O'Donnell were in constant contact. O'Donnell had planted the seed and it grew in the mind of the Clonlara cleric, by then parish priest in Newmarket-On-Fergus. In January of '47, The Canon got to work.

At the Clare county board's annual convention in Ennis courthouse on January 19, he brought forward the idea. It had slipped by unmentioned in the local newspaper, The Clare Champion, who listed 28 other motions two weeks later. What was mentioned in the local press was that The Canon wished to take on the position of Central Council delegate.

He did so, he said, reluctantly but he mentioned that moves were afoot to re-organise the tradition of bringing teams across the Atlantic, which had been common before the outbreak of the war. Indeed, Cavan had travelled three times in the 1930s to the east coast. His friends stateside – by which he meant, of course, O'Donnell – had asked him to bring some pressure to bear, and the best way he could do that, he reasoned, was at Central Council level.

His influence was clear from the reaction of the other five nominees – each immediately withdrew, clearing the way. The Canon was on his way to Croke Park, carrying his almost-ignored little motion of bringing the All-Ireland final to the USA with him. The die was cast.

Every journey starts with a single step, and this one couldn't have been more humble. There was no shock at a leading light of the Association calling for such a radical move. In a seven-paragraph report on the convention, the Irish Independent carried just one line, in paragraph seven: "It was unanimously decided," the paper noted, "to ask Congress to empower the Central Council to resume American tours and to arrange for the playing of an All-Ireland final in New York".

Short and sweet, but The Canon had won the first battle. The war was only starting.

Next stop was Rineanna, as Shannon Airport was then called, for the Munster convention, where Canon Hamilton stepped down as provincial chairman after three years. There, he appealed to members to support his efforts to have the final played in New York.

"The present year is the centenary of Black '47, the year in which the Irish race was founded abroad," he was quoted in the Irish Press.

Stating that there were many obstacles in the way of restarting Gaelic games in New York after the war years, he added: "But we will be there if we and they can find the way".

The response is not recorded, although "many delegates" noted the Independent, "paid tribute to his great work for the GAA". He was a man, seemingly, held in the highest esteem, and he finished the day, as you do, as Hon President of the Munster Council.

It was clear, then, that if The Canon had his mind set on something, even a plan as ludicrous as transporting two teams and the biggest day in Irish sport 3,000 miles across the Atlantic, he would take some derailing.

Rineanna, the priest was determined, would play a bigger role in the GAA story of 1947 than just hosting a convention.

Fairytale in New York

CHAPTER FOUR

The Beginning

MONEY wasn't tight during the Emergency – there was none, not in rural Cavan anyway. Hard times had come against the door, families were huge by modern-day standards and the majority eked out a living.

Footballs were so precious that they had minders, the local schoolteacher or shopkeeper, who kept a diary. Want the ball? Sign for it. It's on your watch now, son...

Some though had left the old sod and made it. Some were old money, landed gentry and the like; others were above what was called the 'peasant class' but nowhere near the aristocracy either. The McDowells from Caughoo, a townland beside Cashel, outside Ballinagh, were one such family.

Caughoo was populated, as is often the way in the border counties, by a cluster of Church of Ireland families and the McDowells were well-known, solid people. Their Protestant work ethic saw the family develop a thriving farm. They kept horses, their womenfolk entered fetes to win prizes for marigolds and laying hens.

One of the clan, William, moved to Dublin in the mid-1800s and established himself as a jeweller, first on Mary St, and, later, on O'Connell St.

The Dublin branch of the family was based in the Howth, Sutton and Malahide areas. They were well-to-do, members of the horsey set, who kept close ties with the old homestead in Cavan.

A descendant, Herbert, was a vet who dabbled in horses. In 1941, at the Ballsbridge Sales, a two-year-old caught the eye of a friend of his, another vet by the name of Jack White. He wasn't sure why but as a horsey man, McDowell took a punt, spending 50 guineas – a significant sum at the time.

He named the horse Caughoo, after his family's ancestral home. It was Herbert's first foray into training racehorses. He must have wondered why he bothered. The horse was small and unsociable, frowning upon all bar its groom, Ted Wright. Even the McDowells themselves weren't welcome in Caughoo's stable.

Initially, the purchase was a disaster. Caughoo's record on the flat showed more duck eggs than the old yard five miles outside Cavan town. At first, it didn't appear to have much aptitude over the obstacles either. Herbert broke the horse and trained it himself and entered it in a bumper at Phoenix Park for his first start. Caughoo was nowhere.

In all, the horse would run four times on the flat in 1942, generally over a mile and a half, placing once behind Mathiola in Listowel. Finally, with Liam McMorrow in the saddle, he got his nose in front in a maiden hurdle at Limerick.

After finally getting some black type after its name, the horse didn't exactly leave its form behind.

As a four-year-old, Caughoo ran 10 times, winning just once and the following year, it fell in a flat race in the Park. There was a small sliver of promise at the Galway Festival in August of '44, when the horse placed third at 10/1 in the Galway Plate, but it was not enough.

Back on the old beat, Cavan footballers had seen off Monaghan by three points in a lacklustre Ulster final but in the same week that Caughoo grabbed the place money in Galway, Cavan were trounced by their old friends, Roscommon, 5-8 to 1-3 – the worst All-Ireland semi-final defeat in the county's history.

As Big Tom and John Joe O'Reilly, Fonsie Comiskey and John Wilson and the rest of the footballers from south Cavan, then the powerhouse of the club game, made their way home through Ballinagh, past the turn-off at Cashel that links Caughoo to Kilmore, the big time must have seemed further away than ever.

For connections of the horse that bore the townland's name, the feeling was mutual.

*   *   *

Among the drumlins of Cavan, hard on a border just a couple

of decades old, New York was the furthest thing from their minds. The population was slowly slipping into a decline – it wouldn't steady for almost half a century. Rationing meant that smuggling along the boltholes that dotted the border around Redhills, Belturbet and the west was a necessity. Life was tough, the county's footballers the sole source of diversion, a guarantee of a day or two in Dublin each autumn at worst.

And even their stock had fallen badly in '46, after an Ulster final setback against an unheralded Antrim.

After years of close shaves, the patience of the supporters was wearing thin. The gruff Hughie O'Reilly was the man in charge and he stalked the sideline, like a scowling general. Hughie hadn't seen the Antrim defeat coming; nobody had.

Unbeaten in Ulster football since 1938, Cavan entered the 1946 provincial final as unbackable favourites to send Antrim scuttling back to the glens.

They had put 13 goals and 23 points past Armagh and Donegal in the quarter and semi-finals. Dispatches from the north had it that Antrim had looked the part against Monaghan and in challenge games against Mayo, Meath and Kerry but this was Cavan, lords of the manor, who refused even to train for an Ulster final. There was never any need before, went the logic, and they weren't starting for a team from the far north who hadn't hoisted the Anglo-Celt Cup since 1908.

O'Reilly, a republican, ran his team along military lines. Cavan had pioneered collective training, taking players off for two weeks to a 'big house' where they would rise at dawn, march in formation and spend the day running through football drills. That was the way Hughie knew best, and it served Cavan well.

He came to prominence as a footballer on the Cavan junior team that won the All-Ireland at Breffni Park in 1927. The following year, he was at midfield on the first Cavan team to reach the senior final, losing to the side they had beaten in that junior final, Kildare.

Hughie hung tough on the Cavan team for another decade, winning All-Ireland senior medals at midfield in 1933 and again two years later. In 1934, '36 and '38, he toured America with the Cavan side.

It was a golden generation but, by the end of '46, it looked as if Cavan's time with Hughie in charge would pass without their chips being cashed. Cavan football's stock had fallen.

They had come close but luck had deserted them when they needed it most. They could have won in '43 and should have in '45, losing both finals. The first loss hurt the most, when a replayed final against Roscommon turned on the dismissal of Joe Stafford.

Where centre-forward Mick Higgins was the playmaker, always thinking a few steps ahead, Peter Donohoe was a gentle giant with a gift for frees and lightning wing-forward Tony Tighe was perhaps the fastest ball-carrier the game had ever seen, Stafford was different. Small, stocky and balding even then, he was the rabble-rouser of the attack. He could be wild but his teammates loved him because he was explosive on and off the field and came up with the goods, making a name for always getting a goal when it was most-needed, including one in the Polo Grounds final.

In '43, he had been unmarkable.

"I was playing mighty football that year. I scored a goal and three points against Monaghan in the Ulster final and the goal that won the game, and maybe a point or two, against Cork in the semi-final. And a goal and four points against Roscommon in the final – but it wasn't enough," remembered Stafford years later.

"Big Tom O'Reilly – the Lord have mercy on him – wasn't fit for Jimmy Murray and John Joe [O'Reilly] played a bad game, too. And the Lord have mercy on Paddy Smith, but he was only disastrous. He was taking 14-yard frees and kicking them wide. I said: 'Paddy, will ye let me take a couple of them?'

"'Oh no,' he says, 'I'm designed to take the frees.'

"'Well,' says I, 'you're making a fucking bad job of it.' The game finished in a draw but we really should have won it.

"They were the better team second time around and made a great start with two good goals. But I got one back after 20 minutes and we went in at half-time just a couple of points down and were starting to get back on terms when it all went sour in the second half. I had a chance… a great chance. I was through on the Roscommon goal. Sackie Glynn was a big long lingle of a goalie but I knew that with a low shot – a grasscutter – I'd beat him. I was sure to score.

"Well there I was with the goal at my mercy when Owensie Hoare – the Lord have mercy on him too – took me down with one of the finest kicks ever a man got in the ankle. And the referee ran over and immediately gave the free but the free wasn't enough. Because I was sore. So sore. And I pulled myself off the ground with the ball still under my arm and looked at Owensie. He was a wee man with curly black hair. 'Ye black fucker ye,' I said, 'I'll kill ye'. And I drew on him with my left hand and turned him upside down."

So, Joe was gone, for the rest of that match and for all of '44, too.

Barney Cully, the best full-back in Ulster, missed the shot at redemption in '44 as well, his suspension arising from the same fixture. An umpire, or so the story goes, was a college mate of Cully, who was studying dentistry in UCD, as was goalkeeper Des Benson. When Roscommon scored a goal, the man with the flag waved it in the full-back's face. When the dust cleared, umpire and flag were in the back of the net and Cully was in trouble. Higgins, watching from the far end of the pitch, would later recall seeing the umpire's white jacket go tumbling. Barney's fate was sealed.

Facing a lengthy ban, Cully was advised to resign from the association. Unfortunately, the powers that be were cuter and barred his re-entry and it was '45 before they relented and the Arva man wore the blue jersey again.

In the Cully family, they tell a story about a day in the early 40s when Barney's parents arrived home to find a note on the kitchen table. Scrawled on it were three words: "Gone to Castlereagh".

The Connacht final was on, see, and Barney wanted a look at Cavan's semi-final opposition and cycled the 50 miles to watch the game. When he returned, he went to the pitch to train. That was the calibre of player the team were losing, and it showed in '44, when Cavan were routed in the semi-final again by Roscommon.

Deprived of Cully's services, Cavan also lost Big Tom O'Reilly, by then the grand old man of the team, who had been a driving force alongside Hughie O'Reilly in 1933 and '35, and got involved in what Michael O'Hehir would surely have termed "the shemozzle" in the replay, and he was forced to sit out '44 as well.

After the humbling in '44, the Anglo-Celt reporter spoke of his puzzlement at how "the traditions of 60 years on the football field should suddenly go wrong".

"Out of evil," he noted, showing a gift for the dramatic, "cometh good... Cavan will rise again."

*   *   *

They did. As the War trundled to a close, Cavan and Hughie were back for more the following year, with a new player on board.

Playing for Cornafean against Mullahoran, Big Tom, brother of team captain John Joe, was given all he could handle by a powerfully-built teenager called Phil 'The Gunner' Brady in the '44 county championship and by the following summer, the Gunner legend was born. He played midfield through the Ulster campaign and against Wexford in the All-Ireland semi-final but was considered too young by the time the final came around. There was a racket in the dressing-room at half-time as the experienced players called for his introduction but the selectors thought better of it and future-Taoiseach Jack Lynch led the charge as Cork, the county of Hughie O'Reilly's birth, held on narrowly on a day of thunder and lightning in Croke Park.

Higgins, an ingenious leader of the attack, had broken down in training at Bingfield House the previous Monday. His loss and the fact that Cavan had what looked a legal goal ruled out after Cork protested to the umpires that a whistle had gone, made the difference in a four-point defeat.

The Celt's headline – "Cavan's bold bid against bad luck" – told its own story.

By 1946, Cavan seemed dead and buried. All the 1945 provincial winners, Wexford, Cork and Galway, had fallen by the wayside and it looked as if Cavan's best chance of winning a third Sam Maguire was past. Spring would be sprung before the corpse started to twitch again, but even then, few expected the deposed kings of Ulster to go very far.

The team, however, had other ideas.

Fairytale in New York

CHAPTER FIVE

Easter Rising

"Nobody took Canon Hamilton's proposal seriously at first but he was determined to succeed and no-one was left in any doubt about that."
Patsy Lynch

CONGRESS came, at last but The Canon was delayed. Easter is the busiest working week of the year for men of the cloth and the principal Clare delegate was finding it hard to get time off from his boss.

Needs must, though; the priest had his mind set on a little piece of history and late Mass in Sixmilebridge wasn't going to derail his plans.

He contacted one of the other Banner delegates, Sean Clancy, and asked that he place a special request: let the show go on until evening time but save a slot on stage for The Canon.

The snow had played havoc with the on-field schedule that year. Pitches weren't so much frozen as buried under feet of it and when it came to making fixtures, all bets were off. The Railway Cup final had been delayed by almost a month and would finally throw-in at Croke Park on Easter Sunday, April 6.

Meanwhile, Congress began, as usual at the time, at the Dublin Corporation council chamber in City Hall, just off Dame St in the city centre and only two-and-a-half miles from the action.

GAA President Dan O'Rourke called proceedings to order just after 10am.

The morning session ran off smoothly, the usual accounts (showing a surplus of £15,765 for the year) to be ratified.

Four counties moved to drop The Ban – the strict rule that members of the GAA, on pain of instant banishment from the association, were forbidden to play in or even attend 'foreign games' – but they were shot down.

The morning session sped along. O'Rourke had announced

that business would be over by 2pm, allowing time for delegates to attend the Railway Cup match, then a huge attraction usually played on St Patrick's Day. The meeting would reconvene in an office space under the tiny old Hogan Stand, he directed, later in the evening.

That was when The Canon, after flooring it from noon Mass, would make his big play. Sean Clancy, an army officer, was a friend of both Canon Hamilton and Padraig Ó Caoimh's. On the eve of Congress, he took a call from the clergyman, asking him to beseech the GAA's general secretary to jig around the agenda so that he could speak on the New York motion in the brief evening session. Ó Caoimh agreed, this was Canon Hamilton asking. No problem, the Corkman said. The rest of the items would be heard in the morning and The Canon would get his say.

It was 4pm by the time Hamilton, parochial duties fulfilled, hit the big smoke. By then, the delegates were assembled in Croker, watching Connacht produce a massive shock in winning their first Railway Cup hurling title, a crown they wouldn't wear again until 1980.

"[At] about half-time, Canon Hamilton arrived from Clare and he joined us in the Hogan Stand," recalled Clancy.

"And we told him what the feeling was among the delegates at Congress and people at the match and we advised him that there was no hope of getting the motion through, everybody seemed to be against it. At that stage, several people approached the Canon and apologised to him for not being in a position to support him.

"And I remember one in particular, Seamus Gardiner, he was afterwards president of the Association, and I recall the words he said. He said: 'Look, Canon, I supported you always in the past in the great things you've done for the Association but I cannot support you in this motion."

Canon Hamilton, however, was a man who got his own way. The iron cleric was not for turning. Clancy: "I suggested to him that he might withdraw the motion but he wouldn't hear of it. He said the motion is going through."

Gardiner's son, speaking to legendary GAA writer Mick Dunne half a century later, would verify the story. "My father said that he told the Canon that he couldn't support him, but some people were afraid that the Canon would get very few votes. He remembered that he and Pádraig Ó Caoimh asked a number of people to give the motion a few votes so that the Canon wouldn't be embarrassed."

Indeed, when, during the recess for the match, Clancy and another friend, Fr Johnny Minihan, then parish priest in Nenagh, asked Ó Caoimh to be allowed in to watch the debate, the official handed both men, neither of whom had any mandate or position, delegates' voting cards, imploring them to support the motion.

"Look, vote for the motion, it's going to be heavily defeated and I'd hate to see the Canon humiliated," he implored.

So, in the pair went, and The Canon began to fire.

*   *   *

Patsy Lynch was the Cavan chairman at the time. The youngest man ever to play in an All-Ireland final, when he lined out in the 1927 junior decider, he was the son of a butcher from Market St, Bailieborough. He won a senior All-Ireland medal at full-back alongside Hughie O'Reilly and Big Tom (then a teenager and referred to as 'Young Tom') in 1933, and, like Jim Smith, was a folk hero by the time he was in his 20s. After the '33 final, tar barrels were lit in Bailieborough and a brass band headed a torch light procession to his home.

His playing career appeared to be over after he wound up in hospital following the 1934 semi-final against Galway, with the Irish Press even speculating in 1935 that he would "never don the blue of Cavan again". Don it he did though, returning in the new role of full-forward late in his career.

By the late 1930s, he was routinely described in the national press as a veteran, despite the fact that he wouldn't turn 35 years of age until 1946.

He had come in as county chairman in 1944, making him

effectively the leader of the group at the top table to whom the Cavan delegates reported. He would later credit The Canon and another Banner man, Vincent Murphy, as the individuals who, more than anyone, brought the final to New York.

"Canon Hamilton and Vincent Murphy operated like a two-man Clare army, knocking over all the obstacles and pushing ahead, with every means at their command, to get their plan adopted and then, put into effect," he remembered.

Hamilton's address certainly was militaristic in its precision; he found the weakness in the delegates – their nostalgic side, their longing to see their relatives again – and he pummelled them with his heavy arsenal of powerful oration. The doubters never stood a chance.

By the time Canon Hamilton took to the stage, snow was pelting down outside and a sizeable number of the delegates had turned for home after the match, content, perhaps, that the preposterous Clare motion wouldn't go through in any case.

So there they were, crammed in a cubby-hole under the creaky old stand, which itself would be knocked 11 years later. The meeting room underneath, recorded in the minutes of Congress as "the secretary's room", comfortably held, it was later claimed, somewhere closer to 20 than the 200 or so that squeezed in.

Tired, uncomfortable and cramped, they craned their necks and listened. As the snow thickened on the ground outside, the motion was called: "That the incoming Central Council take up with the Gaels of New York the question of resumption of tours and that the Congress empower the Central Council to arrange, if found feasible, for the playing of an All-Ireland final in New York. That Rule 92 of the Official Guide be amended accordingly."

The Canon's moment had arrived. In all, he would speak for over 20 minutes, without notes. "The second part of the motion is not such an easy proposal for, in the first place, it requires the temporary suspension of a rule in the Guide Book and, moreover, it would be the biggest request ever made to Congress, namely that in the special circumstances of this year, and to give a much-needed fillip to the games beyond, the 1947 All-Ireland football final be played in New York," he said.

He acknowledged the potential pitfalls but stated: "All I ask today is that this Congress gives its sanction to the principle and empower the Central Council to make the tremendous gesture to help our fellow Gaels in exile in their efforts to preserve the continuity of their racial characteristics and to cherish amongst a rising generation of Irish-Americans the games and pastimes of the Motherland.

"That such an incentive, such an inspiration, is really necessary, there is no shadow of doubt. The Gaelic Athletic Association in New York is in a critical stage of its existence. It has been hitherto sustained by the Irish-born hurlers and footballers that we knew. They are now passing beyond the period of active field service, in fact, many of them have long defied the passage of the years in their efforts to keep the games going.

"The immigration quota is not sufficient to fill the depleted ranks, so there remains but one hope of the survival of the GAA and it is the young Irish-American element growing into manhood.

"The leaders of Gaelic life in New York have come to the conclusion that nothing else than an All-Ireland final can create that stir and give that impulse to new life, which can put the Association once more on a sound footing.

"I could not attempt to express what an All-Ireland would mean to our exiles. There are hundreds of thousands of them awaiting the decision of Congress and if that decision is in their favour there will be a wave of joy and happiness in the homes of our exiles not merely in New York but north to Chicago, south to Florida and west 3,000 miles to San Francisco."

By now, the delegates, tired, huddled together, and glancing furtively at their watches, began to sit up and take notice. The Canon was on a roll. It was time to seal the deal.

"Strong hearts will throb with emotion that only those who have been in exile can appreciate or understand. We are asking you in the name of these exiles to pass the motion, to make whatever sacrifices are involved, we ask you especially in the name of the more humble and lowly amongst them, fortune did not smile on them all, there are thousands who will never see their native land again and there are thousands among them who feel they would die happy if they saw their native county playing in an All-Ireland final.

"This," he said, "is the year 1947, the centenary of that dark and dismal period, when hunted by the spectre of famine and pestilence, the great exodus of our people found a friendly welcome and warm hospitality on America's shores.

"By sending out the best of our athletes, the flower of our manhood, to contest an All-Ireland in New York, we give a magnificent demonstration of the unbroken historical continuity and the wonderful tenacity of our race."

Sean Clancy surveyed the room, which had been transformed. Men were weeping silently. The Canon had struck the right chord.

"He gave his reasons for having that match played in New York and he finished his speech, I can remember it very well, by saying 'every one of you here this evening has some relative in the New York area, a brother or a sister, an uncle or an aunt or someone else'. And he said, 'are you going to deny them this little piece of Ireland? They'll never see their homeland again. Are you going to deny them this bit of Ireland in the area where they're living?'" recalled Clancy.

"Honestly, I could see tears in the eyes of some of the delegates and I could see a change coming over the gathering. That's the line on which he finished his speech."

*   *   *

Better was to come. An ally of Hamilton's, a teacher from Milltown Malbay in west Clare called Bob Fitzpatrick, spoke next, seconding the motion and conjuring from his pocket, like a magician, a heart-wrenching letter he had received from an emigrant, from which he quoted at length about what it would mean to have a final played in New York.

It pulled on the heartstrings and sealed the deal. It mattered little that the letter was a fake, written by Fitzpatrick himself the previous evening – it produced the desired effect.

"The delegate, the rogue, after the thing was passed admitted to all and sundry that he had written the letter himself the night before in Barry's Hotel," recalled Paddy McFlynn. This was later confirmed by Seán Ó Síocháin, a GAA Director General in the 1960s.

There were still questions to be answered, though. In all, 20 individuals spoke on the motion, with Gerry Arthurs and Fintan Brennan (secretary of the Ulster Council and chairman of the Leinster equivalent respectively) speaking vehemently against the idea. Both men, ironically, would later be included in the official party.

Another to speak in the strongest terms against the idea was a Waterford-based Galwegian, Vincent O'Donoghue, who was later president of the GAA. As an aside, in the 1960s O'Donoghue sought permission for the Waterford hurlers to travel to the United States for an unofficial tour while he was Central Council delegate for the Déise. One of his strongest advocates was one Patsy Lynch.

At the time, though, he was adamant. The Canon bit on his gumshield and rolled with the punches. Would this set a precedent? No, he said, we only want this to happen in 1947. Was it for football or hurling? Who would take charge? How would the costs be estimated? The Canon had answers for it all.

"It was clear," said Lynch, "that the Canon had done his homework but there was still considerable resistance as the delegates – remember, this was long before the championship had even started – presented a whole litany of arguments as to why the All-Ireland final should be played at home.

"It was a hot, sticky night and the meeting dragged on to nearly two in the morning... There didn't appear to be a breath of air as the arguments waged, first one way, then the other. The general opinion was, at that stage, that the Canon was going to fail."

There was relief when an adjournment was called for refreshments. While the delegates took a break, Hamilton and his Clare colleague Murphy got to work again, canvassing, imploring, fighting their corner. It was politics at work, coercing and coaxing the weary would-be voters until the plan was nearly over the line.

Lynch: "I don't know who he spoke to or what he said but on the resumption, it became clear that considerable headway had been made in winning opinion over to his way of thinking. It must have been about 2am when the decision to play the game in New York was finally taken."

As the weather worsened outside, delegates, many facing hours of driving in treacherous, dark conditions, must have wished it was all wrapped up. Now, their emotions stirred, their beds calling, they gave in. The vote was called.

"The President said it was the most unusual motion ever to be discussed at Congress in his experience," said Clancy.

"However, he eventually put the motion. Slowly, an odd thing happened. As if by magic, a forest of hands appeared, as virtually all the delegates rose in acclamation and the motion was declared and carried without even counting the handful of dissidents. At this stage, there was a wild rush to congratulate the Canon on achieving something that appeared to be impossible. Everybody agreed that nobody else in Ireland could have won the hearts and the votes of the delegates as the Canon had done. It was, indeed, his hour of triumph."

War whoops and back-slaps done with, heads spinning, the delegates filed out into the night, their coat collars pulled up to protect them against the snow. Many would have a long drive home, not least Hamilton, who must have been content at his day's work.

There was one bridge yet to cross – the motion was only that the idea be explored to see if it was feasible, and the GAA were immediately sending Ó Caoimh and Connacht secretary Tom Kilcoyne to New York to investigate. They would report back to the Central Council meeting in late May, when the decision could well be effectively over-turned.

But, for now, in the early hours of Easter Monday, April 7, things looked very promising indeed.

London Calling

BY 1945, Herbie McDowell had invested four years, and a substantial amount of money, in Caughoo, a trundler on the flat who had been unplaced on his debut over hurdles at his local track, Baldoyle, on New Year's Day that year.

The horse, not temperamental but quirky, was trained on the beaches in Fingal, splashing away in the Irish Sea and rolling in the sand to dry off. They tried him over fences and found that he could leap; maybe the little horse had a future on the track after all.

A breakthrough arrived later that year at the end of May. Starting a "quietly-fancied" 8/1 chance on the tight, undulating Downpatrick course, Caughoo romped to victory in the Ulster Grand National.

Suddenly, everyone wanted a piece of the pie. Suitors lined up for a dalliance with McDowell but Herbie wasn't keen on letting his old friend go. In the end, he sold the horse to his brother, Jack, the jeweller.

It was a tumultuous time. The front page splash in The Irish Press on the day after the horse's success was "British cabinet sits late as guns roar in Syria".

But while Caughoo had turned a corner on his own road to Damascus, the same wasn't happening with the footballers from the county from which his connections came.

Up the road from Downpatrick, Cavan were in action in a challenge match on that same weekend, losing to Antrim. While they would avenge that defeat a few weeks later in Breffni Park when it mattered, and would reach a first All-Ireland final in eight years, Sam still hadn't returned to the drumlins by the year's end.

Not that it would have overly bothered Jack McDowell, proud and all as he was of his Cavan roots. McDowell was more interested in the oval ball. A prominent player with Suttonians and a man with plenty of cash to spare, Jack was a dashing figure and saw something he liked in Caughoo, not much bigger than a pony and not much faster, either. The horse had guts.

He chose the colours of the rugby club he had helped found in 1924 for his silks – the royal blue and white of Cavan, with a dash of green, and Caughoo, now a chaser, was on his way.

*   *   *

It's late in the afternoon on Easter Monday, and Dan O'Rourke has made his way from Congress to London, to watch a tournament match between Cavan and All-Ireland champions Kerry in Mitcham Stadium.

With time ticking away, Cavan are struggling; the Kingdom are dazzling, Dinny Lyne, Teddy O'Connor and Batt Garvey whipping over scores as Cavan, trailing with the clock ticking down and playing into the teeth of a gale, struggle to hold them off. On the sideline, the cameras click – a battalion of English pressmen have mingled with the 16,000 assorted Irish exiles, here for an hour-long trip home, and the handful of bemused locals, who have come to watch the Paddies in action.

Almost seven decades later, it seems a curious scene, but the past truly is a different country – they do things differently there. Before the game, the players bow as Cardinal Griffin, Archbishop of Westminster, strides on to the field, his robes swishing in the wind, to throw in the ball.

Dan O'Rourke, the GAA President, has flown over for the match straight after Congress the previous day, and with him he brought surprising news. The All-Ireland final, if feasible, will be played in New York. The teams are stunned. The champions, we can only guess, already thinking of the Big Apple.

Cavan were no strangers to Mitcham, a ramshackle old ground, which wouldn't see another decade. It was tossed in 1956 after it went to the dogs, literally – the owners, making nothing from humans, tried to attract the greyhound racing community but the venture never got off the ground. Soon, the old stadium, which had catered for 25,000 rugby league fans in its 1920s pomp, was in a similar condition, levelled to make way for housing and then a public garden.

When the developers brought in the wrecking ball, they saved one of the stands and sold it to Leyton Orient Football Club. The Os had never spent a day in the top flight of the English game, but their history was a storied one. Formed by a group of former public schoolboys, they had gone through numerous name changes before settling on the one they use today; the Orient part of their title hinted at something exotic, even if their trophy cabinet didn't heave under the weight of silverware.

Then again, there wasn't much of the exotic about lower-league English football in the years after the War. Arsenal and Manchester United were the glamour clubs, with the great Wolves side yet to hit their peak. The lower leagues were inhabited by a mixture of old provincial clubs, fallen on hard times, and unfashionable small-fry who'd never known anything else.

One club who fell into the latter category, below even dowdy Orient, with their snazzy name and little else, was Lincoln City. In '47, an outlier of a season, they topped the old Division 3 North. The following year, they were back down, rooted stone last in Division 2.

Their side was generally made up of local lads, journeymen and the odd recruit. One season, though, they had a remarkable name on their team-sheet; Willie Doonan, a recent returnee from the war who starred at right full-back against Kerry in Mitcham.

Cavan needed a warrior attitude in London as Kerry threatened to take the Owen Ward Cup back on the boat with them, along with Sam Maguire.

With 12 minutes to play, Kerry, with the wind, were cruising but Cavan's revolutionary short-passing style cut the Munster men to ribbons on the home stretch.

Higgins, the greatest of them all, broke through for a goal (he would finish with a tally of 1-5) and Tony Tighe and Big Tom sent over points. Cavan won by four and their supporters stormed the field at the finish. It was only a tournament match but the significance of a win over the All-Ireland champions, while missing three of their most experienced players in captain John Joe O'Reilly, Barney Cully and TP O'Reilly, wasn't lost on the Breffni exiles in attendance.

The teams shook hands when they left the field. That night there was a function for both sets of players and they spoke among each other, the Kerrymen's lilt mixing with the broad Cavan tones. The teams were stunned when the word filtered through. When they were leaving, Mick Higgins called out to some of his Kingdom counterparts.

"We'll be meeting in New York, we'll see yiz again over there," he grinned. "But just as a joke," recalled Mick, a half a lifetime later, "little did we ever think that the teams would be travelling to New York in the following September."

By then, though, they were daring to dream.

National Question

IN 1946, Caughoo had taken on the field at the Ulster National in Downpatrick again. Again, the horse won. Suddenly, connections had a brainwave – maybe this horse wasn't so bad after all. It jumped, and stayed, and could even make a National runner.

So, in 1947, they set out for Aintree, certain also-rans in the eyes of the racing world, with an eight-year-old with little to go on but hope.

Meanwhile, 150 miles away in Inch, Co Clare, a farmer called John Mungovan was waking up with a strange sensation. The night before, he'd had a dream; Caughoo would win at Aintree.

He approached one bookmaker for a bet of £20 but it was refused. He tried again, hit a couple more turf accountants' offices, and eventually got on. Then, he found a wireless and sat tight.

On the B&I boat over to Liverpool, legendary snapper Billy Merriman was chatting with a colleague, Tommy Lavery, when they bumped into a bullish McDowell.

"Have a bet on my one," said the man carrying the hopes of Cavan. "He's going to win the National. And join me for a glass of champagne afterwards."

One hundred thousand punters had assembled at Aintree, which was covered by a carpet of fog. The big race had attracted a record entry of 57, with Caughoo friendless in the betting market.

The horse took off under Eddie Dempsey at a price of 100/1, a no-hoper in a field which included horses such as Revelry and the 1946 Cheltenham Gold Cup winner Prince Regent. Dempsey held him up off the pace, though, and when the chasing pack behind Lough Conn began to fade, his mount grew stronger.

Lough Conn's jockey Danny McCann, amazingly a next-door neighbour of Dempsey's in The Ward, took his off the bridle but found no more as Caughoo galloped and galloped and galloped.

On the second circuit, Caughoo caught him, and passed him with three fences to go. He pinged the last two, as racegoers frantically scanned their programmes to see exactly what horse this was, and came home 20 lengths clear, a stretch that was further than the distance between McCann and Dempsey's homes.

The crowd were stunned into silence. It was a sensation. McDowell had been vindicated and his unfancied, quirky horse, carrying the name of his father's townland, had just won the greatest race in the world.

On the boat home, McDowell walked into the bar and asked those behind the counter what they thought the stock was worth. They didn't know, he didn't really care. McDowell specified that nobody was to be allowed to buy a drink and gave the barman a cheque for £200, and told him to keep the change. The gesture would later enter the Guinness Book of Records as the largest round ever bought.

Whether or not they crossed paths with the Cavan footballers on their respective journeys isn't recorded, but it's possible. Cavan, on the day after the National, were heading in the same direction, taking the ferry to Holyhead en route to London and Mitcham Stadium for that annual Whit Sunday match.

Back in Dublin, at the North Wall, bands turned out to greet the winning horse and connections and they were paraded down O'Connell St. In Ashbourne, Eddie Dempsey threw a party and at midnight, the pubs in the area ran out of drink. He deserved one – the trip to Liverpool was his first time in England, and he hadn't ridden a winner of any kind in three years. It was a fairytale come true.

Immediately, critics tried to discredit the victory, claiming that Caughoo did not complete the entire course but had instead hidden, concealed by the fog, while the others completed one circuit, before emerging for the run-in. It was nonsense, but the story hung around until finally disproven with the discovery of new footage half a century later.

Maybe it was natural, though, that some cynics would try to find a plausible explanation for the whole thing – when the seemingly impossible happens, it's hard to comprehend.

The only losers were the bookies, who had been cleaned out.

McDowell, it is estimated, made 40 grand and when one Howth bookmaker, hit to the tune of £5,000, found himself out of business, the jeweller, belying the miserly Cavanman stereotype which would become famous in later years, loaned him the money to set up again.

In the old county, the Cavan Drama Festival was in full swing on the same week as the Aintree Festival and the win in the National, by a runner routinely described "a Cavan horse", added to the sense of revelry. (It was a big week for one would-be Polo grounds hero, too. Paddy Smith from Stradone, Cavan and Ulster corner-back at the time, won a gold medal for his acting that same week in the Town Hall in Cavan.)

The McDowells and their horse were toasted throughout the county, and The Anglo-Celt carried the news on their front page, revealing that Caughoo had, for a short time, grazed in the townland after which he was named.

"It is a tribute to the McDowell family that in naming the horse," the Celt said, "they didn't forget the townland where the old homestead remains. The family have always kept in close touch with their native county..."

Oh, and John Mungovan got paid too, but didn't blow his thousands. The 83-year-old Clareman won £3,000 in all, and donated one third of it to the Bishop of Killaloe "to send to the Holy Father for the relief of distress in Europe". This was a man who had been born in 1864, and he was under no doubt that divine intervention had led to his dream, and his win. Thanks to Caughoo, he would die a richer man than he imagined five years later.

For Michael O'Hehir, who commentated on the race, it was a momentous day. For Cavan folk, it was too. Nobody could have imagined that just six months later, it would be topped.

*   *   *

Padraig Ó Caoimh and Tom Kilcoyne, a native of Achonry, Co Sligo, and secretary of the Sligo county board and Connacht

Council, had been sent to New York to assess whether playing the final there was feasible at all. Their mission was one of reconnaissance and they were to report back to the nerve centre on May 23 in a small hall in North Frederick Street, beside the LSE garage, as there were no facilities in Croke Park to accommodate the enlarged Central Council.

The men quickly discovered that there was no room on any boat travelling directly from Ireland and, air travel regarded as fraught with danger at the time, they decided to sail on the Queen Elizabeth from Southampton, leaving Dublin on April 15.

On their arrival in the United States, the men were feted by the Corkman's Association, the Sligoman's Association and New York GAA.

Little did they know the uproar they were leaving behind.

*   *   *

In the days before widespread TV coverage, let alone the internet, information travelled slowly. It took a while for the word to disseminate from Croke Park but, when it did, the reaction was almost universally one of outrage. "They" were taking the biggest day in the GAA calendar away, away from the masses, away from the very nation, and it didn't go down well.

The chairman of the Monaghan county board stated that if Monaghan happened to be in the final, he would not ask the people of the county to send the team out of the country. Eventually, an amendment was proposed, that the final be played in Croke Park and the finalists tour American afterwards and, after deadlock at eleven votes each, the chairman's vote swung it.

Fermanagh county board, by a tight margin of 13-12, expressed the view that the final should be played in Croke Park. In Enniskillen, they weren't even waiting for the return of the emissaries, either – a motion that no decision be taken until the return of Kilcoyne and Ó Caoimh was defeated.

In Wexford, the chairman, a Mr O'Kennedy, stated that if his team made the final "there would be a revolution in the county if people did not get to see it".

At a Dublin county board meeting, a resolution was passed on a 21-5 vote asking Central Council to rescind the earlier decision. Roscommon reluctantly acceded to it, after heated debate.

The Galway county board meeting on May 3 saw a belligerent county chairman, James J Nestor (after whom the Connacht SFC cup is named), claim that a final in America wouldn't have been agreed upon if Congress had heard the motion at midday on Easter Sunday instead of late that evening. And he was right, too.

The issue was hotly debated around the country.

A "bunch of turf workers" from Kerry, based in Kildare, were moved to write to The Kerryman on April 26 expressing their displeasure.

"Like anybody else in the county [we were] dumbfounded when we heard that next year's [sic] All-Ireland football final will be played in America. Now, Kerrymen everywhere think of All-Ireland final day as the one day in the year when they will travel to Dublin. So often have Kerry played in Croke Park that every young lad in the Kingdom saves up his money for months beforehand to get to Dublin for the final.

"We would as soon miss the Puck Fair," read the letter, signed "Three Kerrymen in Kildare".

*　　*　　*

On Kilcoyne's and Ó Caoimh's return, they reported that the idea was a runner, with the main obstacle the fact that the liners were booked out for the dates in question. Someone would have to travel by air.

This, more than anything, almost derailed the plan at the final stage. Finding a venue, too, threw up huge problems.

Ó Caoimh recommended that the best method of transportation was that 25 players travel by boat to New York and the remaining 35 by plane. He and Kilcoyne had, he said, stressed to the relevant people in New York that Central Council would be in control of the whole undertaking and would take full responsibility for all expenses, and that the proceeds would be the concern of Central Council.

While in New York, the pair had met with management of the largest stadia in the city, Yankee Stadium and the Polo Grounds, both of which were baseball grounds. They also met with officials of the main shipping companies, Cunard White Star and United States Lines.

By this stage, it still appeared odds-on that the New York idea would be cast on the scrap heap. The word from the boats, for example, was bleak.

"Bearing in mind," the report stated, "the wishes of the Executive that it was not desirable to transport the players by air, we concentrated on trying to acquire shipping space."

The United States Lines was booked up until December, while Cunard White Star had only 20 berths available, although this later increased to 25 on the way out and 60 home.

The minimum specifications of a Gaelic football pitch then, as now, were that it must be 84 yards wide and at least 140 yards long. To put it in perspective, Croke Park, at the time, measured 155 yards by 80 yards.

Ó Caoimh's report included drawings of four possible lay-outs at Yankee Stadium, prepared by the Yankees' groundstaff, but none were even close to suitable, the longest being 11 yards wide; in effect, the pitch would end at the half-forward line. That wouldn't do and the fact that the only guaranteed date was October 19 due to the Yankees' involvement in the latter stages of the National League ruled it out.

In the end, the Yankees would win the World Series of 1947, their first title in four years, beating bitter rivals the Brooklyn Dodgers in the final. Like Gaelic football's, 1947 was a historic season in baseball, with the Dodgers' Jackie Robinson desegregating the sport. Yankee stadium, which attracted an average of over 70,000 paying fans at four home games during the series between

September 30 and October 6, was significantly larger than the Polo Grounds, home of the New York Giants, but the Yankees' packed schedule and the tight space requirements made it a non-runner.

The Polo Grounds also offered three potential pitches, the most suitable being an irregular lay-out measuring one 137 yards in length with 84 yards' width at one end but only 71 at the other.

The capacity, Ó Caoimh reported, was over 54,000 seats, 10,000 of which were uncovered, and rental was set at $5,000 (or IR£1,250), plus a further £1,000 tariff for insurance and cleaning of the grounds (this would, of course, be on top of the flights and accommodation costs, the latter of which were quoted at approximately $60 per person, or IR£15 per week). If the game was to be played in New York, it quickly became clear that the Polo Grounds was the only viable option.

The Giants' treasurer, a Mr Feeley, with whom Ó Caoimh was dealing, wasn't entirely optimistic as to his team's chances either, with good reason as it turned out – he guaranteed the availability of the ground on September 14. In the end, they would finish a distant fourth in the National League, surprising given that the franchise would win five league pennants in 28 seasons between 1930 and 1957. Maybe there was more to it, though – midway through a tumultuous 1948, in an unprecedented move, Brooklyn Dodgers' Leo Durocher left as Dodgers skipper to manage the Giants, and was later accused of gambling in 1947 and subsequently suspended for that whole season by Baseball Commissioner Albert 'Happy' Chandler.

They would soon get back to winning ways but, in '47, their poor run suited the needs of the GAA. The Polo Grounds it was, then, if the thorny issue of how to get there could be resolved.

Dan O'Rourke was still against the idea, stating that while he "was prepared to travel by air", he "wouldn't vote anyone else to go that way".

It was the intervention of Kerry delegate Micheál Ó Ruairc that helped sway this aspect of the debate. Rineanna had already established a significant reputation for its location as a re-fuelling stop for trans-Atlantic crossings and Ó Ruairc stressed the point that, while Kerry was opposed to the idea, the issue of air travel shouldn't put a stop to the idea.

Vincent O'Donoghue, a future president of the Association, who had spoken out at Congress, did so again. The stage was set.

So, to the final decision, and more drama.

There were two meetings held – one in camera in order to "avoid the press", as Paddy McFlynn later recalled, and a second in the glare of the media.

That structure, unsurprisingly, had prompted a strange result – a small majority voted against rubber-stamping the trip at the early meeting but, helped at least in part by an intervention from the now-hapless O'Rourke, there was a swing when it really mattered.

"A vote was taken and by a very small majority, it was decided against going to America with the final," recalled McFlynn, then a delegate.

"Then the press were allowed in and we started off again and I think one of the things that changed it around a bit was, Dan O'Rourke, whose son was playing on the Roscommon team. He said 'no son of mine will fly to America' or something like this, inferring that Roscommon were going to beat Cavan [in the semi-final were the teams to get there].

"I think some of the Ulster delegates... I can't even remember whether I myself changed over but I know they changed over sufficiently. The first result was narrow and the second one, I think there were about three votes in it, deciding to go to America."

In actual fact, the vote was 23 to 12 in favour. With pressmen in attendance, there was no turning back. O'Rourke, we can only presume, was not happy.

It was, in fact, a rare faux pas by the official, who also happened to be a sitting TD during his tenure as county chairman and was the man credited, more than any other, with dragging Roscommon from junior ranks in the late 1930s to the best team in the country.

O'Rourke had vision – it was he who brought the renowned Tom Molloy in from Galway to train the team and Toddy Ryan as masseur, a key role in those days. He was directly involved in the running of the county team, too – when they went into collective training, they were housed in his home and fed by his family.

On this, though, his pleas fell on deaf ears. His son could be going to America after all.

The vote came and O'Donoghue, with some pockets of support, moved to rule it out. It didn't succeed. A counter-proposal "that the teams travel by whatever means available" was carried by 20 votes to 17, and on a vote of 25-12, the Polo Grounds was confirmed as the venue.

The reaction at the top table, says Paddy McFlynn, then a 29-year-old delegate from Derry, was one of disbelief.

"When the whole thing was discussed, one of the big problems was whether the teams should fly or go by boat. I'm sure when the vote was taken it was very narrowly decided not to go. Then when the press were brought in, they were given the impression that the meeting had only started. So, when it came to discuss the American thing, it was agreed that the discussion be very limited, that there be a proposer and a seconder that we go, and a proposer and seconder that we don't go.

"And by a very narrow majority, the previous decision was reversed and I can see still see the look on Dan O'Rourke's face because this was only supposed to be a case of going through the motions as the decision had already been made," remembered McFlynn.

"The first part of the meeting, which was informal, that's where the real debate took place – a very strong debate about going. Poor Pádraig Ó Caoimh got an awful grilling about the situation and about his report. And the actual meeting later was supposed to be a formality.

"Then, of course, the joke of it all was that there was an executive meeting and when they met they all appointed themselves to go. That was the greatest laugh of all."

There was one exception; Alf Murray, the Ulster chairman, hadn't been in favour of the idea and, presumably on a point of principle, was the only one of the Executive Council, which consisted of chairman and secretary of each provincial council and other officers, who did not travel.

Ó Caoimh had assured Central Council that while expenses would be high, the playing of the final in New York would show a profit. The following day's Indo, though, wasn't so sure:

> It is hoped that the venture will prove successful financially. This will test to the limit the organising power of the GAA for many of the men in New York on whose efforts much will depend are no longer in the full flush of organising vigour, and a great deal of work will devolve on less experienced exiles and on the long-distance control from the Central Council.
>
> The approximate cost for the party of 60 is estimated at £14,400, while ground expenses will be heavy. The Federal tax will take roughly 20 per cent of the gross receipts, and then there is rental (£1,250), labour (£375), cleaning after the match (£250), and insurance fees (£100) to be met.
>
> Further costly items will be the establishing of an office in New York and the general administration of the tour.
>
> Prices of admission have yet to be decided, but it is evident that even at an average of two dollars (10/-) a capacity attendance will be needed if a loss is to be avoided.

The general mood in the country hadn't changed. Roscommon, unsurprisingly given Dan O'Rourke's sentiments, were still dead against it and, ironically, Cavan supporters and The Anglo-Celt made their feelings known, too.

The Roscommon Herald ran a "plebiscite" and from one 1,700 votes, it was reported, just one, "a woman", it was helpfully added, was in favour of playing the final in New York.

The Celt revealed that it had received a number of letters "strongly condemning" the fixing of the final for New York but seeing as a decision has been come to, the publication of these letters would serve no useful purpose".

The paper was moved to comment on May 31, however:

> From the meagre reports published of the Council's meeting, there is nothing to show how the representatives of the counties voted: Information which the supporters of the GAA in this country are justly entitled to. It is the usual course at all GAA meetings that a two-thirds majority is necessary to carry a motion but now we find the Central Council taking this momentous step by a paltry majority of three votes, a decision which may bring about serious repercussions.
>
> It will take a high tariff to make any profit on the final, as transport, hotel expenses, rental of pitch and insurance of players will run into a staggering figure.
>
> However, a financial deficit may be easier got over than the keen disappointment which is expressed by thousands of genuine supporters all over the country, who really lived for this one day in the 12 months... Under such circumstances, how can the people be expected to maintain an interest or bother about inter-county contests?
>
> The players and officials of the two counties in the final may appreciate the trip by sea or air but for the ordinary man in the street, who has made the sport a hobby, this year's final will be remembered as Black '47.

Regardless, the decision was made. At last, there was no turning back.

The Rise

IT was the second week in June, Monaghan were coming to Breffni Park and Hughie was thinking. He had seen his team beaten by Antrim in the previous year's Ulster final and he was desperate for redemption with a trip to New York at stake.

For the visit of Monaghan, he started to tinker. His team had performed well in challenge matches, beating Kerry in London and trouncing Westmeath, and the Farney men's lustre had faded over the previous decade. At home on a beautiful June Sunday, Hughie decided to try something out.

Peter Donohoe, the prince of free-takers, was positioned at full-back. Paddy Smith, a razor-sharp corner-back, played in goal, at the expense of injured regular No 1 Brendan Kelly from Bailieborough. Others were rested, new faces were thrown in, but Monaghan came with a team littered with recent graduates from minor ranks, who had won the Ulster Minor Championship two years previously, and were in no mood to roll over and play dead.

In glorious sunshine and with the hundreds of supporters crouched on the sidelines lending a claustrophobic feel to the clash, Cavan led by 0-6 to 0-4 at half-time but Monaghan, inspired by captain Mickey Finnegan, bagged a goal. With time almost up, Monaghan had a free to win it but their corner-forward, McGrath, inexplicably kicked it wide from close-range.

There was time for more drama. Cavan were awarded a penalty and, with Tony Tighe shaping up to take the kick, John Joe O'Reilly stepped forward. The captain would take it and, surely, tap it over the lath to seal the win.

This was John Joe, however; the noble way was the only option. "We'll not win a game like that," he informed Monaghan goalkeeper Sean Mulligan, a Castleblayney man and father of Dessie, who later played for the county, as he placed the ball. This was the first year penalties were introduced into the championship.

O'Reilly went low to the right but Mulligan saved, carried the ball out to his left and drove it over the sideline. Cavan lumped it in again but the long whistle sounded. Stalemate.

Cavan were bewildered, Monaghan were jubilant. The visiting supporters, The Anglo-Celt reported, "carried their grand little goalie shoulder-high from the pitch". But Cavan lived to fight another day and the following Sunday, they put it right... Just about.

A crowd of 10,000 streamed into St Tiernach's Park in Clones for the replay. The general consensus was that Cavan had been over-confident the first day out and would finish the job with something to spare, and those predictions looked prescient when Stafford goaled; he would raise 12 green flags in the Ulster SFC before the end of his career to send Cavan in 1-6 to 0-7 ahead at the break.

But Hughie's men couldn't get in for another, Mulligan repelling them time and again, and Monaghan grew into the game. With a few minutes on the clock, they led, but a point from Tighe and two from Donohoe saw Cavan escape with the win, 1-11 to 1-9.

And it got worse before it got better. The following week, a weakened side were beaten by a point in a challenge against Sligo in Dungannon and the week after that, a fourth Sunday in succession on active duty for many of the players, they returned to the same venue to take on the locals in the Ulster semi-final. In torrential rain, Cavan found themselves level at 0-2 apiece at half-time. Higgins, Tighe and forward TP O'Reilly had been forced to sit it out, although the latter two travelled anyway, due to injuries picked up in the previous month, while young midfielder Phil 'The Gunner' Brady and Doonan came off with knocks.

It was the second half, in the driving rain, before Cavan, for the first time in the championship, showed a glimpse of the form which would take them to New York. McDyer set Carolan, who along with Doonan, the Gunner and Dan Danaher, had played on the junior team beaten by Down the previous month, up for a goal and Cavan grew in confidence. Tyrone barely left their own half of the field, let alone scored, as Cavan swatted the Red Hands as they would a fly, winning, pulling up, by 4-5 to 0-2.

A handful of Cavan supporters made the trek due to the shortage of bonded cars. Smuggling was rife and security along the border, despite the countless boltholes, was tight and while it was possible to slip through, it wasn't advisable. A few years previously, in Armagh, Cavan had been watched by four spectators. They won anyway, and now they had repeated the trick.

So, it was Antrim, again, in Clones, again, for The Anglo-Celt Cup on Sunday July 20, 1947.

The Scholar

THE dates aren't clear, but it matters little – what's important is what happened. Mullahoran is a rural parish, circular in shape and rustic in nature. Football is the social and sporting outlet in one, always has been and remains so.

Mullahoran's style of play hasn't changed in a century; they are hard men. Around Loughduff and Kilcogy and Killydoon, the game is like a family business, handed down through the generations. Old stagers stay on, young guns, honed in the house style, are promoted to the firing range early and the show stays on the road.

The heartland of Cavan football has always been in the south of the county, despite fantastic contributions from other areas.

The likes of Mountnugent, Cornafean, Mullahoran and, in more recent decades, Crosserlough and Gowna, have hoovered up senior titles since the inception of the competition. That was the case, too, in '47; the Dreadnoughts had the highest representation on the Cavan team that year and back-boned the Breffni challenge.

It's a vibrant place, like no other in the county, and produces mighty people, including four, John Wilson, Phil Brady, Val Gannon and Brian O'Reilly, who travelled in the Cavan panel to the Polo Grounds. Rarely in their history has the club's senior team been ranked outside of the top five of Cavan's 40 clubs.

The greatest handballer ever to play the game, Paul Brady, a nephew of the Gunner, is a son of Loughduff, too. And when ladies football took off in the 1970s, the Dreadnoughts led the way, winning an All-Ireland club title and backboning a Cavan team that won two senior All-Irelands. Football matters in Mullahoran – they revel in life in the trenches and if it's a battle, as their matches frequently were and are – they generally do enough.

The suffix the club chose, Dreadnoughts, tells its own tale. No quarter is asked, none is given. Mullahoran play it ferociously hard but, off the field, the community is close-knit, the people engaging and warm.

"They'd knock lumps out of you and then invite you to the house for tea and bread," recalled Mickey Walsh of Drumalee, a contemporary and sometimes teammate of the Cavan players of the 1940s and '50s who once lined out with the Dreadnoughts in a tournament in that era.

"They were that kind of people, when the game was over, that was it."

Stuck for numbers for a Féis match in Belturbet, they sent word to Mickey, a member of Cavan Harps, and some pals, and collected them en route.

"There were no restrictions in tournaments. They collected Paddy Boylan and big Paddy Brady in the town, word was sent on to them.

"We were playing the Fermanagh champions in a Feis game. They beat us, we [Mullahoran] were the Cavan champions but we weren't taking it seriously.

"They started celebrating and I turned around and they were carrying their players off shoulder-high. 'Jaysus,' I says to Phil the Gunner, 'they're carrying them off'.

"'Well, if I had've known that,' he says, 'they'd have needed a few stretchers!'"

That was the Mullahoran way. The pot simmered and, sometimes, boiled over. Once, it almost tipped and the county board were called in. A melee, the latest in a series of incidents, had alerted the authorities and it looked ominous. There was talk of fines and bans and whispers that the Mullahoran club was on the way out of business.

It was going to take something special, so Mullahoran sent out the best man they had, John Wilson, to plead their case.

Faced by a hostile room of delegates and officials and given little hope of earning a reprieve for his club, Wilson took off, speaking at length, *as Gaeilge*, on the situation. Mullahoran were innocent, he said, of the charges. They were simple people, just playing a game and keeping a tradition alive. There were shades of Canon Hamilton as the mood changed in the room.

To sum up, he delivered the matador's final thrust.

"Who dares," he asked, scanning the room, "to throw mud at the little white-washed cottages of Mullahoran?"

Case dismissed. That was Wilson, truly, a man in a million.

What was it Patrick Kavanagh wrote about Homer making the Iliad, Wilson's favourite book, from such a local row? In Cavan and Mullahoran, gods made their own importance.

*   *   *

Cavan folk are lucky — while many counties' records were destroyed in the Four Courts, much of the Cavan material was held in the county town's courthouse by the Grand Jury. The Wilsons' connection to Mullahoran, thus, can be traced back to the 18th Century.

John was born in 1923, one of eight siblings, and his rare promise was first noticed at Clonoose and Cloncovid national schools, where a teacher, a Mr Savage, spotted his potential.

Encouraged by his mother, a farmer's wife in 1930s rural Ireland but a woman who had lived and worked in the United States, Wilson landed a scholarship to St Mel's in Longford.

There he excelled, as a footballer and as an academic. A strapping lad, standing over six feet tall, he had an enormous intellect. After finishing school, he studied in UCG and UCD, gaining a degree in Classics and picking up a love of languages and of ancient Greece, which he would carry like a flame all his life.

He made his debut for Cavan as a teenager in 1943 and floated around between the defence and midfield for a number of years. Around that time, he had been studying for the priesthood in Maynooth but dropped out, for his own reasons. When his wife asked him years later, he replied that he didn't think he had the humility for the role.

He would finish a career in politics, and this was perhaps his greatest achievement of all, admired and respected by all sides.

Wilson was that rare combination, modest but confident, a

gifted mind and a driven one. Handed the precious chance to gain an education, he grabbed it.

He began teaching in St Kieran's College in Kilkenny, having worked for a short time in St Mary's in Galway and Finchley Grammar in London, and soon graduated to the role of ASTI president, now a full-time position but then something working schoolteachers juggled with their school duties. Often, Wilson would set off straight after the final class, chair a meeting in some far-flung location and drive through the night, crossing the Nore the next morning and striding into the classroom as the first bell sounded.

He was a man forever busy.

He met his future wife, Ita Ward, a Londoner whose mother was from Galway, when he paid a surprise visit to the home of a lady – Ita's aunt – with whom he had boarded in the city. They were married in 1953, by which time Wilson, still in his twenties, had moved on from sport, with two All-Ireland medals, five Ulsters and a Railway Cup gong tucked away, to the next challenge.

He carried his love for Cavan football with him everywhere he went and his remarkable wit, oratory and grace went with him, too. His was a life less ordinary.

In Spain's Zaragoza University, he studied for a year and befriended two former Nazis who told him they had been brainwashed by the regime a decade earlier. "Extraordinary", he used to say, recalling it.

In Moscow, on government duty in the 1980s, he would amaze local journalists and dignitaries by delivering a speech and hosting a press conference in the local tongue, of which he had taught himself the rudiments.

When teaching in St Eunan's College in Letterkenny for eight years, he single-handedly revived underage football in the county, coaching the school to a first-ever Rannafast Cup title, retaining it and leading them to a first MacRory final in 30 years.

Hugh Daly, father of Tom, who went on to be Ulster Council President, had a conversation with Wilson once. Donegal were bottom of the GAA pile yet Wilson, a renaissance man in every sense of the term, was beginning to enjoy unprecedented success in schools football. "I wonder," asked Hugh, "will we ever make it in senior football?"

"Oh your time will come," assured Wilson. "I don't know, John," replied a gloomy Daly, "I think the Queen of England will be in Croke Park before Donegal win an All-Ireland in it."

*　　*　　*

His greatest gift of all, perhaps, was his ability to retain the common touch. In Cavan, and to his old football comrades, whether he was Minister or Tánaiste, he was just Johnny. While serving as a TD, first in the old Cavan three-seater and, from 1977 until 1992, as the holder of one of the seats in Cavan-Monaghan, he held 10 regular clinics.

On trips home to Mullahoran though – he bought a weekend bungalow in Finea, a mile from the old homestead in Callanagh – he didn't bother. The people, noted the Sunday Independent in the late 1970s, "come to his door and meet him at church and crossroads".

He was held in huge esteem in his native county, not just for his football exploits. He was a prince among politicians but brought it all back home, all the time.

"We don't know," claimed John Joe Brady, then-Mullahoran chairman, once, "whether John Wilson has made Mullahoran or whether Mullahoran has made him."

Val Gannon, who played in goals in the Polo Grounds, went further.

"Johnny Wilson has never lost his localism," said Gannon.

"He's a man we are all very proud of and a credit not only to Mullahoran but to Ireland."

A mesmerising orator, Wilson could speak fluent Irish, Spanish, Latin and Greek and was proficient in French, German and, of course, Russian.

He was head-hunted by the renowned Jesuit school Gonzaga College in Dublin, where he taught from 1961 until 1973, when his old football foe, future Taoiseach Jack Lynch, came calling. Politics beckoned.

Influenced by his father, who died that year aged 87 and whose own father had been a Fenian, Fianna Fáil was the natural fit. Being Wilson, he studied the party's history and founding at length before taking the plunge.

He called his wife from school to tell her that he had decided to throw his hat in the ring. "Good God, John, are you serious?" she asked.

"Is that the only encouragement I'm getting?" he grinned.

The couple, a pair of live wires, sparked off each other for half a century, the debates generally ending with a wisecrack from the husband.

He wasn't one to take it easy, to retire to the fairways or the bar, although he was sociable and loved a singsong (despite an awful singing voice) and a glass of 1760 whiskey.

In ways, his life was only beginning when he hung up his boots.

Balancing his love of the arts, sculpture and learning with Cavan football, especially as the county's status descended over the decades was remarkable. Wilson would sit up until 6am, for example, reading in Greek (his contribution was such that the Greek embassy recognised him with one of their highest awards in later years).

At one stage, he had never read the Protestant version of the 'good book', the St James's Bible, and after procuring a copy, would sit up till dawn reading it and calling out the wonderful translations to his restless wife.

"Just listen to this..." he would start, clearing his throat.

"And I would say 'for Heaven's sake John, look at the time'," recalled Ita, "and he would laugh and say 'Philistine!'"

He would freely admit in later years that, as a political greenhorn, his football connections sealed that first nomination. Elected along with former Minister for Agriculture Paddy Smith, Wilson was made spokesman for Education by Lynch, against whom he played in the 1945 All-Ireland final, on his first day in the Dáil.

Four years later, after Fine Gael fell, he was on the front bench as Minister. Speculation as to who would make up the various portfolios was rife and, on the morning of the announcement, Wilson met Lynch passing through a doorway at Leinster House, the Corkman surreptitiously passing over a handwritten note.

On it were two words: "*Bí ullamh*", be prepared. Wilson was in.

In time he would hold seven minsterial portfolios. He was Front Bench spokesman on Education and the Arts from 1973-77; Minister for Education from 1977-81 and spent a year as spokesman in the same department in 1981. He was later front bench spokesman on Communications from 1982-87, and was Minister for Transport and Post and Telegraphs from March-December 1982, and Minister for Tourism and Transport from March 1987-July 1989 before his last Ministerial post in the Department of The Marine in the Fianna Fail/PD Coalition Government of 1989-92.

Wilson wasn't one to court the media, maybe to his political detriment, but could take criticism with a shrug. His reluctance to stick to the speech issued by a department and distributed to the press – Wilson spoke off the cuff and never, ever used a script – meant he was often misquoted completely by the hacks. He would let it slide.

And his one-liners, delivered often in Latin and razor-sharp, were legendary.

On one occasion in the Dáil, the tyro Labour TD John Horgan, a former editor of the Education Times and himself a very capable debater, hammered him for two hours about the lack of investment in eduction. Later, as Wilson passed him on the steps of the house, he delivered a line from Cicero which cut the upstart in half: "*Proviniebant oratores novi, stulti adulescenti*", which, originally delivered in relation to the Roman Senate, translated as "New orators rush forward [to air their views], stupid young men." Ouch.

If Wilson had said it in English, he would have been hauled up by the Ceann Comhairle. That was the genius of the man, the skills of the best courtroom senior counsel and as sharp as a dagger.

In 1977, while Minister for Education, he was due to speak at a function in Trinity College. There was a student protest on the event, activists and hangers on making their feelings known on education cuts. The provost of the college approached the minister and suggested it might be a good idea if he entered via the rear of the building.

Wilson smiled, and his retort summed up one side of his character: "No Mullahoran man goes round the back way. You go straight in!"

The speech he delivered, engaging, eloquent and verbose, summed up the other. He went to the top in everything he ever tried, and football was no different.

As 1947 progressed, he was determined to win back his place in the team. As in all aspects of his life, it was going to take something formidable to stop him.

CHAPTER TEN

The Olympian

WITH the trip of a lifetime at stake, Cavan were taking no chances. Before the Ulster final against Antrim, for the first time in the county's history for a provincial match, they decided to train. Antrim were good, and would take beating. There was nothing else for it.

So, the word went out. Secretary Hughie Smyth sent cards to the players' homes and they duly reported for duty in Ballyjamesduff in July.

The collective training was overseen by Hughie O'Reilly, and his selectors in '47. They comprised of his own brother Tommy (or 'TJ'), MJ Mullen from Mountnugent, Jimmy Dalton of Mullahoran, Smyth himself and chairman Patsy Lynch, but another man behind the scenes completed a formidable back-room team.

That man was John McGeough, nominally "masseur" but the individual who oiled the wheels of the Cavan machine.

* * *

McGeough was no ordinary old codger, brought along to play a small role. He had scaled the mountain and knew what the ascent was all about. Not many Gaelic football teams of the time, or even now, could boast an Olympic medallist in their corner.

McGeough – often misspelled in the papers at the time as "McGough" – was a native of Annaglaive outside Castleblayney who had emigrated to Glasgow with his family as a six-year-old in 1882.

As a boy, he got into running, and at 17, he threw his lot in with the Bellahouston Harriers. Three years later, he was Scottish one-mile and four-mile champion and, in the same year, was barely beaten into second on a sodden track at Ballsbridge in an international meet by Galway-born John J Daly, after running 4:27 for the mile.

A year later, he ran away with the Scottish 800m title and he would win the national championship over the mile again in 1904, '05, and '07. In 1907, at Ibrox Stadium, he clocked 4:22.2 for the mile, an Irish record which would stand for over 50 years.

By then, though, he had already peaked as a runner. He was selected to compete for Great Britain in the 1906 Olympics in the 800m and the 1,500m but suffered badly from sea-sickness on the boat to Athens, spending his days vomiting and sweating in his cabin.

He arrived in Greece weight-drained and listless, but his training beforehand had him in fine fettle. McGeough came through his heat, holding off Englishman Reginald Crabbe, who would be ordained an Anglican bishop the following year, to qualify for the final.

Trailing for most of the race behind six of the world's greatest milers, who qualified out of 20 from eight nations, McGeough grew into the race. On the final circuit, he passed Hellstrom from Sweden, American JP Sullivan, Australia's GA Wheatley and Great Britain's Cohn, to find himself six yards behind Pittsburgh legend Jim Lightbody.

McGeough put on the burners and left the field for dead, but ran out of track, as the American broke the tape two and a half yards in front.

The Irish press didn't pick up the significance of the Monaghan man's run. While they reported joyously on gold in the Hop, Step and Jump and Con Leahy's second in the same event, they ignored McGeough's silver, presumably not realising that the man listed as British was, in fact, Monaghan born and partially bred and one of the many thousands of Irish who had made Glasgow their home.

McGeough retired from running in 1910, having also competed, carrying a bad ankle injury, at the 1908 Olympics in London, but his sporting story wasn't done yet. By this time, he had jacked in his job with the Scottish postal service and was working full-time as a trainer for Glasgow Celtic.

Word spread, and Manchester City came calling.

So, John was off to Lancashire, where he was employed by the club for a decade before returning to Ireland and Annaglaive to work the old family farm. He fitted in easily when he came back to 'Blayney, the Olympic hero and former aide to cross-channel superstars. The locals showed a gift for understatement and McGeough wasn't one to brag anyway, so he became saddled with a new nickname – it's debatable whether those who knew 'The Runner McGeough' at the time really appreciated the enormity of his achievements.

Cavan's players knew his worth, however.

*   *   *

On his return, he started training Gaelic teams, a new departure at the time. County sides were beginning to carry masseurs – part trainer, part physio and kneader of muscles – a position more important in the set-up than is held in the modern game, and Cavan quickly snapped him up.

McGeough was on board as early as 1928, when Cavan lost their first All-Ireland final, against Kildare, and was still there in 1933 and 1935, when they finally got over the line after almost 50 years of heartbreak.

He took a step back but was back with the squad for the All-Ireland final appearances in 1943 and two years later. By 1947, he was 71-one years old, but his experience would be vital.

By the time Hughie and The Runner were through with Cavan, well, Antrim wouldn't know what had hit them...

"The previous year Antrim beat us," remembered Higgins.

"In 1947, we were the outsiders all the time. But what Antrim probably forgot was we never trained for the Ulster final. We always trained for the semi-final, collective training, and for the final if you got there.

"But as this trip to New York was coming up, we went into training for the first time ever for an Ulster final. The first and only time I think."

Fairytale in New York

CHAPTER ELEVEN

The Gatecrashers

CAVAN were readier than ever, but they would need to be. The previous year, they were gunning for eight Ulster titles in a row and had kicked 13-23 in two games before facing an Antrim team who were appearing in their first final in 20 years.

Defeat was unthinkable, but Cavan were over-confident and were beaten by four points. Antrim, without an Ulster title since 1923, had gatecrashed the private Breffni Ulster party.

They carried their form through the spring of '47 and the papers made the Ulster final a pick 'em match.

Hughie and his band of selectors knew it, too, and tinkered with the team again. The Gunner was left off due to injury, TP O'Reilly slotted in at wing half-forward and a young man from Killinkere called Terry Sheridan, who had made his name in a recent Leinster Colleges final, was handed his debut on the opposite wing.

"This time last year Antrim sprang into the limelight by defeating Cavan in the Ulster final at Clones, and now these same two counties meet again at the same venue, each a year older in experience," noted The Irish Independent's reporter.

"In the 12 months I think Antrim have progressed the more and they have gradually eliminated faults which no title-holders could afford."

Andy Croke, in the Sunday Indo on the morning of the game, couldn't make up his mind.

"The Breffni midfield players, Tighe and McDyer, are on the light side but as they have speed and experience, their partnership may be a winning one," he wrote.

"Antrim usually stake all on attack and I expect it will be so today. Despite the presence of expert score-getters on each team, this game is likely to be won from midfield and here O'Neill and Gallagher will take beating."

The Cavanman's bible, The Celt, confidently predicted a win, but what was more notable was a few paragraphs which accompanied the verdict. In the next column to the match preview was a comment on Paddy McNamee's reconnaissance trip to New York, and some damning criticism of the whole exercise.

Noting that McNamee had, in a speech on his arrival, paid tribute to Canon Hamilton for his role in the project, the Celt couldn't conceal its outrage.

"Mr McNamee is badly informed if he considers that any person deserves credit for this colossal blunder. With very few exceptions, the Gaels of Ireland are entirely opposed to taking the final out of this country," it railed.

The Big Apple buzz, clearly, was already growing...

*   *   *

With New York looming on the horizon, the interest in every championship match was magnified and this was the most hyped Ulster final there had ever been. The talk all week in Cavan centred on whether Higgins would be fit. When word leaked from the camp at Byers' Hotel in Ballyjamesduff that he would be, having missed the Tyrone win, the county breathed a collective sigh of relief. Willie Doonan was also carrying a knock but, outstanding as he was, he was replaceable; Higgins was indispensable.

The entire panel were in training bar one; Paddy Smith, then a bank clerk in Granard, was unable to get the time off. It mattered little as Smith, small in stature but an excellent, tenacious defender, started at corner-back anyway.

In Bally'duff, the players followed Hughie's tried and tested routine: an hour's walk in the morning before breakfast, then physical training, followed by football practice and sprinting in the evening and an hour's walk again before retiring at 11pm.

"It has," commented O'Reilly, "brought a vast improvement in the speed and stamina of the 21 men here."

The man with the stopwatch, McGeough, announced himself "very pleased" with the performance of the players, and expected a win.

On Sunday morning, the team rose in Ballyjamesduff and looked out of their windows. "Greasy pig, boys," announced Stafford – a wet pigskin. It was indeed wretched, rain teeming down and no sign of it lifting.

When the team bus hit Clones, the town's arteries were clogged with drinkers and merchandise sellers and revellers from all over the province.

The old town was thronged. The game attracted a record crowd of 34,009, more than double the attendance at the previous year's final and a special 12.30pm mass had even been arranged for those travelling long distances.

For supporters, the trek from Cavan town had begun that morning at 7.30am, donkeys, carts, vans and traps ferrying half a dozen at a time. Thousands cycled, and two kids with notebooks recorded that 755 cars passed back through Butlersbridge that evening. It was extraordinary; unknownst to themselves, the public had bought in to the American dream.

*   *   *

Cavan were primed and, on cue, they detonated. Within 12 minutes, the game was over as a contest after a goal from Donohoe (direct from a 14-yard free), an own goal from Antrim and a daisy-cutter from Stafford helped the underdogs into a 3-2 to 0-0 lead.

Antrim were reeling; they had walked into a Breffni haymaker and couldn't cope with the bombardment in the driving rain.

They settled, landing a couple of points but the loss of Kevin Armstrong before the break threw their plans asunder again. With the wind, they upped it on the restart but Cavan, and in particular Doonan, who pulled on loose, skidding balls and sent them 60 yards downfield to the roars of the crowd, held steady.

Eventually, the Antrim pressure began to pay off. Doonan's injury flared up and he came off, with PJ Duke following him. John Joe Cassidy and Owen Roe McGovern came in, but Cassidy, too, got a knock and was replaced by Big Tom.

The changes upset Cavan's rhythm and Antrim pressed, with Val Gannon in goal keeping Cavan in the game. When they goaled five minutes from the end, their supporters threw drenched coats and hats in the air, exploding into life. There were now only three points between them – game on.

But Cavan had the final say, and ran out four-point winners.

"No final in the long history of the association in the province got such a grip on the populace as that of Sunday," commented The Celt.

And the fun was only starting...

Bad Blood

CAVAN and Roscommon had history. It had been festering since '43 with the Cully and Stafford incidents and, four years later, the fire was still burning.

Early in 1947, they had played a not-so-friendly match in Castlereagh. The challenge match circuit for fundraisers and pitch openings was a lively one at the time and Cavan, with their dashing forwards and their central location, were in constant demand. Things there had got a bit heavy.

Cavan won, Stafford raising a couple of green flags as was his wont, but relations between the counties weren't good.

Maybe Cavan were envious – while they'd let Sam slip from their grasp on a couple of occasions and by the end of '46, were no longer even rulers in their own province, Roscommon had clocked up two All-Irelands in '43 and '44, lost a replayed final in '46 and were second favourites after Kerry to win a third in '47.

Cavan against Roscommon, then, for a place in the Polo Grounds, was a delicious appetiser to the following month's final.

There was more cause for needle, too. Dan O'Rourke, the GAA President and a Roscommon man, albeit one born in Leitrim, hadn't endeared himself to the delegates in Cavan, or Ulster for that matter, when he spoke at the Central Council meeting in late May which would ratify the earlier Congress decision to award the final to New York.

His comments about his son not going to New York had raised the temperature of the Ulster delegates on that occasion, and it was threatening to spill over.

Against that backdrop, the teams took the field on August 3 before 60,075 spectators at Croke Park.

Cavan made one change, the Gunner moving to centre-field for Cavan in place of Tony Tighe, who played right half-forward, with Terry Sheridan the man to miss out.

Cavan, it was reported, had prepared better than ever and

John Joe O'Reilly didn't over-elaborate when he spoke to The Celt's reporter at the training camp in Ballyjamesduff. "We will get there this time," was the only line from the captain carried in his local paper.

Opinion as to who would win was split. Cavan, mesmerising in the rain of Clones a fortnight earlier, were moving well but Roscommon, in that era, were an awesome outfit, compared decades later to the Down team of the '60s.

Andy Croke, writing in The Sunday Independent, did nail his colours to the mast and they were primrose and blue. The match-up had Gaeldom "buzzing with excitement" but, admitting Cavan's stock had soared after the Antrim performance, he still came down on the side of Roscommon.

Analysing the Cavan team, he made some interesting observations.

"Gannon is an opportunist who is inclined to take his understanding with young [Brian] O'Reilly too much for granted," he wrote on the morning of the match.

"[Paddy] Smith's forward experience helps him to hold down the left full-back berth with distinction, but the live-wire of the rearguard is Doonan. Fully recovered from his injury, his first-time kicking is a treat. I have seen enough of Deignan, JJ O'Reilly and Duke as individuals to hazard how devastating they will be in company as a half-back line. On this trio, Cavan's hopes of victory are mainly built.

"In the Cavan attack, Donohoe, whom many thought a stopgap, has developed full-forward tactics of the true Blessing tradition. He is ably supported by Stafford, always good for a score, and the promising newcomer Carolan."

Crucially, though, he believed he had found a chink in Cavan's armour – and it came in the form of their brightest light.

"One of the highlights of the game should be the duel between the Cavan half-forwards, Tighe, Higgins and TP O'Reilly, and the Roscommon half-back line. Good as Higgins is, I believe he will meet his master in [Bill] Carlos. And with Higgins subdued, the Cavan attack loses some of its sting," he concluded.

One man Croke gave special mention to, as it happened, was

Columba McDyer, a Donegal native whose transfer to the Breffni county came as a result of some opportunism on the part of Cavan officials, and who, amazingly, would have a direct, posthumous link to his native county's second All-Ireland win in 2012, too.

"I still have visions of McDyer's red head dominating the scene of Ulster's Railway Cup win in 1942," Andy Croke wrote in the Independent.

"Since going to Cavan, he has retained his early brilliance and I fully expect him to hit it off with Brady."

Hit it off they did. McDyer, commonly known as Colm, was a special talent and was, in a way, the missing link on the Cavan team of '47. A very clean player, he was tall, athletic and blessed with a great engine and a tremendous burst of speed.

When Ulster won their first Railway Cup title in 1942, McDyer was a key man, as Croke pointed out, and, working in Sligo, he would declare for the Yeats men in time, playing club football for Craobh Rua and winning a Connacht League title against Galway in the Showgrounds in 1945.

A carpenter by trade, he came to work in Monaghan in early 1947, Cavan got wind of it and, despite lobbying from Monaghan, he began working for Elliott's builders of Church St, Cavan, while living 16 miles away in Clones.

Alongside the Gunner, McDyer shone. The Mullahoran man sorted out any rough-housing and McDyer hoovered up ball around the middle, dominating in the air and bombing forward.

Years later, Higgins would laud McDyer as "an outstanding player".

"He was a gentleman on and off the field and was fortunate to have a midfield partner in Phil 'Gunner' Brady who looked after anything that was needed to be looked after," said Mick, showing a fine line in understatement.

"I played against him when he was playing for Donegal. He came to Cavan at a time when we were having centre-field problems.

"We found him to be an outstanding player and he solved our problems in this area of the field in partnership with Phil Brady.

"He was a great athlete with wonderful fielding. His chief asset, at least I felt, was his fetching. He was a fine fielder of a ball and never relied on punching, he always caught it.

"Columba was a genius, too, to launch an attack. He didn't play defensive football as was commonly understood and he always managed to get scores at vital periods.

"He never resorted to rough play and was always skilful and naturally fit throughout his life. We used to train only for finals at that time and he would always be supremely fit. He had a tremendous attitude overall."

He would show as much the following month when he waved goodbye to his new bride Peggy, cutting short their honeymoon, to join up with the rest of the Cavan panel in Ballyjamesduff and hit the road for Rineanna.

McDyer signed for Cavan Slashers to legalise the move and despite not having an array of medals like some of the Breffni galacticos of the time, he immediately won their respect.

Mickey Walsh, a regular on the Cavan junior team and an oft-time senior panellist who wasn't far off the '47 squad, remembers McDyer regularly being asked to referee matches in Cavan, his roots in far-off Donegal perhaps rendering him somewhat neutral.

Weeks before going to the Polo Grounds, Walsh ended up making up the numbers in Butlersbridge in a challenge match between the home team and Cavan Slashers and having a run-in with Willie Doonan, his own Cavan Harps clubmate, also there to fill out a team.

McDyer was the man in the middle. There had been a collection for Doonan around the local shops and businesses for his trip to New York and, later, the lads set out to watch the match in the 'Bridge and were roped in to play.

"It was an oul challenge thing," remembered Mickey.

"Jaysus, Doonan hit me a kick in the back of the leg. Colm McDyer was refereeing the match... I went for Doonan and I said 'if I get you, I'll bloody kill you'.

"McDyer says 'you know that man is going to America?' I says 'well not if I can feckin' help it!'

"So after the game we went up to Con Smith's for a drink and Doonan felt so bad, he was trying to give me half the money. Oh, a big eegit!"

That was Doonan – a different man to his teammates, but still a teammate. And that was McDyer – helping out and playing his part in one of the greatest footballing journeys of all time.

He played just one year but was the greatest transfer Cavan ever had. And, almost seven decades later, his legacy touched on another momentous All-Ireland success. When another Glenties man, Jim McGuinness, took the Donegal team through their warm-up before the All-Ireland final against Mayo, in his hand was a whistle, in the Cavan (and Glenties) colours, given to him 20 years beforehand by McDyer.

"Me and Columba would have been fairly close," McGuinness remembered before that final.

"He was an absolute gentleman to the fingertips, very well-educated. He went on his travels when he was young, played with Cavan and Sligo before returning to Donegal, playing first and then managing the team. He came down to the field one night with his wife Peggy. I was out with the young fellas when he called me aside. He handed over a whistle, a blue and white whistle and said: 'I think you are going to be a coach. I want you to have this whistle'.

"Jesus, that's at least 21 years ago but I have never lost that whistle. Oil has been spilt on it. The pea is probably gone in it, and the boys slag me about it. But there would be panic in the dressing room if I mislaid it. It actually happened one day. All the boys could hear was 'where's the whistle? Where's the whistle?' Now they know the full significance of it."

All of that, though, was well in the future. On the morning of August 3, 1947, McDyer and his teammates, in a convoy of cars, were headed for the Big Smoke with just one thing in mind – to even the score with Roscommon and book their seats for the greatest trip of all.

The match was an epic, that swooped and soared and, played in an almost-unbearable tension, threw up a multitude of mini-dramas.

The exodus had begun at dawn in Cavan town, with The Anglo-Celt remarking that smoke was seen from chimneys in the county town as early as 5.30am, "evidence of preparations for breakfast", it helpfully explained.

Cavan's support out-numbered Roscommon by two to one in what was a remarkably-high attendance of 60,075 for the double-header. Cork beat Antrim by 7-10 to 0-5 in the hurling semi-final on the undercard as the gate smashed the previous semi-final record by 9,000. Such was the size of the crowd that The Irish Press carried a photo of a section of them over four news columns on their front page the following morning.

Gaelic games correspondent Traolach, writing in The Press, would describe the match as "a grim grueller, replete with iron knocks in which men threw every ounce of strength into the issue, eschewed fancy frills and played themselves to a standstill".

Cavan tore into their opponents from the start and with Donohoe kicking three points, opened a lead, but Roscommon finally settled into the game and were level with 10 minutes left in the half. Tony Tighe was everywhere, the Independent's reporter noting that, at times, he thought there were "two A Tighes playing for Cavan".

The turning point came just before half-time when Cavan made an unusual switch, bringing both Higgins and Tighe to midfield in place of Brady and McDyer. There, Tighe was rampant, gobbling up breaks and running directly at Roscommon.

His trademark was dashing solo runs. He had the acceleration of a 100-yard sprinter but uncanny control with it.

The son of a bank manager from Ballyjamesduff, at the time Tighe was renowned as the fastest ball-carrier in the country. Years later, when acting as a selector with the Cavan team in the 1960s, he would let Steve Duggan, another earth-scorching forward, in on one of his trade secrets.

When you gather the ball, he said, take a few steps and bounce it before soloing.

"If you get a big run and hop you can go 20 yards with one hop if you do it right," Duggan smiled, remembering his words of wisdom. "And I used it many times."

On this day, Tighe was unmarkable. In the second half, at full tilt, he burst through the middle, playing one-twos with TP O'Reilly for 15 yards, before unleashing what the Indo described as "an astonishing goal".

*   *   *

Roscommon had pressed for a goal of their own early in the second half but Cavan goalkeeper Val Gannon, the farmer from Mullahoran who only came into the team when Brendan Kelly got injured before the Monaghan match and was paying his first visit to Croke Park, made a great save.

The hits were hard, too. Bill Carlos was forced to leave the field after shipping a heavy tackle from Donohoe, Tom Collins, too. Their captain and centre half-forward Jimmy Murray, the great man from Knockcroghery, went off as well. It was awfully unlucky for Murray in particular. The previous year, Roscommon looked to have the final won, even after Murray got knocked out. As the medics revived him on the sideline, readying him for the presentation of the Sam Maguire, he could only watch in frustration as the aristocrats from the Kingdom bagged two late goals, and an unlikely title.

The following year was more of the same. Cavan's goals and the loss of Carlos and Murray knocked the fight out of Roscommon. Little did anyone know it but that great team from the West would never hit the heights again.

Incidentally, half a century later, the same Murray still kept the football from the '43 final hanging by a chain from the roof of his pub. One night, the building caught fire and a man broke from the crowd which had surrounded it, trying to fight the flames, and dashed inside, emerging moments later triumphantly crying "I've got the ball. I've got the ball!"

Not that Cavan, on August 3 1947, were mourning for them, as one supporter in the stand, Lavey man Johnny Cusack, remembered.

Cusack was a regular on the Cavan junior team at the time and would, in time, secure his place at corner-forward on the senior side, winning an All-Ireland medal in '52. That day, though, he was in the stand, watching, having blown out his knee earlier in the year.

The win over Roscommon couldn't have been sweeter.

"In '43 Cavan drew with them and Joe Stafford was put off. He hit some fella and there was a bit of a ruck, Barney Cully and a few of them were in it. Sure the replay came then and they hadn't Stafford and Roscommon beat them well.

"So there was bad feeling. And then in '47, in the spring time, there was a match, and the prize was travelling bags. And the heading in some paper said 'last year's All-Ireland finalists and probably this year's All-Ireland finalists in Croke Park'. Roscommon and Kerry. It was some time around Easter."

It didn't sit well with Cavan.

"Roscommon thought after beating Cavan so often and after the bit of a ruck before it that they'd beat them easy again but it was a great victory for Cavan to get their own back on them."

Cavan won by 2-4 to 0-6 – their lives would never be the same. And one man almost missed out in what would have been the cruellest twist of all – the Gunner.

Brady had been magnificent, throwing his body on the line all afternoon in a titanic tussle with Roscommon's Eamon Boland. With five minutes to go, the ref called the pair together – he had seen enough, and pointed to the line.

The pair looked at each other, and maybe to the scoreboard. Cavan weren't going to be caught. Boland spoke up.

"Don't send him off," he pleaded with referee Dowling from Kildare, "I'll go but don't put Brady off. He'll not get to New York."

Both men stayed on, and when the long whistle sounded, Cavan's players were chaired off shoulder-high by their supporters. They were about to get a bite of the Big Apple after all.

The Buzz

THERE was to be no triumphant homecoming for Hughie O'Reilly's troops after the Roscommon game, however. Their task completed on the field, the job of work in preparing for the logistics of the trip to New York the following month began in earnest immediately. Some of the players – like Donohoe, Owen Roe McGovern and PJ Duke (who had been replaced by John Wilson for the Roscommon game) among others – were based in the capital but the rest stayed on to apply for passports, obtain visas from the American embassy and receive vaccinations against smallpox.

The staff at the consulate began work at 7am to process the visas while the Department of External Affairs hastily prepared the passports. The Cavan panel stayed in Barry's Hotel on Sunday and Monday nights, a crowd of well-wishers clapping them off on Tuesday afternoon. For 21 of Cavan's travelling party of 25, it would be a first time to cross the water, but football had taken four men, chairman Patsy Lynch, trainer Hughie O'Reilly, and the O'Reilly brothers, John Joe and Big Tom, to the USA before.

When Simon Deignan's brother Jim, a seminary student, was refused permission to travel, Cavan had to scramble for a replacement. They turned to Brendan Kelly, who had lost his place in goal to Gannon, who quickly proved himself to be a fantastic goalkeeper, after getting injured, and sent word to him in Bundoran, where he was on holiday.

There was an interesting postscript to The Anglo-Celt's report, too.

Under the heading "Why not a broadcast?" the paper asked:

"If at all possible, Cavan county committee GAA , in justice to their thousands of loyal supporters, who, of course, cannot travel to New York, should leave no stone unturned to have the final against either Kerry or Meath broadcast.

"As none of the American radio officials could be expected to do so, because they have no knowledge of the players individually, the position points to Mr Michael O'Hehir, Dublin, who stands alone as a football commentator.

"No time should be lost in sending a cablegram to Mr P O'Keeffe, Sec Central Council, who is in New York, to have the matter adjusted at that end so that Mr O'Hehir could be one of the parties to travel with the teams."

Little did the well-meaning local journalist know that the wheels were already in motion...

*   *   *

Before O Caoimh had gone to America in July, he had booked 25 places on a Trans World Airline (TWA) flight from Rineanna and Cavan decided that their party would be made up of the starting team plus Hughie O'Reilly and John McGeough.

There were two exceptions: Willie Doonan, after his experiences in the war, refused to fly and he alone of the Breffni starting side would take the boat along with the remainder of the subs plus Patsy Lynch and Hughie Smyth, while John Joe O'Reilly, due to army commitments, would fly separately, with his wife Olive, on the morning after the rest of the playing contingent took off.

There was one lucky traveller on John Joe's flight. Charles Dobbin from Belfast had won a free trip in the popular magazine GAA Digest. The draw had been presided over in Tralee by Dan Spring, TD, who had captained Kerry to the 1940 All-Ireland title.

Kerry sent players who were familiar with the sea, Dingle men mainly, and the rest would also go by air on the same flight as the Cavan players. Before that, though, Hughie O'Reilly's men would endure a week of hard training. On the Sunday morning, August 31, they assembled in Ballyjamesduff and began to plot how they would scale the mountain. Hughie worked them hard.

The players rose at 7.30am and walked five miles before breakfast. After that it was ball drills, physical exercises, seven-a-side games and, sporadically during the day, sprints and longer runs. Lights out was at 10.30 at night. There were no exceptions.

Two men, TP O'Reilly and Mick Higgins, the solicitor and the Garda, couldn't attend the whole week's training due to work while one other had a good excuse to slip away on the Tuesday evening – Colm McDyer was due to marry his fiancé Peggy on Wednesday morning, over 100 miles away in Ballina, Co Mayo.

The hum of chat centred mainly on one thing. New York. Players were excited, but apprehensive, too. Flying was new, and viewed with suspicion.

One day, Paddy Smith, one of the characters on the team, lightened the mood.

Hughie was thinking, and wondering aloud.

"How many passengers do these airplanes hold anyway?" he asked, to nobody in particular.

"Sixty-five," came Paddy's reply, quick as a flash.

"How do you know?" someone asked.

"Because," Paddy smiled, "whenever there is a plane crash, they always announce there was 65 killed!"

His teammates hooted with derision but Paddy grinned, and so did they, eventually. Innocent devilment was the currency and, when groups of footballers got together, the trade was brisk...

Fairytale in New York

The Men of Cavan, 1947

13 clubs, 22 players, one manager, three countries in one year on a single magical journey. There has never been an All-Ireland winning team like them.

1. V. Gannon (Goal)
2. W. Doonan
3. B. Reilly
4. P. Smith
5. P. J. Duke
6. Comdt. J. J. O'Reilly (Capt.)
7. Lt. S. Deignan
8. C. McDyer
9. P. Brady
10. T. Tighe
11. M. Higgins
12. T. P. O'Reilly
13. J. Stafford
14. P. Donohue
15. E. Carolan
16. J. Wilson
17. T. Sheridan
18. O. R. McGovern
19. J. J. Cassidy
20. D. Donagher
21. T. O'Reilly
23. E. Tiernan

Hughie O'Reilly

*The man described as 'the old reliable'. Asked by a reporter before
the 1948 All-Ireland final how Cavan would do, he replied: "well*

The head and the heart: With his captain, John Joe, at training in Ballyjamesduff

Ready for action: Hughie during his playing days.

Reluctant star: Signing autographs after yet another famous win.

Eyes of a legend: Hughie O'Reilly pictured at a Cavan match in the late 1970s.

John Joe O'Reilly

"John Joe belonged, not to Cavan only, but to all of us no matter what county we come from, who appreciate a gentleman, a soldier and a Gael."

Tony Myles, The Irish Press

Wedding bells: John Joe on the day of his marriage in 1945.

Men of honour: John Joe with Michael O'Hehir and Kerry captain Dinny Lyne.

Glory days: With trainer Hughie O'Reilly, chairman Patsy Lynch and Mr Sam Maguire in 1948.

The greatest: After being named on the Team of the Millennium in 1999, John Joe was honoured with his own postage stamp. There was some surprise that An Post got the great man's name wrong.

John Joe O'Reilly *(continued)*

The youngest Commandant in the Irish army, John Joe was ear-marked for the very top from the day he entered the Cadets, as these internal military memos show…

❶

Cadet School,
The Military College,
Curragh Command.

2nd May, 1938.

Confidential Report : Easter 1938

No.76322 Cadet O'Reilly, John J.

GENERAL CHARACTER

Conduct — Excellent.

Personality — A very fine type. Industrious, conscientious, and thoroughly reliable.

EDUCATIONAL PROGRESS

Ability — Above average.

Application — Good.

Class Standing — Above average.

PHYSICAL CHARACTERISTICS

Appearance — Good.

Athletic Standard — Very fine all-rounder.

Health — Good.

GENERAL REMARKS

This is an excellent type who should prove an acquisition to any Unit.

_____ Major
(L. Egan)

Cadet Master : Cadet School

❷

...retary.

(.copy) ...mitte...r...h.tiag.
Cutped liuut. ....cuugeon.

The above-named officers who are members of the teams playing in the all ireland football in ...s...ch 14th september have applied for 14 days leave under the provisions of para-16(2) which remain...

...in very exceptional circumstances the Minister may authorise the granting of special leave up to a maximum of fourteen days in any one financial year provido. that ordinary leave is not available.

...he leave provides for in this paragraph of the regulations is normally granted for the purpose of international athletics and it is recommende. that the all-ireland football final is now one he regarded as an international event for the purpose of granting the leave.

All the officers will be granted their full entitlement of annual leave(s) and Carry-over leave(s) before they avail of this special leave.

...flias. .elonel.
Adjutant General.

23rd August, 1947.

(Major for the purpose of travelling to ...s.A.)

S.6

For nece-sary, action, please.

...h. Aj.G.-y.

Brigadier.

General.

Will you please see minute above from the Adjutant

...eneral. In my opinion as Cadet regard the event mentioned as an internationol one. The question of special leave is not therefore covered by regulations.

❸

COP.

B.A.G.A. F... ... COL...E... IN SA... ... ...N...AL...A...
SPECIAL REPORT ON CADET – No.8 BATTLE COURSE

– Capt J.J. O'Reilly – race ja*

A very good leader, forceful and full of character. Displayed great keenness and goes easy with a good grasp of what has been taught at the school. "ants to be a little more clear Ra...lic, an he could be really first class.

(signed); ... ... Gibbons, Lieut-Col.
Commandant, B.V.N.I. Junior Leaders' ... ...
(CO-OOL.

...Capt. J.J. Reilly
On the 29th November 2/Lt. C. Gleeson returned from Northern Ireland and was admitted to St. Bricin's Hospital suffering from a leg injury.

(Sgd.) T. O'Higgins. MAJOR
26.11.1942.

❹

...retary.

(.copy) ...mitte...r...h.tiag.
Cutped liuut. ....cuugeon.

The above-named officers who are members of the teams playing in the all ireland football in ...s...ch 14th september have applied for 14 days leave under the provisions of para-16(2) which remain...

...in very exceptional circumstances the Minister may authorise the granting of special leave up to a maximum of fourteen days in any one financial year provido. that ordinary leave is not available.

...he leave provides for in this paragraph of the regulations is normally granted for the purpose of international athletics and it is recommende. that the all-ireland football final is now one he regarded as an international event for the purpose of granting the leave.

...flias. .elonel.
Adjutant General.

23rd August, 1947.

(Major for the purpose of travelling to ...s.A.)

S.6

For necessary, action, please.

...h. Aj.G.-y.

Brigadier.

General.

Will you please see minute above from the Adjutant

...eneral. In my opinion we cannot regard the event mentioned as international one. The question of special leave is not therefore covered by regulations.

In the granting of leave to an officer, I suggest we approach it on the merits of the case and request sanction ... ...internal... leave required.

Mick Higgins

A brilliant schemer who, at 25, returned to the city of his birth, New York, to lead the Cavan attack against the Kingdom.

"I won't keep you out long in the rain": Mick Higgins accepts Sam as captain in 1952.

The brains of the team: Mick Higgins surveys his options (right).

The Men Behind Maguire

Booking their tickets: The Cavan team which played Roscommon in the 1947 All-I
Tony Tighe, Peter Donohoe, Terry Sheridan, Eunan Tiernan, Jim Deignan, Phil Brac
Front row: Joe Stafford (partially hidden), Willie Doonan, Simon Deignan, John Jo

semi-final.. **Back (from left):** John Wilson, Columba McDyer, Edwin Carolan,
Hughie Smyth, Brian O'Reilly and Paddy Smith.
Reilly, TP O'Reilly, Mick Higgins, Val Gannon, Owen Roe O'Reilly and Dan Danaher.

The journey begins

Sailing away with a precious cargo, bound for New York, the group left on September 1.

Plain sailing: The group of Cavan and Kerry players and officials set off from Cobh on the Mauretania.

All clear: Paddy Smith's letter from the doctor to confirm that he had received his vaccinations.

Full deck: The Cavan and Kerry parties on the Mauretania.

Ship shape

The Kerrymen who sailed were sea-faring types, the men from land-locked Cavan far from it. They got along famously.

Boys of Liverpool: Players pose on the way to New York on the ship.

Board game: Patsy Lynch displays his skills to John Joe Cassidy, Eunan Tiernan and, standing, Big Tom O'Reilly on the Mauretania. The original caption for the photo was headed "IRISH SOCCER PLAYERS ARRIVE".

"Then the turbulence started and it was horrific. The plane shook and jolted, drinks were spilled and stomachs jumped. Sleepers were awakened. It was dark outside and nobody had been on a plane before. The best and bravest footballers in Ireland were frightened."

All aboard: The parties board the plane in Rineanna on September 6, 1947.

Phil 'The Gunner' Brady

'Jaysus,' I says to Phil the Gunner, 'they're carrying them off'. '"Well, if I had've known that,' he says, 'they'd have needed a few stretchers!'" **Mickey Walsh**

Just the ticket:
Phil 'The Gunner'
Brady's passport
and his boarding
pass to New York.

CHAPTER FOURTEEN

The Trip

THOSE travelling by boat left Cavan first, skipping town from Bally'duff early on the morning of Monday, September 8, en route to Dublin. There they stayed the night, taking the train to Cork the following morning. For Patsy Lynch, the journey south was particularly memorable. On the way down, he met his future bride, Ms Lilian Farrelly, from the Old Cabra Road in Dublin, who was on her way to Cobh to embark on a holiday in the US.

The pair would be married a couple of years later and had three children.

On Wednesday, the Cavan delegation reached Cobh and finally boarded the Mauretania.

Back on home turf, their teammates were counting down the hours before they too hit the road. It was Sunday before they did, leaving from Ballyjamesduff with the cheers of hundreds of supporters ringing in their ears.

The county board had hired a handful of cars from Flood's of Cavan town for the first leg of the trek.

The first stop was Dublin, and Croke Park, where the players took in the All-Ireland hurling final between Kilkenny and Cork. In a portent of things to come, the match was a classic and was instantly recognised as the best All-Ireland hurling final of all time.

Kilkenny had lost the previous two finals, having been trounced by the Rebels in the '46 decider, and 61,000 packed into Jones' Rd to see if they could win a first decider since the 'Thunder And Lightning Final' eight years earlier.

The Cork defence was more or less impregnable when it came to goals, so Kilkenny opted for points, and shot some amazing scores from long range to move 0-7 to 0-3 ahead at half-time.

With 10 minutes to go, Terry Leahy sent Kilkenny two points clear after weathering a Cork storm but a Mossy O'Riordan rocket to the net nudged Cork in front for the first time. Tom Walton and

Leahy, twice, pointed for Cork but with time almost up, the Rebels goaled again.

From the puck-out, the Cats attacked and Leahy converted a free and on the stroke of full-time, Leahy, from Urlingford, held his head to fire over from 30 yards for the winner.

The crowd erupted, and Leahy was chaired off the field. There was a Polo Grounds link, of course – Leahy's sister would marry reserve Cavan forward John Joe Cassidy, then on the Mauretania halfway across the Atlantic as his teammates watched a wondrous match unfold.

*　　*　　*

The Cavan party had a light lunch in the city before driving to Naas, where they stopped for tea in Lawlor's. Then it was off to Limerick, where they were greeted by Col JP Murphy, a Cavan player of old, and a few of his army colleagues.

In one of a thousand neat tie-ins in the story of this final, the colonel had played for Cavan against Kerry 22 years earlier in Tralee, a game which resulted in a famous objection which saw Cavan and Kerry both thrown out of the championship.

Nothing was booked in Limerick and, on arrival, there was no room at the inn. Kerry were already in situ at Sadlier's Imperial Hotel, which sported the colours of both counties alongside the Stars and Stripes, so Cavan, accompanied by a handful of supporters including Tony Tighe's sister and Bailieborough doctor Phil Carroll, the team medic at training, took off for Ennis.

The Kerryman's report on the journey outward contained some prophetic words.

> "When we left Tralee on Sunday afternoon, Donal O'Keeffe, young son of Kerry's famous goalkeeper 'Danno', was among the cheering kids who gave us a hearty send-off," the paper noted. "Donal, though he does not know it now, witnesses the start of an event which in later years

he will look back on and boast of having witnessed. And when we all grow old – those of us who will get time to grow old – we will tell future generations of how the first teams to play an All-Ireland final in New York took off by plane, away back in 1947, when flying was still an adventure."

The greatest adventure in the history of the GAA was only starting.

*   *   *

The groups were due to fly from Rineanna the next morning at 11.30am. The usual journey time was 12 hours but the flight had scheduled to land in the Azores en route for re-fuelling, due to a heavy load.

And the man who, more than any other, made it all happen was waiting in Limerick.

Canon Hamilton, who incidentally couldn't be persuaded to make the trip, despite the best efforts of officials in the preceding weeks, delivered a typically stirring address to both teams, stating that they were "going out to engage in the match with intense rivalry but would act as a united body to uphold the grandeur of their Irish games".

The players finally boarded the TWA Skymaster 'Moulmein Padoka', but high winds, and a dispute with pilots over the weight of the luggage, saw the flight delayed.

It was 6.25 in the evening when the party of 40 footballers, officials and press finally took to the skies, and left their lives behind...

Meanwhile, on the Mauretania, all was well. The ship had been too large to dock at Cobh and passengers boarded a tender to take them out.

Players from both sides mingled freely, relaxed, had an odd drink but there were no sessions. Patsy Lynch did some light training with the Cavan players – running on the deck and swimming in the pool

– but mostly, it was a case of relaxing, writing postcards and enjoying the trip.

The weather was fine, although in the middle of the ocean, the seas got rough and some passengers struggled with sea-sickness. On the third night, they were especially bad.

The Kerrymen, though, weren't affected. When they had met to decide who would travel by air and who by sea, the likes of Paddy 'Bawn' Brosnan, a fisherman, Batt Garvey and the other west Kerry players chose the boat. They loved the water, and sea-sickness was never a worry.

On the fourth morning, after the rough weather, Garvey and a few others came down for breakfast and while their table was full, most of the passengers were too ill to eat. Garvey was amused by the sight and, tucking into their breakfasts, asked an English waiter who would win if there was a prize for eating most food on the trip.

"If you stopped eating now for the rest of the journey, you would still win," came the reply.

*   *   *

It was 17 hours before the footballers and their entourage left the confined spaces of the plane for a significant length of time again. At the start, songs had been sung but the novelty soon wore off and some slept.

Then the turbulence started and it was horrific. The plane shook and jolted, drinks were spilled and stomachs jumped. Sleepers were awakened. It was dark outside and nobody had been on a plane before. The best and bravest footballers in Ireland were frightened.

When the flight got jumpy, the men looked around at each other. Maybe Paddy Smith was right. They shuffled in their seats, grasped the hand rests. Finally, TP O'Reilly, not a religious fanatic by any stretch, took out some beads and started the boys saying the rosary.

"We were more tense travelling on the plane than we were playing the football. It was more nerve-wracking," recalled Higgins.

At 1.40am, Irish time, the plane landed at Santa Maria on the Azores. They were allowed 45 minutes to wander around the airport, where the officials had difficulty with the Irish names (Tony Tighe was rendered as 'Tiggy', a nickname which stuck) but at Gander, in Newfoundland – often referred to as the most Irish place outside of Ireland and the only one to have its own Gaelic name, *Talaimh an Éisc* – the party disembarked and took breakfast, most opting for tea and muffins with maple syrup.

Hughie O'Reilly was a man of habit, though, and he ordered eggs. Asked by the waitress how he wanted them, sunnyside up or turned over, he boomed "Sunnyside up, me giirrrlll!"

The group laughed. They were tired but in good spirits; it was all new. Standing beside the footballers in Gander Airport were a delegation of five Arabian princes, in full desert dress, carrying swords and guns. This really was a new world.

* * *

The worst of it was over (little did the players know that for four hours on the way over, the plane had lost all contact with air traffic control). The back was broken in the journey. Surely, it wouldn't be long now.

Except it was. When they reboarded, they were informed by the crew that one engine wasn't functioning properly. Off they got again and returned to the airport to play the waiting game.

After three and a half hours, they eventually took off for a third time, but there would be another stop, this time in Boston, where the parties were greeted by city officials, including some of the Kennedy family.

When the wheels touched down, it was 11.25pm on Tuesday night and a cheer rang out among the passengers. Finally, they had made it.

Big Apple

ONE man didn't hang around the Big Apple. Martin O'Neill, the veteran tasked with reffing the most famous, and perhaps most important, All-Ireland final of all time, had been the first man to leave Ireland, departing from Cobh in mid-August.

The day after he arrived, O'Neill made his way to Grand Central Station and, eventually, far from the madding crowd, to Chicago to where his father's brother was employed in construction.

While the hype grew in the Irish enclaves of New York, O'Neill relaxed in the Windy City. He would stay 10 days with his uncle to avoid mixing with the teams and the entourages, which were growing by the day as the eyes of the east coast became fixated on the match.

He wasn't the type to get excited in any case. As full-time secretary of the Leinster Council, a job he would hold for over four decades, he had seen it all in the association.

A tall, thin man, he was an excellent all-rounder in his youth. As a child in Ferns, he started to play handball against the wall of the castle. When the family moved to Bray after Martin's father began working in the GPO (he would commute from the seaside town to the city centre each day), his handball career took off. With a friend, Luke Sherry, they would take off on summer weekend mornings to enter doubles tournaments in Talbot's Inch and Green Street, Castlebridge, Delvin and all the other hamlets where the game prospered, bringing home trophies and suits of clothes as prizes.

At 21, he won a Leinster SFC title with Wexford and 11 years later, in 1936, he would captain Wicklow to an All-Ireland junior football crown. O'Neill also found time to win three Railway Cup medals, to represent Ireland in football in three Tailteann Games and to win an All-Ireland senior handball doubles title, then a very, very tough championship to annex.

In the late 1920s, he married a girl from Croghan, outside

Boyle, a lady called O'Dowd, and built a house on Bray Head and, shortly afterwards, was appointed full-time Leinster Council secretary. In time, the couple would have seven sons, all of whom kicked football or hurled. The eldest two, Micheál and Martin, excelled with the big ball and would represent Wexford in the 1950s and 60s.

By then, Martin was back home. In 1944, a Mrs Sweetman, an elderly Catholic woman who was living in Ferns, had died and, at a time of "a love divided" as the film termed it, when there was a certain amount of competition between religions in the region, it was deemed essential that her farm mustn't fall into Protestant hands. A priest approached O'Neill and he acceded, buying Charlesfort House, near Townbracken.

By September '47, the wheel had come full circle. Martin's uncle had been born less than a mile from Charlesfort, the ancestral O'Neill home, where Martin now lived. As uncle and nephew whiled away the days before Martin's return to New York, they would have spoken about the old country, about family and, more than anything else, about football and hurling.

The games were in the O'Neill DNA. Martin's father had been a delegate at the very early Congresses of the GAA in the late 1880s, and played with Ferns. He, in time, had a houseful of children, 12 of whom survived. Martin was the eldest of eight boys and four girls. In 1945, two of his brothers, Des and Joe (who was the youngest) won a Leinster SFC title, Des at centre half-back, Joe in goals. They were fancied to go further but ran into Cavan in the semi-final.

Before a record attendance of 44,526, a full 4,000 more than the previous record set in the Kerry v Carlow clash in '43, Cavan, inspired by Simon Deignan and with a goal from Joe Stafford (who else?), won a dour match by 1-4 to 0-5. For the O'Neill boys and Wexford, for whom Nicky Rackard lined out at full-forward, it was a bitter day; up to 2013, the county would never win the Leinster senior football title again.

Another O'Neill brother, Paddy, would in time become sports editor of The Anglo-Celt newspaper, writing under the name PJ

O'Neill, before going on to edit the Waterford News and Star. The family's tentacles, then, spread far and wide in the Association. They were steeped in it.

At Christmas, the brothers would meet up and, over a whiskey or two, the chat would turn to who was the best footballer the clan had produced. Des generally got the nod, with another brother, Colm – a nifty full-forward with Wexford in his day – gaining an honourable mention.

The trip to New York, during which Martin celebrated his 43rd birthday, was his first time in America, and it was a poignant one. Meeting old acquaintances and viewing at first-hand the impact of emigration on the displaced masses affected him greatly.

"I honestly think I cried more in New York than I did in my whole life at home," he would recall later in life.

"It was very touching to see the strains of emigration at close range and to watch the effect the game had on those exiles who, probably, would never again set foot on our Irish shores."

He played handball in the Tailteann Games, too, running into Clare-born Mickey Maloney on all three occasions, a man he would, by coincidence, bump into in the Woodstock Hotel on the night before the final in New York.

Although he played club football until he was in his 40s, O'Neill had by then been refereeing for almost two decades and had been the man in the middle in the 1932 Kerry v Mayo All-Ireland final and the following year's decider between Cavan and Galway.

It was a shock, though, when he was appointed to ref his third decider 14 years later, as he admitted himself. He had effectively come out of refereeing retirement for one night only; the difference was, this wasn't the entertainment business. The GAA needed a firm hand and turned to a man who had served them maybe better than any single official to that point in their 60-year history.

"I was a bit surprised when both counties agreed to my appointment. I often wondered afterwards if it had anything to do with the fact that since I, as provincial secretary, was entitled to go in any case, their agreement to such an appointment enabled both counties to take an extra substitute," he remembered.

One thing was for certain – Martin O'Neill wasn't going to be overawed by the occasion.

*   *   *

At the other end of the spectrum were the young guns, Duke, Tighe, Eunan Tiernan and a man who, possibly more than any other from the Polo Grounds, became a by-word for heroic, old-school football – Phil 'The Gunner' Brady.

The Gunners came to Mullahoran from Crosskeys, 12 miles away to the east.

The origin of the name is clouded in doubt. Some say it was because the old people of the Bradys were great hunstmen, which they were, or because they were active in the Fenians in the middle of the 19th century. Others prefer to recount the story of Danny Brady and the Black and Tans.

Danny fought on the Republican side during the War of Independence, during which he spent time on hunger strike in Ballykinlar. Later, he would be interned in the Curragh during the Civil War.

During that time, he was a wanted man, looking over his shoulder. One evening, word reached the homestead in Loughduff. The Black and Tans are coming for Danny, or words to that effect.

The hated 7,000-strong British militia, rounded up mainly among the dregs of unemployed World War One veterans and despised for their violent reprisals against innocent civilians, had been after Brady for a while and set off from Ballinagh, seven miles away.

Brady, they say, scarpered out the back door and vaulted a wall, just as the Tans arrived and opened fire. His hand was still resting on the wall and a bullet smashed it, taking the tops off a couple of his fingers, the blood gushing like a set of geysers, as he took off up the fields. The intruders didn't get their man.

The ordeal wasn't over, however. Blood poisoning set in and

Brady's comrades had to sneak him to a sympathetic doctor in Cavan.

Lesser men would have folded but the Gunner kept on going, raising 13 children with his wife and playing football for two decades after.

His last big game was the junior championship final of 1940, when he lined out at corner-forward. Coming on to the team at the time was his son Philip, then a big-boned 16-year-old. Mullahoran won and the old man retired; his sons carried the torch.

Phil was the third youngest and coming in the middle of a run of six girls, spoiled rotten.

He first came to prominence as a footballer in the 1944 county championship when he eclipsed Big Tom, then a veteran but still one of the best midfielders in the country.

The following year, he won his first Ulster senior medal, but, even by '46, he was still regarded as a *gasun*, albeit a ferociously strong and competitive one.

All that would change the following year. The arrival of young guns like Tighe, Carolan and, especially, the Gunner, completed Cavan's jigsaw.

His reputation as a combative player was carved out immediately on his arrival to the senior team. He fitted in like a hand in a glove. The Gunner, it quickly became clear, was born for the big stage.

* * *

It was known, at the time, as the Wonder City.

America was rejoicing in the post-War period; it's always darkest before the dawn and that's what the period immediately following World War II was – America had never been brighter, or more optimistic, and New York City was a glittering jewel in the crown.

It couldn't have been more different to dreary old Ireland, still hemmed in by church and politics, the great haemorrhage of the young and confident and ambitious only beginning to reach full flow. In New York, emigrants were arriving by the thousand, attracted to the jobs, the excitement and the genuine allure of the American dream. It was a land hewn from fairytale, almost. For two groups of footballers and their entourages, it wasn't so much the New World as a dream world, and they were living it.

In 1950, what writers would term 'The Long Boom' would begin in earnest but the seeds were sown immediately after the war and had grown into saplings by '47. Between October of '45 and November '48, employment growth was almost 18 per cent.

As EB White wrote in the New Yorker, then in its pomp, "no-one should come to New York to live unless he is willing to be lucky". Luck, a life, a pot of gold at the end of the rainbow, it was all there for the taking...

* * *

He was a struggling square-jawed young actor when he arrived at the broken-down hovel in Provincetown, clad in Levi's, notes in hand.

He had borrowed the fare from New York, setting off with hope and not much else in his luggage.

When he arrived at dusk, he met Tennessee Williams at the door. "Come in," said the author, waving the kid in to a house strewn with people, the plumbing busted, the light switch flickering. He dropped his bag and rolled up his sleeves, fixing the overflowing toilet bowl, sorting out the fuse box. An hour later, the house was ticking like a clock, and he cleared his throat and read his lines.

It was the most magnificent reading Williams had ever heard, and the part of Stanley Kowalski was his. The kid curled up on the floor in a tattered quilt, exhausted, and next morning, took off. By December, A Streetcar Named Desire was the toast of Broadway, playing to packed houses at the Ethel Barrymore Theatre in Midtown Manhattan. Stanley was smouldering; a star was born.

That was the story of Marlon Brando in 1947; in many ways, it

was the story of New York in that year, too. If you had the pluck, and
the luck, anything was possible.

* * *

America was booming and New York was the torchlight at the
head of the procession, a landing place for emigrants, a place
apart.

In early March of '47, an American businessman had arrived in
the city by bus from Mexico. Within days, he was dead, bowled over
by the dreaded and highly-contagious smallpox. Panic spread but
the NY Health Department's response was incredible for the time.

Police, fire and health departments were mobilised after Mayor
O'Dwyer recommended that all 7.8 million inhabitants of the city
get the jab. A catch cry of "Be sure, be safe, get vaccinated" was
plastered on billboards and the problem was nipped in the bud.
Within days in April, over a million were vaccinated and the total
would run to over six million that month. It was staggeringly
efficient, a confident, assertive response the like of which no other
city in the world in that era could have mustered.

* * *

Mack Robinson was one of six kids raised in abject poverty by
a single mother in rural Cairo, Georgia, a poor little town of a few
thousand nicknamed, perhaps ironically, the Syrup City. He showed
an aptitude for sports and in time would make the American track
and field team, winning a silver medal at the 1936 Olympics in Berlin
in the 200-metre dash, with only Jesse Owens beating him to the
tape (by 0.4 seconds) as Adolf Hitler looked on.

He should have returned a hero but this was America, and this
was the 1930s. Old feelings died hard – Mack returned to Pasadena,
to where the family had moved, filed away his medal and found that
the only employer willing to give him a job was the owner of a refuse
collection company. So, one of the fastest men on the planet was

back on civvy street, reincarnated as a hired hand on a battered old garbage truck.

Jackie was five years younger than Mack and just a 17-year-old kid when big brother won his medal. Watching the family's Olympic hero bring out the rubbish for a living hurt. He was determined he wouldn't walk the same path.

Inspired by Mack and another brother, Frank, he soon began breaking records, lettering in four sports – basketball, football, "track" and baseball – in high school and junior college. Towards the end of his time in the latter, Frank was killed in a motorcycle accident. Jackie, who had already been given a two-year suspended sentence for protesting against what he saw as a racist decision by police to detain a friend, threw himself into college, and sport.

He was destined for the summit and he got there the hard way, never sacrificing his principles. After being drafted, he ended up court-martialled for refusing to sit at the back of what was ostensibly a non-racially segregated bus.

He spent time playing football and coaching basketball before signing for the Kansas City Monarchs team, plying their trade in the Negro Leagues in early 1945. The New York connection, for which he became most famous, began that August 28, 10 days after Cavan had beaten Wexford in the All-Ireland semi-final, when Branch Rickey, club president and general manager of the Brooklyn Dodgers, met him for three hours to discuss a contract.

Chief among Rickey's concerns was whether Robinson could handle the inevitable racist abuse without reacting angrily, as he had done in college and the military.

In a famous exchange, Robinson asked Rickey: "Are you looking for a Negro who is afraid to fight back?" to which the baseball chief is said to have replied that he needed a black player "with guts enough not to fight back".

Robinson wasn't necessarily the best player in the Negro Leagues, but he was of flawless character and Rickey took the plunge.

Jackie was originally shipped out to the Dodgers' farm team, the

Montreal Royals in the Minor League, where he suffered a torrent of bigotry, some of it from inside his own dressing-room, all of which he ignored. After a season, the Dodgers, then so hapless that they were nicknamed 'The Bums', needed Robinson and in April 1947, he became the first black player to line out in the International League since the 1880s.

On the 15th of that month, he made his Major League debut at Ebbets Field before 26,623 spectators, over 14,000 of them black. Initially, rival teams threatened to strike if he played and even some Dodgers players warned that they would sit out rather than play with him.

But the club stood tall. A week after his debut, the Philadelphia Phillies manager Ben Chapman called Robinson "a nigger" from the dug-out and suggested he should "go back to the cotton fields". Rickey would later recall that Chapman's comments caused the Dodgers to rally around Robinson.

"When he poured out that string of unconscionable abuse, he solidified and united 30 men," he said.

Robinson was an instant hit and his arrival heralded the dawn of the greatest decade in New York baseball history, during which a team from the city contested the World Series every year bar 1948 and New York, as in most aspects of life at the time, led the nation.

By the end of the 1947 season, Robinson received the inaugural MLB Rookie of the Year award and was the toast of New York. Two years later, he was named as the league's Most Valuable Player. He helped the Dodgers win six pennants and a World Series and would be inducted into the Hall of Fame in 1962, by which time his courageous stance was already being cited as a launchpad for the Civil Rights Movement.

On April 15 1997, 50 years to the day since he played that first game at Ebbets Field, Major League Baseball would retire his number, 42, the first athlete to be honoured in such a way.*

Three thousand miles away, on that same Tuesday morning, incidentally, Liam Horan in the Irish Independent broke the story that Cavan and Kerry would play a National League match in

New York that October to commemorate the 50th anniversary of the Polo Grounds final.

"There is huge interest in the game in the United States. Already, 700 people have booked to travel from Cavan and 500 from Kerry," New York GAA official Terry Connaughton told Horan.

*   *   *

Since 2004, every player on every team wears the number for one day only, Jackie Robinson Day.

He now has a day, but in 1947, he had a year and New York had it all. And in September, to Brando and Robinson, you could add Higgins and Lyne and Donohoe and Tighe. It was a city of characters and the cast had never been more colourful.

CHAPTER SIXTEEN

Hero Returns

FOR one man, New York was something new and yet, it was nothing new at all. Mick Higgins was simply returning home.

Cavan's centre half-forward was born in New York on August 22, 1922, the day Michael Collins was shot dead in Béal na mBláth. Higgins' father, John, was a native of Kiltimagh, Co Mayo.

To make ends meet in a foreign city, John took a job driving a bus. For a while, he worked a bar, learning to deal with the wisecracks, the drunks, happy and angry. These were the men who spent the grocery money, the emigrants who would never return.

Higgins didn't fall into any of those traps. He was a placid man and when he wasn't working, he would run. He joined an athletics club. He liked the running and soon was picking up medals.

In 1927, John loaded up the family and decided to make a clean break for it. John's wife Mary was one of the Farrellys from Kilnaleck. They headed for Cavan.

When they arrived, they stayed a short while and got restless, moving to Kiltimagh, and then back to Kilnaleck, where the family bought a pub from a man called Sheridan. John got into building, putting up a row of houses on the Church Road.

They had a family, five boys and one girl. Mick was the eldest. He started kicking around on the field in his local village, fetching balls from behind the goals when the great Jack Smallhorne, a hero of 1928-33, went down to practise.

When it came time for him to leave the national school in Kilnaleck, where Peter Donohoe was a classmate, Mick was sent to board in the Marist College in Dundalk, where he came under the tutelage of Derry-born Fr MacOscar. In 1938, at 15, he played wing half-forward as the school won its first MacRory Cup. A nascent star had begun a journey which would become stellar.

What separated Higgins from the rest was his smarts. Off the field, he was laid-back and unnervingly modest but on it, he was a winner who could think his way out of trouble.

The year after the Polo Grounds, Cavan would play Louth in the All-Ireland semi-final. At one point, the Louth captain Jim Quigley found himself backing up, eyes on a high ball which had been hoisted towards his team's goal. Quigley was brilliant in the air but this ball was sailing and he'd misjudged it and he ended up leaning back like a man stretching out his window to see was there a fire on his roof.

After an eternity, it dropped and Quigley had it in the left half-back position. The crowd erupted but the Louthman was on the deck and had lost his bearings, the Hogan Stand above, the sky below, the ball still in his grasp. In the second it took him to find his bearings, Higgins appeared.

Now, Quigley, like Mick, who had lined out for St James' Gate on the wing during his time as a bar man in Dublin, had played some soccer under a false name and, to his teammates, his nickname was 'Soccer'. Higgins was by this stage stationed in Drogheda and had heard the name used in passing on the beat, at work and on the pitch where he lined out with the Geraldines, and filed it away in his brain.

With a place in an All-Ireland final at stake, the Louth crowd on their feet after a heroic fetch and their captain taking a second to steady himself, Higgins pounced.

"Soccer, now," he yelped, racing down the line. 'Soccer', dazed and frantic, as footballers are, to off-load before being blown for over-holding, obliged with a hand-pass. The Louth supporters groaned – Mick was away.

He was cute, a schemer whose brilliance allowed him to run a game from the 40, and yet he was one of the cleanest players ever to play the game. Asked in 2008 how he would like to be remembered, Higgins paused a moment and, eschewing his three All-Ireland medals (one as captain), stated earnestly: "That I never hit anybody. I was never put off."

After three years in Louth, the young Higgins left and headed to school in Celbridge, where an uncle-in-law lived. In 1940 he was chosen at midfield on the Kildare minor team, ironically losing the

Leinster final by a point to Louth, who would go on to win the All-Ireland.

The following year, he was working in Louth and played for them and, almost inevitably, they reached the Leinster final again. This time, they played Kildare, and Higgins lost his second final.

He would lose plenty more in his career but it was for the wins, and his brilliantly cool demeanour, that he is remembered.

Peter Brady, a former Cavan county board chairman and publican in Higgins' home town (Kilnaleck, not the Bronx) tells another story to illustrate Higgins' cunning. He wasn't nasty in any way but he carried himself like a champion on the field – the bigger the game, the better he played. It was in an era when Cavan usually just turned up for Ulster fixtures. Training started after that.

"It was easy keeping fit because you had no money," explained Higgins in 2008.

"You went out and played football. It was a different time... there is more money now. In our time there was no money involved. It was just a pastime, that's how you looked at it till you came to the semi-finals. There'd be a bit of pressure on you then."

And that was when he thrived, as Brady discovered when he met Paddy Dixon, a former powerful, old school centre-back for Meath, in Trim Golf Club one night and the talk turned to Higgins.

"Higgins had the ball and he was being marked by Dixon out close to the line," recalled Brady, taking up the story.

"Dixon was a big man and he had his two big hands out like that [extends his hands in front of his chest] and his body spread and Higgins had nearly nowhere to go. It was either get pushed over the line or foul the ball. Next thing, Tony Tighe came running up on the outside very fast and shouted 'right Mick!' and as soon as he did, Higgins put the ball out between Dixon's legs. Now, it was what happened next that ruined Dixon.

"Higgins just gave Dixon a little tap on the jaw. Dixon took it into his head that what Higgins was saying to him was, 'not alone could I have played the ball but I could have broke your jaw as well'. And he said it ruined him for the rest of the game, Higgins psyched him out of it just like that. Just a gentle tap. Ball gone, you're finished. Dixon was an old man at the time and he never forgot it. Never forgot it."

Inside the velvet glove was an iron fist – he was silken on the ball but tough as hell. In an era when forwards received little or no protection, Higgins was as hard as a coffin nail. He needed to be. By stroking Dixon's jaw, he was sending out a message – I'm too fast for you, so don't even think about it.

He was powerfully built but with dancer's feet; he could ship a hit and keep his balance.

And ship them he did – as well as scoring himself, he was the man who loaded weapons for Stafford and Donohoe to fire, and he was singled out. He missed the 1945 All-Ireland final due to injury, and with him went Cavan's chances. The following season ended early when Antrim gate-crashed Cavan's private Ulster party.

By '47, though, Cavan were taking no chances. "We got a big surprise [when the New York decision was announced]," Higgins would recall.

"We couldn't believe it. It was on the go for a while the previous few years but it was always defeated in Congress. We were glad to hear about it, it was another thing to get to it. That was the only time we ever trained for Ulster... We generally won the Ulster Championship and went into collective training for the semi-final. No training for the Ulster final.

"But Antrim beat us the previous year and we decided we'd do a bit of work and not let them beat us again."

His take on the semi-final epic against Roscommon is revealing.

"Roscommon were hot favourites. We beat them too and that was that. They were sure of winning but it didn't work out that way, everything went right for us. It was a good game of football, it was supposed to be one of the best for a long time.

"When you'd be playing it you'd never think whether it was good, as long as you were winning (laughs) I didn't mind. But you couldn't say you got excited about it."

That was Mick's attitude – he was a household name with the

expectations of thousands resting on his shoulders yet, on the big days, was probably the most relaxed man in Croke Park.

Because while Higgins was a football immortal before the phrase was even coined, he retained a remarkable modesty. He was witty and engaging yet shy and quiet, too. His friendship with Doonan, the Garda sergeant half-forward from the country sitting beside the townie, gregarious corner-back, soaking up his infectious confidence, was remarkable, but typical of the man.

His first appearance at Croke Park came in 1942, when he came on as a sub for Cavan against would-be All-Ireland champions Dublin. The Ulster winners were a young team and not given much chance in the papers.

Doonan was having none of it.

"Billy Doonan was a character, he was right full-back," remembered Mick, "and Billy called out as we were about to go out on the field 'come on lads, if you can't play football in Croke Park you can play it nowhere!'"

Higgins loved to talk football but it was the craic from the dressing-room he savoured, funny anecdotes rather than bragging or recalling heady wins. For that as much as his skills, he was universally respected.

When Joe Keohane died in the early 2000s, Higgins and Peter Brady drove to Tralee for his funeral. The ceremony was attended by thousands of Kingdom diehards and, over half a century after the Polo Grounds final, Higgins was mobbed. A group insisted on his accompanying them to a hotel for a drink, where Brady was astonished to see grown men, Kerry football fanatics, sizing Higgins up, some walking behind to check out his build.

Like many a great footballer, you see, Higgins togged out bigger than he looked in his street clothes. He was tremendously muscular, an athlete to his fingertips, but in his Garda uniform or his civvies, his physique wasn't spectacular.

"Chrisht," one of the Kerrymen noted as Brady looked on, amazed, "he's not a big man. How the hell did he get by Joe and Bawn and Dinny and Jackie?"

*　　*　　*

When Cavan needed Higgins most in the Polo Grounds, when their hopes looked to be in the grave, it was he who resurrected them, ghosting behind the defence as the dust rose from the rock-hard earth, picking out passes others couldn't see and tormenting a brash, hard-hitting Kingdom defence.

The bigger the challenge, the better he would perform and they didn't come bigger than this, the most momentous day in the history of the GAA to that point.

It had destiny stamped all over it, and 25-year-old Higgins, back in the city of his birth, history and cheers echoing in his head, played like his life depended on it.

The Week

WHAT struck them more than anything was the heat. It hit the Irishmen like a sledge hammer when they came ashore in Manhattan and, later, when the door of the jet slid open.

The players' shirts clung to their backs as they stepped on the dock to be greeted by a horde of well-wishers and pressmen.

The New York Times were on hand to capture the 14 players and 11 officials, noting the names of only two of the footballers – Lieut Joseph Keohane and William Doonan who "was an infantry machine gunner in the British Army during the war and was wounded three times while serving in North Africa and Italy, where he was attached to the United States Fifth Army".

"Do we have to play in this heat?" one incredulous player, who remained nameless, was quoted in The Irish Press.

When the other party landed at the airport that evening at 6.30pm local time, suited and booted in shirts and ties, they were equally struck by the 85 degree weather.

Said Higgins: "It was overcoming, the heat. If you opened a window, it was warmer."

The delays had thrown the reception arrangements out of sync but Ó Caoimh had quickly re-organised things. After a good night's sleep, the players rose early on Wednesday morning and began to take in their surroundings. The city was alive.

*   *   *

"The sight of skyscrapers was not a surprise because we had seen them in the cinema," remembered Wilson.

"Instead, the culture shock arrived in smaller ways. The city was full of lights, the shops were full of food, unlike the rationing that had been endured in Ireland and England and the bars all had televisions. The whole city carried an air of prosperity; everything was just go, go, go."

Nothing could have prepared the groups for the welcome that awaited them.

They made their way to City Hall, where a crowd of 2,000 had assembled, to be greeted by the man referred to as "the boy who put the 'r' in Mayo", O'Dwyer.

The Bohola man was in ebullient form.

"When the Dodgers win the National League," he began, only to be drowned out by the rapturous cheers of the crowd.

He soaked it up for a moment and then continued.

"When the Dodgers win, if we were to suggest playing the World Series outside Brooklyn and taking it to Ireland or any other country, I would not accept responsibility for the peace of this city.

"Well, that's parallel to what the GAA are doing in playing this great game in New York, and New York should be proud to welcome this generous offering of the best Ireland has in sport to this country."

Songs were sung and the mood was a carnival one. The New York Police Band played Irish airs and John Feeney, a magnificent tenor from Swinford who was by then huge in the States and commanding 100 bucks a night, belting out The Rose of Tralee with Sean Ryan singing Come Back Paddy Reilly to Ballyjamesduff in response.

From there, the group motored the seven miles, through Riverside Drive, under Manhattan Bridge and up South St, to the Hotel Roosevelt, on 45th St and Madison Ave, and literally brought the city to a standstill. Along Broadway, the wide avenue running north to south down the middle of Manhattan, they were escorted by 18 bright red police motorcyclists, their sirens wailing. Thirty cars carried the Irish party as the rush hour traffic came to a halt. The sidewalks were crammed with crowds straining for a look, while bare-chested workers on scaffolds and high-rise buildings downed tools to cheer and wave.

Confetti and ticker tape rained down from 40-storey-high buildings, a reception usually reserved for July 4 or the election of a new president. "The Irish appeared to have taken over New York," it was reported. "Everywhere, crowds were stupendous."

The brilliant Anna Kelly in the press captured the scene.

From the sidewalks, Irish voices cheered, Irish faces smiled, wistful faces, happy faces, all lighted with love for the country that will always be home. Women wept and waved handkerchiefs.

"How's the turf at home?" some cried.

"Ah, 'tis fine and dry," shouts Mick Finucane.

"Anybody here from Cork, Galway, Mayo...?" and so on.

Two nuns thrust forward. "Any Killarney boys here?" Teddy Sullivan replied.

"Now don't let Kerry down," said the little nuns.

After lunch in the Roosevelt, the players, under the wing of both counties' welcome committees and a Galway man, Commissioner Nolan – chairman of the Police Department's Athletic League – took in some of the sights before returning to rest for the night.

Next day, they trained, Cavan in Van Cortland Park in the Bronx, Kerry in John Kerry O'Donnell's Croke – later Gaelic – Park.

But the heat was ferocious, and training had to be curtailed. The hype was building, too, hurtling towards Sunday like a steam train. The Cavan players, ensconced in the Hotel Empire, found it hard to get a minute's solitude.

"I remember the many meetings with callers and friends; the difficulty to get a peaceful period for rest before the game," Columba McDyer would write.

Fans poured into the city and made tracks for the team hotels, where the squads were inundated with callers, autograph-hunters, strangers and old friends. Kerry, based at the Henry Duson Hotel, could take no more and took off for two days as guests of the New York Athletic Club to Travers Island, where the temperature was cooler, away, wrote Kelly, "from the intense humidity and the burning sidewalks".

While they were gone, Cavan took their place in Croke Park but their training schedule was light.

It needed to be. Edwin Carolan was struggling to overcome an adverse reaction to the inoculation he received at home while the Gunner was taking penicillin for an injury. The news was worse in the Kingdom camp, as they sweated – literally – on the fitness of midfielder Paddy Kennedy, who had been taken off injured in both the Munster final and All-Ireland semi-final win over Meath.

After Wednesday's reception, there was no further contact between the camps, and there wouldn't be until Mass on the morning of the match. Both were struggling to adapt but Kerry, the older of the teams, were finding it particularly hard, as Mitchell Cogley noted in The Irish Independent.

"Popular opinion among Irish-Americans is that neither side have had time to acclimatise themselves and certainly the weather here is something we never experience at home. From early morning to late night, the city is baked in dead and damp heat... I will say I have seen more sign of weather-distress in the Kerry camp than in the opposition..."

The clock ticked on...

*   *   *

All was calm until Friday. A few boxes had been ticked during the week and ticket sales were lively, with all media back at home confidently announcing that the Polo Grounds would be a 55,000 sell-out.

It was announced that a film would be made of the game, to be flown as the first and only cargo on the three new Aer Línte – a sister company to Aer Lingus – planes two days after the match and, after a meeting of the official delegation, the match officials, barring the referee obviously, were selected. The umpires would be Gerry Arthurs and Tom Kilcoyne, secretaries of the Ulster and Connacht Councils respectively and the linesmen appointed were two Irish priests who had come to New York in the previous three months, Fr Hickey from Dublin and Fr Burke, a Corkman.

Malachy Doyle and Tom Burke, two Croke Park officials, would supervise the lining of the pitch.

On Friday morning, then, Cavan followed Kerry's lead and boarded a bus, heading upstate to get away from it all. When they returned, they got a look at the pitch for the first time, and couldn't believe what they were walking on.

At home, it would have been deemed unplayable. There was barely any grass and the ground was concrete-like. It was small, too, and seemed smaller than the bare measurements looked on paper but the most bizarre feature was the pitcher's mound, eighteen feet in diameter and ten inches high in the centre.

"It wasn't real high but when you were going for a ball you had to go up on it," was Higgins' description. "Anyway, some of the pitches in Ireland at the time weren't that great."

Peter Donohoe also played it down.

"It wasn't something you'd trip over. You knew it was there. I wouldn't think it put anyone out of their stride. But when you came from a place like Kilnaleck in Cavan you came across plenty of bad fields and bad football pitches."

The big man, however, conceded that compared to Croke Park, "it was a big disappointment."

Batt Garvey went further.

"It was ridiculous to play a game of football on it," he said, years later, "it was rock-solid, like concrete."

When Martin O'Neill had seen it, he immediately said it wasn't suitable and the mound would have to go. The reaction of the groundsman? "The lad went berserk."

So, the hump was staying, and the teams would make do.

*　　*　　*

That evening, however, another crisis was developing behind the scenes, one that threatened to derail the success of the whole project.

When Michael O'Hehir was shown around the commentary

position early on Friday, his heart skipped a beat. The place was bare, no lines, no equipment and, seemingly, no hope of sending back any type of commentary on the game.

"To my astonishment there were no wires to be seen anywhere to suggest that the required broadcast lines from the international telephone exchange had been installed," he reflected.

"Panic. The caretaker knew nothing about a broadcast, so I hastened back to the hotel and immediately told Paddy O'Keeffe [Ó Caoimh] that no provision seemed to have been made for the broadcast. It even looked as if I might not have anything to do on the Sunday."

Born in Glasnevin, O'Hehir was 27 years old by the time of the Polo Grounds final and already established as "the voice of Gaelic games." While Radio Éireann had first broadcast a live match commentary as far back as 1926, the first station in Europe to do so, on any sport, it was when O'Hehir took over on the microphone that a new tradition was born – hundreds of thousands gathering around the nearest radio set.

He had applied for an audition with the broadcaster as a teenager and was handed his first major gig, the All-Ireland semi-final between Dublin in Monaghan in Mullingar, aged just 18 in 1938. While his technique was described as "folksy", he had an ingenious ability to capture the imagination, rolling his tongue around exotic club names and playing up the sobriquets of footballers and hurlers.

When a radio commentary from America had been first mooted and to put it in context, when Cavan played Kerry just 20 years earlier in Tralee, the first word on the game to reach Breffni was via carrier pigeon, O'Hehir's name was immediately mentioned. It had to be him. When Cavan formally requested it, the GAA wheels started to turn, but they faced significant resistance from the off.

Ó Caoimh reported to Central Council that he had had "consultations with the broadcasting authorities here with a view to having the running commentary of the game broadcast" but the path was not a smooth one.

Money, as always, was the main stumbling block; Radio Éireann were working off a tight budget and the cost of the commentary from New York, estimated at around £300, wasn't part of it.

At the time, the broadcaster was answerable to the Department of Posts and Telegraphs.

As luck would have it, Radio Éireann's Director of Broadcasting at the time was Seamus Ó Braonáin, a Kilkenny native who had won four All-Ireland football championships with Dublin in the early years of the century, back when he was known simply as Jimmy Brennan.

Ó Braonáin, a GAA fanatic who helped draft the first ever set of rules for camogie, was strongly in favour of the broadcast and approached Sean Moynihan, then Secretary of the Department of Finance and a man with zero interest in the association.

The story goes that Moynihan's reply to Ó Braonáin was: "Tell me, Seamus, does anybody listen to these football matches?"

The money wasn't being released, then, and the negotiations started. Eventually, it was agreed that Radio Éireann would send O'Hehir so long as the GAA covered his flight, hotel and expenses. Deal done, they relayed the news to the commentator, who was equally famous as a horseracing announcer.

After receiving his vaccinations, O'Hehir, not unusually for the recently-vaccinated at the time, fell ill and in mid-August, he had to leave the races at Tramore, where he was working, due to sickness.

Luckily, he recovered in time, but, two days out from the game, it appeared that all the effort would be in vain. That was until Ó Caoimh got to work.

His report on the trip told the story succinctly.

As I wished to determine where on the field to place the commentator's box, I tried to ascertain who on the New York side had charge of the arrangements for the broadcast," he reported to Croke Park.

I cabled Radio Éireann for the name of the responsible

party and, on receipt of their reply, contacted the Columbia Broadcasting System, only to be told that they knew nothing of the matter. A representative of that body informed me that they only supplied equipment and had nothing to do with the relay lines, the American Telephone and Telegraph Company being responsible for that end of the work. However, ATT also informed me that they knew nothing about a broadcast of our proposed game.

This was late on Friday afternoon, and panic was beginning to set in. A broadcast, which would eventually attract a million listeners, was almost still-born.

"Time was running out and after exhausting my patience on the phone, I went to the CBS at 5.30pm on Friday evening to ensure that the equipment would be available, as my informant told me their staff did not work on Saturdays. From there, contact was again made with an ATT official, who agreed to arrange the lines when I promised payment. I returned to the office and decided to ring Ireland to find out the position there. I also cabled Radio Éireann to ring me so that the position could be clarified."

Ó Caoimh, unbeknownst to the hundreds of thousands of supporters at home, was a worried man on the Friday night but, at 1pm (local time) the following day, the word he had been praying for arrived.

A cable from Radio Éireann's offices on the top floor of the GPO re-assured him that all was sorted. Then, ATT got in touch to say that it was all systems go – the match would be broadcast and Radio Éireann had promised payment for the supplying of equipment at the ground. The Secretary General breathed a sigh of relief.

*   *   *

Meanwhile, something was stirring in the Irish Independent newsroom back in Dublin. All of the to-ing and fro-ing, the worried expressions and the whisper of problems had alerted their reporter

Mitchell Cogley, who was also staying in the Woodstock Hotel along with the official GAA party.

So, Cogley wrote the piece at its height and filed his copy. The Evening Herald dropped on Saturday evening, carrying word that the broadcast was in doubt, and the Sunday Indo carried the story again the following morning.

"A last-minute crisis developed among the GAA contingent when they were informed late on Friday night by the Columbia Broadcasting System, who are handling the technical details here, that certain vital details had been overlooked by Radio Éireann and there might not be any broadcast of the game possible," said the Independent.

Hearts sank in Cavan and Kerry and everywhere else. By the time the problems were fixed, a statement was rushed out which made the later editions of the Sunday paper confirming the commentary would go ahead.

The match was set to begin at 8.30pm and, not only that, the coverage was to be preceded by a special documentary looking back on 60 years in the GAA.

By late Sunday night and with an enormously-successful transmission behind them, Radio Éireann would hit back. The station would refute the newspaper's story that there had been a hitch or that the broadcast was ever in doubt, with Deputy Director of Broadcasting Roibeard Ó Farachain denying there had been any uncertainty. By that stage, though, it mattered little. The day, for the million people huddled around the wireless back in Ireland, had been saved.

Fairytale in New York

CHAPTER EIGHTEEN

The Stadium

FAST-forward three years to July 4, 1950 and Barney Doyle was up early, pottering around his home in Fairview, New Jersey.

A burly, 54-year-old Dublin native, Barney had been living in the US for over three decades. A ship's carpenter by trade, he was between jobs and had plenty of time to indulge his hobbies of baseball and boxing.

The big man had once managed fighters in small hall shows in Jersey, with James J Braddock, a future world heavyweight champion at a time when the title may as well have read 'world king', once a name on his books.

Today was a big day. After early Mass and a hurried breakfast, he left his home at 8.30am, stopping to collect a freckled, goofy kid called Otto Flaig, 13-year-old son of a friend, and the pair headed for the Polo Grounds. It was Giants v Dodgers today, you see, and Barney was a Giants man, through and through. Unlike Braddock's, though, there would be no Cinderella story.

The duo took their seats in the upper grandstand, facing home plate, and, above it on the horizon, perched atop Coogan's Bluff, a cluster of dingy apartments.

Unknown to the thousands of baseball fans, 49,000 in all in the stadium, in one of the houses, a 14-year-old black kid was playing with a new toy. It was a .45 pistol he had found in Central Park. In the chamber was one bullet, one bullet he had saved to fire on July 4.

At 12.20pm, as the teams took to the field, the boy, Robert Peebles, clambered on to the grimy roof, pointed the gun and squeezed, aiming into the air, just for fun, just to see what would happen.

Five hundred metres away in Seat 3, Row C, Section 42, Barney was turning to speak to Otto, the kid he had brought with him as a treat to see Willie Mays and all the rest. The bullet entered his skull via the left temple and lodged in his brain. He dropped his scorecard.

Barney was gone. As the police removed his body, fans who had been standing in the gangway nearby, thinking he had died of natural causes or fallen ill or, maybe, not thinking on it at all, scrambled for his seat.

*　　*　　*

The Polo Grounds was always an ugly baseball field, its idiosyncrasies not lending it any particular charm. It was shaped like a bathtub.

Its heyday came in '47, but by the '50s, it had become like the rest of the city, a faded beauty, a pretty old dame with a busted nose. Crime rocketed in the area. Urban blight came quickly, quicker than the authorities anticipated. Neighbourhood kids would offer to mind your car for a buck – if you didn't play ball, you'd be out the price of a tyre.

Originally, the ground was used for polo, and the moniker was an informal one – in fact, amazingly, it wasn't until the Mets (not to be confused with the 19th century team of the same name) put up a sign in 1962 that the name ever figured prominently at the stadium. It hosted its first game of baseball in 1882.

According to legend, John B Day, a wealthy tobacco and owner of the Metropolitans known as 'John B', was unhappy with the poorly-maintained Capitoline Grounds in Brooklyn, where, before the building of the bridge, Mets fans were forced to cross the East River by ferry to see the team play.

While shining his shoes, the boy with the shammy – a bootblack, as they were known – overheard Day's complaints and suggested a site in Manhattan where polo was played. Day checked it out and took out the lease and the Polo Grounds as a baseball field was born.

Day's Mets were invited to join the American Association in 1883, and he created a new franchise – the New Yorks, later called the Giants – to join its competitor, the National League, in the same year. Both teams played at the Polo Grounds before the Metropolitans went out of business.

The first of the Polo Grounds was located north of Central Park adjacent to Fifth and Sixth Avenues and 110th and 112th Streets in Harlem, a tract of land owned by New York Herald publisher James Gordon Bennett.

After the 1888 season, the Giants were evicted and played on various fields between 155th and 159th Streets, on the border of Harlem and Washington Heights, on the southern parcel of Coogan's Hollow, below a large cliff called Coogan's Bluff owned by real estate tycoon James J Coogan, the Manhattan Borough President. The stadium that would become famous was finally constructed in 1890 on the neighbouring Brotherhood Park, and the Giants moved in the following year. The Polo Grounds name stuck.

In 1893 John sold the Giants franchise. The grandstand would be destroyed in a fire in April 1911 but was re-opened that June. The Giants rose from the ashes along with their ballpark, winning the National League pennant in 1911 (as they also would in 1912 and 1913).

The team tried to change the name to Brush Stadium for their new owner, John T Brush, but the name did not stick. The Giants remained at this site for 46 years.

*   *   *

The stadium's connections with Ireland were storied. In the early decades of the Giants, half the team was of Irish descent.

Bill Joyce, the Giants' manager in the late 1890s, once declared: "Give me a good Irish infield and I will show you a good team. I don't mean it is necessary to have them all Irish, but you want two quick-thinking Celts to keep the Germans and [other players] moving."

Twenty-seven years earlier to the day that Barney Doyle would fall victim to a freak bullet, Kerry played New York there in a challenge match, losing 0-12 to 0-3. John Joe Sheehy's team had played an Exiles side that included Johnny McGoldrick (Leitrim), Eddie Roberts (Waterford) and Joe Stynes (Laois) five weeks earlier at the same venue, losing 3-11 to 1-7, and weeks of training in New Haven hadn't improved them.

Cavan had also lined out in the Polo Grounds long before 1947, drawing with New York in 1934 with a team that featured Big Tom and Hughie O'Reilly at midfield and Patsy Lynch at corner-back.

"With mixed emotions," wrote Arthur Daley in the New York Times of that game, "the crowd watched the stirring struggle. Cavan is the first North of Ireland team ever to make the transatlantic trip and there were pleading exhortations throughout the struggle that the New York 15 turn back the Far Downers. But the Ulsterites were out in force as well and every point was greeted with exultant cheers."

In 1938, when Kerry refused to travel, Cavan joined Laois and played a three-team round robin, which they won, John Joe O'Reilly lining out at centre-back, Daley figuring that the wet weather suited Cavan more than New York when the sides met.

"The invading Irishmen are used to rain, while their New York foe-men have formed the habit of cancelling frays when the skies open. So the transplanted Gaels were at a decided disadvantage..." he bemoaned.

*   *   *

The greats of Gaelic football may have played there but there was no chance of the locals becoming star-struck. Practically every early 20th century American sporting idol had strutted their stuff on the hallowed turf.

On September 14, 1923, exactly 24 years to the day before the most famous Gaelic football match of them all, 80,000 paid into the stadium to see then-world heavyweight champion Jack Dempsey, a hero of Irish-America, defend his title against Argentina's Luis Ángel Firpo.

'El Toro de las Pampas' ('The Bull of the Pampas') dropped Dempsey with a right at the start of the first round but Dempsey recovered to knock him down seven times in the same round, before Firpo sent the Manassa Mauler sprawling out of the ring, where he hit his head on a typewriter and opened a gash. After being helped back between the ropes by the writers at ringside, Dempsey went on to floor his opponent three times in the second en route to a KO victory.

In 1951, fans danced in the streets of Harlem when Sugar Ray Robinson avenged an earlier loss to Britain's Randy Turpin in 10 rounds in front of 60,000 to win back the world middleweight title, while Floyd Patterson would become the first man to win back the heavyweight crown when he beat Ingemar Johansson there in 1960.

A year after decimating the world's best in the decathlon and pentathlon at the 1912 Stockholm Olympics, Jim Thorpe, often mentioned as the greatest athlete of the 20th century, lined out at the Polo Grounds when he played for the Giants at the start of a six-season Major League Baseball career. And even Johnny Hayes, the New Yorker with roots in Nenagh, who became one of the biggest track stars in the world, attracted 25,000 to the grounds for a race in 1909.

Fairytale in New York

CHAPTER NINETEEN

The Leader

IT'S hard to describe John Joe O'Reilly without resorting to cliché. He was the greatest leader of men the GAA has ever seen.

There were seven boys and six girls in the O'Reilly home at Derries, Killeshandra, with John Joe arriving on June 3, 1918, bang in the middle. The O'Reilly's weren't rich but they were comfortable, having made some money producing butter and keeping a large farm.

His older brother, Big Tom, remarked that John Joe "played football as soon as he left the cradle". That was the way – every evening, the eldest five, Michael, Tom, Brian, John Joe and Vincent went up the Derries lane to Young's to kick football.

Their father was John, known as The Horse, who had played in goals for Cavan, winning an Ulster Championship in 1904 and playing a memorable game against Kildare in Croke Park in that year's All-Ireland semi-final. He won a Cavan Senior Championship with Killeshandra two years later before joining the newly-formed Cornafean club, winning eight more county medals.

His nickname came, they say, from his physical strength and bravery on the field in the days when goalkeepers were afforded no protection from referees ("severals used to hit the goal man that time," recalled Johnny Cusack). The Horse would gather the ball and drive out from his goal with forwards literally clambering on his back to slow him down.

He played in his last final in 1925 at the age of 42, the Reds going down by two points to Cavan Slashers.

By that stage, his sons were starting to play schoolboy football.

Big Tom was born in 1915 and was the first to follow in his father's footsteps. He came to prominence as a 16-year-old, towering at midfield on the Cornafean team which hammered Bailieborough in the 1932 county final. The following year, he began the Ulster Championship at midfield as a 17-year-old along side Hughie

O'Reilly, turning 18 that August and winning a first All-Ireland medal with Cavan the following month.

He was ferociously strong, well over six feet tall and barrel-chested but gentle and laconic off the field. His entertaining personality, his precociousness and his sheer physical presence made Big Tom, so-called in his early days on the Cavan panel in order to distinguish him from Tom O'Reilly of Mullahoran, a household name before the era of television, radio or even mass media interest in GAA matches.

In 1950, two years after he had retired from inter-county football, an Irish Press article on the rise in popularity of swimming in England noted that "young boys in this country grow up wanting to be Big Tom O'Reilly or Johnny Carey". Dubliner Carey, of course, was then captain of Manchester United; that's the esteem in which O'Reilly was held.

In 1990, when the O'Reilly clan came to electing an honorary chieftain, Big Tom was the automatic choice.

It's hard to imagine, then, that John Joe was even more beloved among GAA followers. He was a warrior, a sportsman, an ancient hero brought to life. Three years younger than Tom, John Joe was always extraordinary. He began school in Corliss, a half-mile off the main Crossdoney to Killeshandra road and then, as now, a two-teacher school, in 1923.

As a child, he would help his mother in the house, unheard of by boys at the time, and would get up at dawn to bring in the cows before the rest of the house had stirred. His sister Annie remembers John Joe, five years her senior, always making time to stop and talk to her. In most large families, the little ones were ignored, but this was John Joe, an extraordinary man in every way.

There were around 90 pupils on the roll and John Joe and his siblings walked the two miles each day. When he was 12, he moved to live with his mother's brother Michael, a bachelor in Drumcoghill, Cornafean, near where McSeain's pub is situated today.

Michael had found himself alone in the house when his sister, and later brother, were married and left, and the boy was company.

His evenings were spent studying and playing football on the old Cornafean pitch in the same townland.

In time, he won a scholarship to St Pat's and enrolled in 1932, immediately making a mark as a footballer. He won successive MacRory Cup medals in 1935, '36 and '37, captaining the team in the latter year. The inter-provincial colleges competitions were a big deal at the time, covered by the national newspapers, and he captained Ulster to the title in '37, too.

*   *   *

After completing his Leaving Cert, he applied for a Cadetship in the Irish Army in 1937, enclosing his references from John Reynolds, merchant, Killeshandra and Fr J Young, CC.

Asked on the form how long he had known John Joe, Reynolds replied "since he was a child". In answering the next question, "do you consider the applicant to be quite suitable in respect of character to be appointed to a cadetship in the Forces?", the shopkeeper was even more concise: "I'd consider him," he wrote, "to be suitable in every respect."

John Joe was accepted, and soon began to make heady progress in the military.

A confidential report from Easter 1938, signed by Major Liam Egan, Master of the Cadet School, described his conduct as "excellent" and his personality as "a very fine type. Industrious, conscientious and thoroughly reliable."

In July of the following year, in another report which was cross-signed by Major General Eoin MacNeill, the 21-year-old was described as "a fine, straightforward type, absolutely reliable and self-conscious." His application, the report stated, was "intensive", his athletic standard "excellent, All-Ireland footballer and all-round athlete". The officer had "no hesitation in recommending him for commissioned rank".

Poignantly, the final heading on the report, health, was summed up in a single word, too: Excellent.

*   *   *

In 1942, he was commissioned as an officer and in 1945, at 27, he became the youngest Commandant in the history of the Irish army.

By that stage, John Joe was a married man, having tied the knot on September 7, 1943. Five days later, he was back in camp with the Cavan team in Cherrybank House, Cornafean for collective training ahead of the All-Ireland final against Roscommon. Not only was he centre half-back and a rock on which the team was built, at 25, and assisted by his old clubmate Willie Young from Cornafean, O'Reilly was in charge of the physical training.

That was the type of him. More so than anything else, John Joe O'Reilly was a born leader.

A British army report in 1942, written after he had been sent to train with them in the north, described him as "a very good leader, forceful and full of character".

Lt Col F Tummon maybe summed him up in an annual confidential report on officers in 1949.

"What," asked the report sheet, "are the outstanding qualities and/or defects in this officer's character?"

His answer could as easily have been written by any footballer in Cavan.

"Conscientious and loyal in the performance of his duties. Temperate in his habits. Considerate, but firm, in his dealings with subordinates."

He wrote an essay in Cadet School in 1938 which foretold with amazing accuracy some of the major military movements of World War ll.

*   *   *

The bare footballing facts don't do him justice, but they're worth listing in any case. He stood just 5' 8½" yet played at the heart of the defence, winning 11 Ulster Championships, two All-Irelands and four Railway Cups. He played his first senior championship match with Cornafean in June 1934 and his first final, against Mullahoran, the following year. He won championship medals in 1936 and 1937 while still a teenager and played his last game in January 1938 a match which, local historian George Cartwright has discovered, was a replayed senior league final and took the place of the championship that year.

The match was also Brian O'Reilly's last for Cornafean; later in 1939, he would be ordained a priest. "It was an awful pity," commented Big Tom, "that Brian left because Brian was, or could have been, better than John Joe."

On moving to Kildare, he played football with the Curragh team, losing Kildare finals in 1947 and '49 and winning one, against Sarsfields, in 1948. He also found time to win a Kildare senior hurling championship medal, excel in basketball and win the army 100-yard and 200-yard sprints.

All the while, he was lining out for Cavan and Ulster, driving the couple of hours north from the Curragh for matches. He had played minor football for the county in 1935 and 1936 and was on the junior team that defeated Down in the Ulster final in '36. His senior debut came the following year in the Ulster final win over Monaghan, when he lined out at right half-back, with Big Tom in the centre, as Cavan won the Anglo-Celt Cup for the seventh successive year.

*　　*　　*

The minors, en route to the All-Ireland final, trounced Armagh on the undercard to that game in Castleblayney. Included in their ranks were Barney Cully at full-back and TP O'Reilly, who would line out in attack 10 years later in the Polo Grounds, at midfield.

Cavan ultimately lost the All-Ireland final to Kerry in a controversial replay but they, and John Joe, would bounce back to win Ulster titles every year from '39-45, and in '47, '48 and '49.

But that was all in the future. Here in New York, it's 11 o'clock in the morning on September 14, 1947 and, for the World War II veteran, Doonan, the leading Irish Army officer and his comrades, D Day has finally arrived.

The Manager

YOUR name is Hughie O'Reilly. You are 43 years old and unmarried. You have a few passions in life, in no particular order – Cork hurling, nationalism and Cavan football. It is the latter that has taken you from Cootehill to America three times, and has you waking on a clammy Sunday morning in a swanky American hotel.

It's been a long journey. It began in Cork, on the Ballinlough Road on the city's south side, where you were born in 1904. Your father was from Drumnagran near Tullyvin, a couple of miles out the Cavan road from Cootehill. He was an RIC man, unusual given your later leanings, and he died when you were a child.

How did you take it? We don't really know. You are a private man, a household name in GAA circles but not interested in publicity, or attention.

Your mother died in 1918 and yourself and your brother Tommy, or TJ, headed home to Cavan, to live with your father's brothers.

Later, you'll move into Cootehill itself but continue to farm the old ground out in Kill, also working as a ganger with the council on the roads. TJ will work in insurance.

You grow into a strong man. An athlete with a huge heart on the field. Nothing will stop you. They say you play better when you're losing than when you're winning.

In 1927, you made your name as a footballer, playing midfield on the Cavan junior team which won the All-Ireland.

Cavan beat Sligo and Kildare and Kerry, after a row, were thrown out. Cavan were awarded the title but refused to accept it. In June 1928, the final was finally played. You were the best player on the field as Cavan won Ulster's first All-Ireland. Patsy Lynch, chairman here in New York, played full-back that day as a 16-year-old. You minded him.

A year later, you played in a senior final, losing to Kildare, but five years later, you made amends, winning a senior All-Ireland at midfield alongside Big Tom, then a teenager. You minded him, too.

You saw the impact a fearless kid could make. You remembered it.

The following year, you went to America for the first time, heading off from Cobh on the Manhattan with your Cavan buddies and the Limerick hurlers.

You picked up experiences then. How to prepare, how to carry yourself. How Irish-America works and how the top teams from the south are perennially so good. You stored them. They'll come in handy here today.

In '35, you were back again at midfield. Cavan win it. You were the captain but you couldn't make the homecoming on the Monday evening. People to meet, maybe, things to do. You pass on your apologies and the party goes on anyway.

You're not a talker. You're stern, you're dour, you bark at players and, they say, make them run bare-footed through thistles, but you are a winner. You want to win and you believe that hard training is the way to go about it. So you'll shout and roar and keep shouting in that Cork accent that you never lost, but you will make sure they are ready to win. Your training camps are run on military lines; then again, that's what you know, isn't it?

Maybe, this morning, you pause to look back. Football has brought you places, shown you things. So has life.

You're not the sentimental type, although you're known to sing a rebel ballad after a drink or two in Jemmy Donohoe's, which is a rare enough occurrence anyway. But as you think of the Kingdom and how to beat them and whether Wilson will be fit for Garvey, if the Gunner will keep his cool in the heat, if the bounce of the bloody ball will go your way, maybe your mind wanders to another hotel of sorts, a less luxurious one where you spent a longer stay.

Tintown, they called it. It was at the Curragh Camp, a jail, effectively, for internees, a makeshift, hastily-thrown together jungle of corrugated iron and concrete which housed 1,000 republicans at one time. It was seven years earlier and the Emergency was raging. Republicans, maybe, could seize on an opportunity like it.

So the government took action and rounded up anyone who might have been that way inclined, and probably some who weren't. Camps were set up and Irishmen were interned by Irishmen. Yourself and the brother and another local man were sent to the Curragh with houses full of men deemed to be threats to the nation.

Conditions were wretched. Food was scarce – men, they say, squabbled over bones and there were schisms and in-fighting. Men went on hunger strike. Morale sunk to such an extent that a majority of internees gave up on the struggle when they were released. The only way to get out was to sign a form abandoning your beliefs, sit tight till the war was over or dig.

So, you and your comrades dug. Once, they started a fire in protest at something and it spread to a hut where tunnels were in progress. The tunnels were discovered. Beatings ensued.

But you survived and after six months, you got out. They say there was a riot, and you saved a guard's life.

So, you were home. You had never hid your allegiances – in 1937, you spoke at a meeting in Cathal Brugha St, calling for the release of political prisoners alongside John Joe Sheehy, the old Kerry captain – and you never would.

You returned to Cavan after the Curragh, and to football and soon your team were moulded in your image; resilient, tough, winners. Your brother is a selector with the team but he's not here in New York; the only selectors brought were yourself, Lynch and Hughie Smyth. No matter, there's a job to do.

Later, your team will win more. You'll lead them to three more All-Ireland finals and win two of them. You'll get over the loss of PJ, and John Joe, rebuild a new team to win in '52, but eventually you'll pack it in.

You'll play football till your late 40s, too, trying to win the only medal you never picked up, a county championship. But you don't, so you start training Cootehill. They've won one league in 50 years by then and words like Mullahoran and Cornafean are used for scaring children round your town.

They don't scare you, though. No way. With you on the line, Cootehill will win the junior championship in 1952 and win the next three senior ones, too. You'll carry on for a few more years with Cavan and then, and only then, will you give it up, step back and do a bit of refereeing.

You won't be that old when you do, but you'll have lived a lot. You have already married Alice Rice, though you'll have no family. You won't have many close friends but that's true of many greats – you are held in a level of respect close to awe. You still follow the Cavan team and you journey south for Munster hurling finals. You'll live on Market St in Cootehill, where you'll spend fine afternoons sitting out and watching the world pass by. You'll be celebrated in song.

You'll draw up your 25 golden rules for footballers, all sensible, ending with the one to sum them all up: "Go out and win, but for God's sake play the game."

Nobody in Cavan will ever master it like you and, when you're gone, so will the county be.

But that's all in the future. For now, you're confident. The hoors have the work done. You know they have, but they'll need it. An All-Ireland final against Kerry is a challenge like no other.

Before you left your camp in Ballyjamesduff, you told the press they were a "loyal lot of lads" and were "in smashing form, most enthusiastic and confident and determined to make themselves as fit as men can be".

You told the supporters to look out for bright news on the night of the 14th. There's no way you're coming home, all that way, as a loser.

They'll not be beaten.

Dawn peeps in through the curtains. Time to go to work...

CHAPTER TWENTY-ONE

The Game

AT mass in St Patrick's Cathedral on Fifth Avenue, said to be built out of the savings of Irish working girls, Monsignor Flanelly, who is accompanied by six other Irish priests, address the football party from the pulpit with rousing words.

"You are sporting ambassadors of Ireland whose sons and daughters have built this great Cathedral which is a monument to the faith and generosity of the millions of Irish that sought refuge in this great land," he intoned.

"The altar speaks of 700 years of religious persecution for our faith and as visiting Irish athletes you can be proud of the great Irish people who came here and built this great cathedral."

Later, Cardinal Spellman was introduced to the delegations, asking each from which county he came as they stooped to plant a kiss on his bishop's ring. As he presented each with a miraculous medal, AWOL Irish army man Doonan turned to Garda Higgins and grinned.

"I'll hope we'll be getting a better one this evening, Mick," he smiled as the men's shoulders heaved with the wonderful, half-suppressed laughter which can only be provoked in a chapel.

Emerging into the light, the clouds had parted.

When they looked out of the windows of the Roosevelt Hotel that morning, what they saw would have been totally different to home, and not just in terms of the architecture and the multitudes milling around. In Cavan, the morning was bright and sunny but in the Big Apple, it was misty with a light drizzle coming in from the bay.

That would change while the men were cooped up in the big house; the afternoon would be almost freakishly warm, the mercury hitting 86F (30C) at one point, which was the highest temperature since the Cavan and Kerry players arrived, the hottest day in September and, in fact, hotter than all bar two days in the preceding August. The pot was simmering nicely...

*   *   *

After lunch, the entourage hit for Harlem, then, as now, a predominantly-poor, almost exclusively African-American neighbourhood at the top end of Manhattan, which, in 1940, had a 20 per cent infant mortality rate.

Harlem was run, essentially, by gangs of black criminals who had taken over from Italian organised crime syndicates in the early years of the century, involved in the numbers racket, an illegal lottery of sorts, the proceeds of which ran into billions.

Tucked in the corner of the locality was the stadium, where the delegations rocked up at 2pm and were greeted by the sight of spectators streaming in early from all corners, in along the river and down the Brush Stairway from Edgecombe Avenue, many having travelled from other Irish outposts as far away as the west coast.

Three thousand came on an excursion train from Boston and large contingents from Detroit, Pittsburgh and Chicago. There were specials from Hartford, Springfield, Hollyoke and Newark, too. For one day only, this was the most Irish place, on foreign soil, there had ever been.

The erudite Anna Kelly in The Irish Press, a specialist colour-writer who was chosen ahead of other luminaries for the trip, was under no illusions as to the importance of the occasion.

"This is much more than a football game," she wrote.

"It is a rally of the scattered Irish... In a big way it is Galway Races, Punchestown, Puck Fair. But longer years divide the exiles' reunion; longer memories hold dear every little turn on the road home.

"For the few that can afford to go back, there are thousands who cannot, who have been working here 40 years and are still unable to put enough together to go home. Many don't care who wins, for the occasion is bigger than that. Many have come to town but not all to the match."

Outside the stadium, in the shadow of Coogan's Bluff where the miserly or the impoverished used assemble to watch Giants' games, pennants of the Cavan and Kerry teams were selling well. Also being pushed were gramophone records of De Valera's speech on partition the previous St Patrick's Day, which also came in booklet form at two bucks a pop.

There were two curtain-raisers on the programme. Two minor teams made up entirely of New York-born players took the field first, Good Sheperd seeing off St Luke's, a game Ó Caoimh described as "a very creditable exhibition of Gaelic football". What was most noteworthy on the day that was in it, as they say in Cavan, was the identity of the scorer of the winning point for Good Sheperd, one Kevin O'Donnell, son of John Kerry.

While John Kerry O'Donnell himself hadn't been much of footballer, by Kingdom standards anyway, Kevin, and his brother Brendan, who also represented New York in later years, had a good pedigree. Their father's placid younger brother Tim – opposite in temperament to his fiery sibling – won All-Ireland medals in 1929, 1930 and 1937 (the latter against Cavan) and missed out on two more due to injury in 1931 and 1932.

Second on the agenda was an intermediate game, St Pius' beating St John's by two points.

*   *   *

September 14 found Cavan town buzzing. The sun was shining and there was a palpable sense of expectation, and not just for the match, due to throw-in at 8.30pm local time. This was consecration day at Kilmore Cathedral, and that was a big deal in 1947 Ireland, big enough, as it turned out, to share equal billing on the front page of the Irish Independent the following morning with the football in New York.

Among the huge crowd assembled were 200 clergymen, the top cleric in the country Cardinal Dalton, the Minister for Agriculture (Cootehill man Paddy Smith), William T Cosgrave and General Mulcahy.

It's easy to imagine the congregation yawning and squirming in their seats in the stifling heat as the Cardinal delivered a tub-thumping speech, railing against idolatry and materialism.

"In the circumstances of the present time, the consecration of the cathedral has a significance that goes far beyond its immediate purpose," he said.

"It is a challenge to an unbelieving world and to all who refuse to acknowledge the kingship of Christ or to recognise his prerogatives."

The irony was that the ceremony didn't even include the actual consecration; it had taken place privately the previous Monday, as it would have unduly prolonged the public function it carried through.

As part of the ceremony and towards the end of the afternoon, his eminence raised a symbolic chalice, a piece of silverware first forged in the 1620s by an old Archbishop. His name? Hugh O'Reilly.

*   *   *

Night was approaching and Cavan had gone indoors – all of them. Young and old clustered around the nearest radio. In the towns, the streets were emptied ("Cavan town", said the Irish Press, "was like the Deserted Village", save for little pockets of men and women huddled around the windows of neighbours' houses.

Those who owned a wireless found their homes full, inside and out, and most opened their windows, placing the radio on the sill, so those who couldn't fit inside could hear.

At the caretaker's house on the grounds of Breffni Park, John Sexton was joined by a group of followers. A former Cavan and Monaghan footballer, he was also a noted referee and had cycled to Killydoon that morning to referee a league match between Cornafean and Mullahoran.

Unknown to him, the sides had cancelled the match themselves. No matter, John got back on his bike and spun the dozen miles home in time for throw-in.

In Ballyconnell, a crowd maybe 50-strong had gathered outside a house on Main St, all inching closer to hear the crackling reception.

As Peter Donohoe placed the ball to take a free, the crowd surged forward.

"Get back will yiz!" yelled the man closest to the window, "and give Big Peter room to take the feckin' free!"

*   *   *

The broadcast, carried by transatlantic cable from New York and then via transmitters from Dublin, Athlone and Cork, attracted, to that point, the largest audience in Radio Éireann's history. In Dublin, groups gathered in restaurants and cafés and on random street corners where some drivers pulled over, rolled down their windows and turned up the volume dial for the benefit of the masses.

"Almost every household in the country" tuned in, it was reported.

In Ballinameen Garda station, Co Roscommon, Joe McManus was pacing the floor. A young man from Lavey, he was desperate to hear the match but equally desperate not to rock the boat in his first Garda posting. When his sergeant asked him what time the broadcast was starting, he told him an hour earlier, 7.15pm, than the truth, hoping he would go out and someone would bring in a radio.

The man in charge was anti-GAA and a strict disciplinarian – which meant no radio in the station, and no-one leaving.

Around 7pm, the sergeant headed off to a neighbour's house to hear the match in any case. Joe sat tight, his mind racing on whether to stay and miss the game, or go and risk incurring the wrath of his superior.

Suddenly, the latch on the door clicked and the sergeant came back, announcing that the radio in Eddie Carlos's house was broadcasting just crackling. The Cavanman's heart sank, but rose again when his companion headed out the door for Frenchpark, to Garda Gibson's.

Joe thought of the Polo Grounds, of the consequences of abandoning his post. Duty called.

"Oh, I was in a bad state now," he recalled.

"I kept pacing up and down the narrow day room. There was awful silence except the clock ticking and I couldn't help thinking of my friends PJ Duke and Tony Tighe and all the rest of them in the Polo Grounds.

"So for the first time ever I broke the barrack regulations and took the keys and went down to the nearest shop where there was a radio, Kelly's, and I went into the sitting room there. I had locked up the station."

*   *   *

Paddy Donohoe was working in Cavan Post Office, a few hundred yards from the cathedral. A future county board chairman, at the time he was a footloose 20-year-old, a goalkeeper with a local team who had once saved a penalty from Big Tom.

The post office was buzzing.

"There was a huge gathering in the town," he remembered.

"There were church dignitaries and politicians. It was a very big event in the town. Then as the day went on, the excitement grew ahead of the final. We were working away and it was busy, the pressmen were trying to get their reports away. We didn't even have a radio where we were working and we were dying to hear how the match was going."

Updates were sketchy.

"I well remember the then-postmaster DT Duane coming down and saying in his funny accent 'another goal for Kirry'. And as the thing went on it started to improve and the reporters were coming in filing their reports and they didn't come in empty-handed. I wasn't drinking at the time but some of my colleagues were, and a great night was had by all, as they say!"

Before the game, oddly, Ó Caoimh visited the teams in the dressing rooms. His directions to the teams were unusual, if one Kerryman's recollection of events is accurate.

Joe Keohane

The late Pádraig Ó Caoimh came into the dressing-room and he said that he wanted an exhibition of football, something that the Yanks would remember – in other words, to depart from our usual brand of football.

Now I got the feeling that his remarks were directed at me, particularly, I'm sure they weren't but I had to leave my own particular brand of football behind me in the sense that I believed in not taking prisoners at any stage in my career. I'm not saying that boastfully or anything like that, it's just an expression to prove that I wanted to win at all times.

But somehow or other he didn't tell the Cavan fellas that because I do remember that Tony Tighe came in with a ball one time and normally I would have hit him a fair shoulder but this time I refrained, listening to the wise words of the late Pádraig, and they got a goal out of it.

Keohane would say later that had that incident taken place in Croke Park, he would have sent Tighe "into the top of the Hogan Stand".

Simon Deignan

We were there to give of our very best and some of the officials may have even suggested to us that we do just that.

Fairytale in New York

CHAPTER TWENTY-TWO

The Play

FIRST out was the referee, O'Neill, along with his umpires, Gerry Arthurs, JP Brennan, Henry O'Mahoney and Tom Kilcoyne. Dinny Lyne would next lead the reigning champions out first, John Joe O'Reilly coming behind him a couple of minutes later in front of the Cavan team. John Joe won the toss and chose to attack the wider end. The tension grew as the sun grinned on the pasty Irishmen and women. Supporters wore napkins and programmes on their heads.

Humidity was 58 per cent and, a breeze "brought no coolness". It was, said AP Quinlan in The Irish Press, "pitiless, broiling sun [which] made the Polo Grounds a melting pot".

The three tiers of stands looming high over the scorched field gave players the impression of playing at the bottom of a deep barrel.

And there was anxiety everywhere, rising from the dusty earth, there in the clammy faces of the patrons, the nervous tics of the players. After everything – Congress, the flight, the boat journey, the hullabaloo, it would come down to this.

Joe Keohane
The hush immediately before they played the two anthems... When we stood for the Irish anthem, there was a tremendous roll of drums... The place had been abuzz with excitement and then there was an extraordinary hush and it was played and sung as well I'd ever heard it sung anywhere.

The teams paraded behind the combined New York Police brass and pipe bands, almost 150 musicians in total, opening with Come Back to Erin, The Minstrel Boy and O'Donnell Abu before leading into the ubiquitous Faith Of Our Fathers and the respective national anthems. The crowd fell into an almost-eerie silence.

It's easy to imagine John Kerry, watching his dream of transporting a massive chunk of Ireland to his adopted city coming

to reality, smiling as he hummed the lyrics from the third track –
"Strike for your country – O'Donnell Abu".

By now, the temperature had risen to almost 30C and the pitch
was "concrete hard", so much so that it had been watered before
throw-in.

By the time Mayor O'Dwyer, surrounded by a pack of press and
photographers, had performed the ceremonial throw-in, the game
was behind schedule. When O'Neill launched the leather for the real
throw-in, it was 3.38pm.

Every player bar the backs and goalkeepers, as was customary
at the time, contested the throw-in but Kerry won it and set the tone
early.

Kerry knew how to win All-Irelands and their way was tried and
trusted – they generally timed their run from just off the pace and
made sure that, even if it took a replay, it was they who were in front
at the winning post. They had done it 14 times already by the
summer of '47 and would repeat the trick another 22 times
subsequently. This was different though – in every way.

The Kingdom tore into the match from the start, Paddy Kennedy
creating a chance which Brian O'Reilly cleared to his clubmate
Wilson.

Simon Deignan

They came out full of bounce. Usually when Kerry walk
into Croke Park – of course they're so used to it I suppose
– they saunter on, don't they? There's no kind of
'gallumphing' on to the field, celebrating the occasion of
being in Croke Park like most teams do when they're there
for the first time, understandably. But with Kerry, normally
their approach is very moderate, they come out and it's just
another match for them, another final so to speak.

But this was different. They came out full of bounce and they
were into their stride like a flash.

The Kerryman

Kerry in this game completely upset tradition by starting off so well; generally we expect from them a slow start and terrific finish. We got the lightning start and finish and no middle to sustain it.

Lyne, the Kerry captain, broke up Cavan's attack and launched one of his own. Kennedy launched the ball towards Tom O'Connor and 'Gega' grabbed it, held off two tackles, paused for just a split-second and drop-kicked it high to Val Gannon's left for a goal. But no. O'Neill's whistle had sounded. A free was awarded and Gega tapped over the opener.

From the kick-out, Kerry attacked again.

From O'Reilly's kick-out, which never rose more than six feet off the ground, wing-forward Batt Garvey got possession 50 yards out. The dark-haired Ventry man was known as one of the best solo-runners in the game and he took off, scorching the brown turf and unleashing a rocket to the Cavan net. The underdogs were reeling.

AP Quinlan (Irish Press)

The roar was deafening. The attack was so quick, it left us gasping.

A minute later, Donohoe settled Cavan's nerves with a free but Kerry were first to everything. The prize at stake, the size of the pitch and the speed of the ball, which was bouncing as if on concrete, meant the tempo was furious, the football travelling the length of the field in a handful of seconds.

And the Kingdom were at full tilt. Eddie Dowling was ruling the skies at midfield and in the seventh minute, he tore through the heart of the Cavan defence and fired an unstoppable shot to the roof of the net. Gannon was transfixed, Cavan were stunned and the crowd – men in white shirts, women in white dresses to stave off the sun – were raucous as Kerry led by six.

Michael O'Hehir
Eddie Dowling dodges and battles his way past the Cavan defence and sends a rasper to the net!

Mick Higgins
We were out-played everywhere. You couldn't describe it. We were beginning to wonder how we ever got there. I'd say the spectators were starting to say to themselves, how the hell did this crowd ever get out here.

Michael O'Hehir
By this time, many fans were wondering just how Cavan got to the final. They soon found out.

Simon Deignan
In the first 10 or 15 minutes Cavan were in a different world altogether... I'll tell you, certainly Kerry's reflexes were much faster than ours and I don't know why. I couldn't tell you. In spite of the fact that the team were kept together for so long before the match, the prior training, the whole idea of keeping us on the plane together and all this sort of thing.

Kerrymen were pouncing on breaks like wasps on a jam jar and they came at Cavan in waves. A foul on O'Keeffe was punished by O'Connor and Kerry led by seven.

On the sideline, the Cavan selectors consulted. Garvey was unmarkable, Dowling playing like a god. Hughie took a gamble and repeated one of the switches which had helped beat Roscommon in the semi-final, moving Higgins and Tighe to midfield.

PJ Duke went to wing-back and picked up Garvey and the Gunner and Wilson took up roles in the attack. The team was transformed, but it would take time for the changes to bear fruit.

Kerry broke again and after a perfectly-weighted hand-pass, Garvey took the ball at full flight. It was knocked from his hands but he controlled on the ground, soccer-style, and blasted past Gannon for a magnificent goal to send Kerry nine up.

Sam, waiting at home in Dublin, would winter again in deepest Munster, surely. Not quite – O'Neill intervened. He had blown for a foul before the goal was struck, said the Wexford man. Free-in.

O'Connor pointed, but Kerry disputed the decision bitterly.

Batt Garvey

The history books show that I scored Kerry's first goal, after four minutes, but I don't remember much about it. Far clearer in my mind is another goal I scored... one that was disallowed.

We had a dream start. We were seven or eight points up when I got the ball out the field. I ran in towards goal. Their backs came out to meet me and I side-stepped them and scored a goal. But the referee disallowed it.

Why? Well, because I had not been touched by any back, to my mind it could only have been a free out for over-carrying. Everybody else seemed to think so too because they started to run out the field for the kick-out but no! The referee signalled a free in. 'Twas a very strange decision.

Eddie Dowling

In my view there was no goal disallowed. If Martin O'Neill took down the scores as they came, the match would have ended in a draw... 4-5 to 2-11, 17 points each. That was the actual score on the day. The goals weren't disallowed. Batt Garvey scored his second goal after a great solo run and he told me afterwards that no back touched him and he thought he was punishing him for over-holding and it would be a free-out. Instead, the ref gave a free-in, which the Gega, the Lord have mercy on him, pointed. So... we got a point instead of a goal.

A few minutes after the same thing happened to the Gega himself, he scored a goal and the ball was brought back and he pointed another free. So actually he gave us two points and he took four points off us, which was exactly what Cavan won by.

I scored the fourth goal and the ref happened to be feeling good that time and marked it down (laughs).

Martin O'Neill
Sure the rule is quite clear. In fact, I see now in the Football Immortals where our friend Raymond Smith had the advantage rule again rearing its ugly head. But Raymond should know that there is no such thing as an advantage rule when the whistle blows. That stops everything... I didn't disallow the goals. When the whistle blows, that stops the play.

Peter Donohoe
I suppose you would have to say Kerry could feel a bit hard done by maybe with one of them, alright. But it happens, the same thing happened us in the '45 All-Ireland, we got a goal and it was disallowed. These things happen. I think that all in all, Kerry really should have held on to their big lead.

Regardless of the legitimacy or not of the goals – and the video clearly shows the second was harsh – Cavan's reaction on the sideline to Kerry's amazing start would win the match for them. Duke was mesmeric on the wing, his best position, and Tighe, showing the fearlessness of youth, revelled in the extra space.

*　　*　　*

In Ballinameen, Joe McManus had his head in his hands. Kerry were seven points up, and cruising. An old man called Patrick Beirne, from the townland of Acres, was in the company and he had faith in the Blues.

"He started searching his pockets and I thought he was looking for a match to light his pipe or something. But he pulled out a five pound note, and they were very scarce at that time, and he placed it on the table and he defied anyone to bet against him, he said that Cavan were going to win."

*　　*　　*

Simon Deignan

They moved PJ Duke back into his natural position. The three of us in the half-back line, we got on very well together. And as soon as he moved back, he closed the gap.

Their team re-jigged, Cavan got back to work. Colm McDyer, one of three Cavan players not born in the county along with Carnaross native Brian O'Reilly and New Yorker Higgins, eased some of the pressure with a fabulous point at the other end after a beautiful catch and pass from Tighe but the Kingdom came roaring back again, Gega pointing from play.

But the corpse was starting to twitch. Cavan's forwards, dining on crumbs to this point, began to take on their men; although they were still seven points down, there remained a glimmer of hope.

Mick Higgins

From the first two points when we got the ball up, I thought if we got enough of the ball we could get within touching distance of them.

Peter Donohoe

Cavan had a very bad start. Nothing went right for them in the first 10 minutes or so and we did feel a bit down. But once or twice the ball came up and we could see that the Kerry defence weren't that confident. They seemed a bit shaky. When Tony Tighe or Higgins got the ball, they seemed to be at sixes and sevens.

The comeback was almost underway. Paddy Kennedy pointed for Kerry to send them eight in front but the game spun off its axis in the following 10 minutes.

Jackie Lyne felled Tighe, a will o'the wisp to that point, gliding across the turf, with a shoulder charge into the chest and the Kerry defence were visibly put off by the booing, unknown in Ireland, which followed. The neutrals in the crowd, from there on in, were on Cavan's side.

Mitchell Cogley (Irish Independent)
From that instant, though knocks were hard and frequent on both sides, the crowd was behind Cavan. And the support of a New York crowd is quite a tangible asset.

The local press in the Kingdom may have seen it differently when it came time to write the story of the match but, regardless, the fact remained that the neutrals were by now screaming for Cavan.

The Kerryman
Paradoxically enough, it was the early scores which turned the sympathy of the crowd to Cavan, for apart from the fact that it's human nature to see a champion dethroned, from Joe Louis to the Kerry footballers, few in the Polo Grounds thousands wanted to see Cavan get the pulverising Kerry seemed about to administer.

Roared on from the stands, Cavan upped the tempo. Donohoe stroked over a free after being fouled himself and then another, after Tighe, tearing through at full tilt, was dumped backwards again.

When the big man fielded and took a return pass, a goal looked likely but Dan O'Keeffe saved with his boot and the ball screwed over the bar.

Cavan were trailing by four, 2-4 to 0-6, but had all the momentum, and Kerry were left reeling when a shirtless Dowling was helped off the field by John Kerry O'Donnell, dazed, confused and unsteady

The Polo Parade

Behold the sons of Ulster marching towards the Sam

POLO GROUNDS 157th STREET and 8th AVENUE, N.Y.C.

SUNDAY SEPTEMBER **14** 1947 3:30 P. M. RAIN or SHINE

ALL - IRELAND GAELIC FOOTBALL FINAL

LOWER STAND $3.60

SECTION 39 ROW N SEAT 14

RAIN OR SHINE Polo GROUNDS Lower Stand $3.60 SECTION 39 ROW N SEAT 14 Polo GROUNDS SEPT. 14

Game faces: The players parade for the final on the arid Polo Grounds surface.

Inset: A ticket stub for the Lower Stand at the stadium

The boy who put the 'r' in Mayo": Mayor Bill O'Dwyer takes his seat for the game.

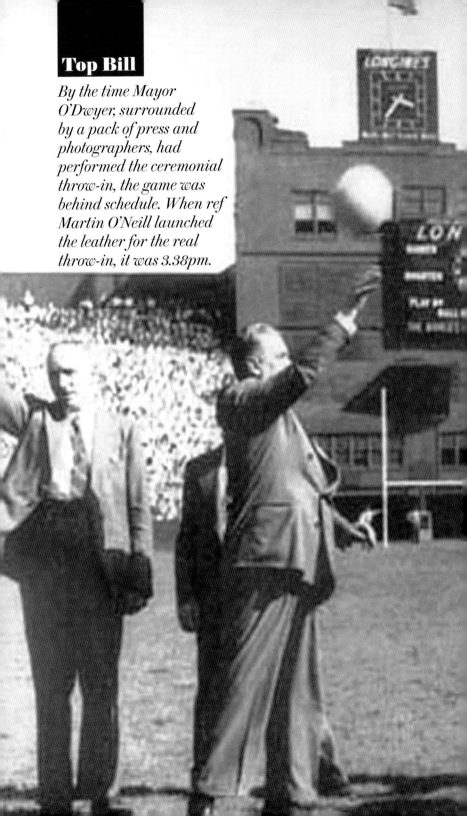

Top Bill

By the time Mayor O'Dwyer, surrounded by a pack of press and photographers, had performed the ceremonial throw-in, the game was behind schedule. When ref Martin O'Neill launched the leather for the real throw-in, it was 3.38pm.

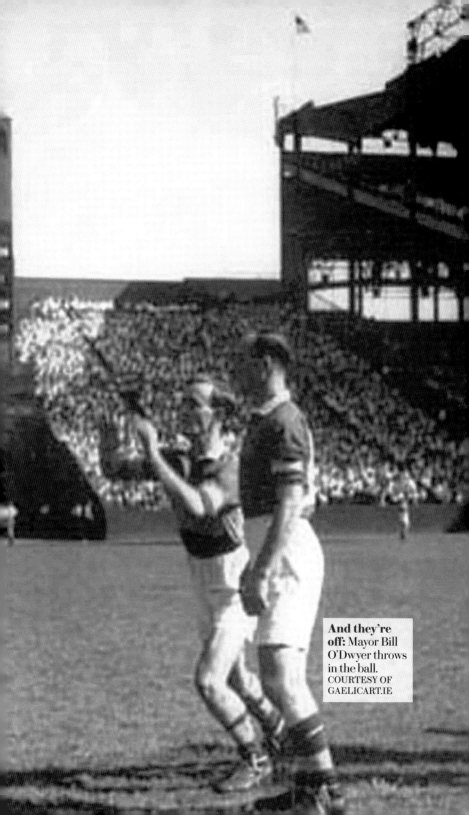

And they're off: Mayor Bill O'Dwyer throws in the ball. COURTESY OF GAELICART.IE

Celebrate good times

Somehow, Cavan found a way to win against all odds. The players were chaired from the field and then made their way to the cool of the dressing-room. There was no presentation, just a moment of exultation before the heroes were mobbed again.

Kerry for Sam? Batt Garvey 'scores' a goal which was disallowed.

Game on! Mick Higgins' goal revitalised Cavan.

Kings again: Cavan players celebrate on the pitch and in the dressing room after the final whistle.

Portrait by an artist, and the missing man…

Art attack: No team picture was taken on the day, even though there were press photographers present. In later years, this painting was created, using the image from the semi-final – with Joe Stafford, obscured in the original, slotted in – and the Polo Grounds super-imposed behind. This painting hangs proudly in homes and pubs in Cavan and beyond.
PAINTING BY IRISH ARTIST BRIAN O'FLAHERTY, COURTESY OF GAELICART.IE

It wasn't all sport...

MAYOR'S RECEPTION COMMITTEE
OF THE CITY OF NEW YORK
MAYOR WILLIAM O'DWYER
Cordially invites you to be present at the Reception
to the

ALL IRELAND FINAL FOOTBALL TEAMS
COUNCIL CHAMBERS AT CITY HALL
WEDNESDAY, SEPTEMBER 10, 1947
AT 12 NOON

ADMIT ONE
Use City Hall North Entrance

GROVER A. WHALEN,
Chairman

Feted: Players and supporters sit for dinner in the post-match banqu at the Roosevelt Hotel.

Left: An invite to a reception in City Hall, hosted by Commissione Nolan.

Right: Players suit and boot up for another Stateside shindig.

LUNCHEON TENDERED
TO
KERRY AND CAVAN TEAMS
BY THE
GAELIC ATHLETIC ASSOCIATION
HOTEL ROOSEVELT

'FIVE MINUTES MORE!'

What Michael O'Hehir (below) asked the American network CBS for so he could continue broadcasting back home to Ireland from the Polo Grounds.

On the mic: Michael O'Hehir at the Polo Grounds.

50,000 WILL WATCH IRISH FINAL TODAY

Kerry and Cavan Counties to Meet for Gaelic Football Title at Polo Grounds

The transplanted All-Ireland Gaelic football final will be staged at the Polo Grounds this afternoon with Kerry, defending titleholder and winner of sixteen All-Ireland championships, meeting the strong Cavan County team. Mayor William O'Dwyer is expected to throw in the first ball.

Encouraged by the large advance sale, Paddy O'Keeffe, general secretary and manager of the Gaelic Athletic Association, which is sponsoring the event, is expecting a turnout of some 50,000 fans for the game, which is Ireland's counterpart of our world series. The classic, played in former years in Dublin's Croke Park, is now in its sixty-third year.

Kerry, which has been Irish champion more than any other team, is the favorite for today's match, although many experts feel that Cavan has the stronger team. The latter has won the crown only twice, but usually has been up among the leaders.

Expected to help the defending champions is Dan O'Keeffe, one of Ireland's all-time goalies who has been on seven championship teams. Leading the Cavan contingent will be John O'Reilly, a major in the Irish Army, who is the team's center halfback and a pillar on defense. Also starring for Cavan is expected to be Jim Donahue, full forward, who will be the biggest man on the field. He is well over 6 feet and scales 210 pounds.

A great deal of interest will center on the activities of Mike Higgins, high scoring ace of Cavan, who will be the only performer who was born in the United States. Higgins went to Ireland about twenty years ago.

Fans watching the conflict will see the cream of Ireland's Gaelic football players. Some 250,000 players in Erin's four provinces and thirty-two counties were in the original starting field. To reach the final, the two teams had to battle their way first through the provincial championships and then through the semi-finals in which the four provincial titleholders engaged. This year's finalists are said to be the best two teams since the beginning of the war.

The probable line-up:

CAVAN.		KERRY.
Gannon	Goal	D. O'Keeffe
Cloonan	R.F.B.	D. Lyne
Reilly	C.F.B.	Keohane
P. Smith	L.F.B.	Brosnan
Duke	R.H.B.	T. Lyne
J. O'Reilly	C.H.B.	Casey
Deignan	L.H.B.	Walsh
McDyer	C.F.	Dowling
Brady	C.F.	E. O'Connor
Tighe	R.H.F.	O'Sullivan
Higgins	C.H.F.	O'Donnell
T. O'Reilly	L.H.F.	Garvey
J. Stafford	R.F.F.	T. O'Keeffe
P. Donohue	C.F.F.	T. O'Connor
Carolan	L.F.F.	Kavanagh

Clockwise from left: The Anglo-Celt, The Kerryman and The New York Times report on the Polo Grounds match

MORE ABOUT U.S.A. TRIP

DETAILS OF AIR VOYAGE AND RECEPTION

Supplementary to write-up of the Cavan-Kerry final in New York, published on Page One of this issue, the latest information is that the journey occupied 29 hours and not 22 as stated. There were three stops—at Santa Maria in the Azores, off the coast of Africa;

Press on: The Irish Press's front page the day after the match. The paper boasted that their pictures were 'sent by wire'. The Irish Independent (left) had no live pictures, so used a cartoon of John Joe O'Reilly with Sam Maguire (above left).

Top of the house: A group of Cavan players, along with the chairman, pictured on the roof of the old Independent House in Abbey St, offices of the Irish Independent, on their return. It was a common custom at the time to bring successful stars to the roof, over-looking the city, for a photo. Back row: Mick Higgins, Big Tom O'Reilly, Peter Donohoe, Phil Brady and Patsy Lynch. Front: TP O'Reilly, Val Gannon, Terry Sheridan and Tony Tighe.

Homeward bound

"On the broadcaster's announcement that Cavan had won, every door was thrown open and the people hurried into the streets. Bonfires were lighted and children and their parents joined in singing local ballads and cheering."

All together now: The Cavan and Kerry contingent outside New York's City Hall.

Below: PJ Duke's programme from the Queen Mary on-board banquet, signed by players and officials

Cheers: A group of Cavan and Kerry men raise a toast on the Queen Mary.

All smiles: John Joe O'Reilly, Paddy Smith and, peeping out, Joe Stafford arrive in Dun Laoghaire.

Right: A dapper Peter Donohoe (centre) poses for the camera at the homecoming in Dublin.

Home, sweet home

*"It was then [when we saw the celebrations at home],"
remembered Mick Higgins, "we began to realise that
there was a big difference between victory and defeat."*

Guard of honour: The Cavan team bus arrives in the county town, flanked by
members of the FCA.

Stand-in: Joe Stafford carries the Sam Maguire Cup into the Farnham Gardens.
Captain John Joe O'Reilly missed the reception due to commitments with the
Curragh team in Kildare.

Stars earn their stripes: The Cavan panel pose for a photograph on their return. Back (from left): Eunan Tiernan, TP O'Reilly, Big Tom O'Reilly, Peter Donohoe, Tony Tighe, John Wilson, Phil Brady. Middle: John McGeough, Willie Doonan, Terry Sheridan, Val Gannon, Colm McDyer, PJ Duke, Hughie O'Reilly. Front: Hughie Smyth, Joe Stafford, Owen Roe McGovern, John Joe O'Reilly, Edwin Carolan, Paddy Smith, Patsy Lynch. Missing were Mick Higgins, John Joe Cassidy, Brendan Kelly and Brian O'Reilly.

Glory days: The team which reached the final again in 1949 (below).

The legacy

The Polo Grounds final and the memory of men like John Joe O'Reilly, his life cut short at the age of 34, left a legacy like no other in Gaelic games.

50 years on... Kerry's Liam Hassett and Cavan's Stephen King lead their sides out before the 1997 NFL game, played at the Downing Stadium, Randall's Island, New York, to mark the 50th anniversary of the Polo Grounds match.

Lions in winter: Cavan's Mick Higgins and John Wilson, Kerry's Teddy O'Sullivan and Mick Finucane, Simon Deignan and Tony Tighe of Cavan, and Gus Cremin of Kerry photographed in 2005.

after knocking himself out when colliding with the turf. It would be a mortal blow for the Kingdom.

Mick Higgins
Coming up to near half-time, Eddie Dowling went up for a high ball. He was having a brilliant match for Kerry in the middle of the field. As he went up for a high ball he over-balanced and came down on the hard ground and dislocated his shoulder and he was taken to hospital.

So I'd say that could have helped us, we got a grip on the game then around the middle of the field and the longer it was going on, the more we were scoring and the better we were getting.

Eddie Dowling
The full-back placed the ball on the 21-yard line and he kicked it out the opposite side from me... And I says, I'm going to get it. And that's what knocked me out. I crossed the field, made a mighty jump for the ball, caught it and was a bit over-balanced. The ball was gone a bit beyond me. I pulled it down to my chest and somersaulted in mid-air and hopped my head off the ground.

The ground was rock-hard and my head came out second best. I knocked myself out stone cold and spent a week in St Mary's Hospital in Brooklyn.

Patsy Lynch
As I saw it, Dowling went soaring up for a ball and came down heavily on the bone-hard pitch. It was an accident, pure and simple.

Batt Garvey
When he fell after jumping for a high ball, he landed on his back and was taken off on a stretcher and that was the end of him.

Martin O'Neill
Eddie Dowling was playing a magnificent game.

*   *   *

It was a cruel blow for Kerry but Cavan had already grabbed the initiative and within seconds, they had stunned their opponents again. Higgins soloed through the Kerry full-back line but his shot on goal was half-blocked and the fearless Stafford flung his body towards it, connecting with his boot and sending the ball hurtling past O'Keeffe from point-blank range.

Suddenly, Cavan were back within two, Stafford bounding away in celebration, the substitutes, white towels round their necks, leaping for joy.

The Kerryman
The Kerry goalkeeper gripped the leather alright and then experienced what must have been a most painful experience for him – being bundled into the net with the ball.

Where were our Kerry backs – big Joe Keohane, the Lynes and Bill Casey? They were completely caught off-guard by the fast-playing Cavan forwards and we had only touched against the fringe of disappointment.

Michael O'Hehir
Stafford finished a Higgins shot to the net. Cavan are jubilant but more is to come...

With two minutes remaining in the half, Cavan were rampant. PJ Duke was attacking at will, eclipsing Garvey, and when he combined with the Gunner and Tighe to create a half-chance, Higgins cut inside and sent a bullet to the bottom left-hand corner of the Kerry net. The stadium rose as one; Cavan, impossibly, were in front.

Mitchell Cogley
Higgins swerved his way through the Kerry defence and gave O'Keeffe no chance with a shot to the net.

Mick Higgins
I remember coming down and I got a pass from Tony Tighe and two of the Kerry fellas came for me. I went one way and I side-stepped the two of them. I was 25 to 30 yards out and I said to myself, a point isn't much good, here's a chance for a goal. And I let bang, and it went into the corner of the net. O'Keeffe dived for it and just got his hand to it and it went in to the corner of the net and I'd say it helped the turning of the game too.

John Wilson
Somehow we fought back from eight points down to level but to my mind the turning point arrived before half-time with Mick Higgins' goal. It was outstanding. A rocket from 25 yards which Dan O'Keeffe, the master goalkeeper from Kerry, just got his fingers to but the ball flew into the bottom corner.

Both the Press and the Kerryman used the same phrase to describe Cavan's goals: "an atom bomb" – and dropped at precisely the right time.

AP Quinlan
They were two of the most sensational goals that ever marked a final.

Cavan pressed more before the break and could have been further in front, O'Keeffe saving brilliantly from Donohoe. The game had changed, utterly, and as the teams headed for the dressing-room, their emotions couldn't have been more different.

As the players left the field, Stafford had a bone to pick. When he had buried his goal just before the break, the American announcer – the custom was to 'call the game' over the tannoy, as in horseracing – mistakenly attributed it to TP O'Reilly.

"Come here," he said to TP, "I scored that goal, not you." TP, ever the diplomat, shrugged it off. It was Joe's goal and, in any case, he hadn't been the one to claim it...

At half-time, O'Hehir, in the gantry, was asked how it would go. "Cavan. But Kerry are never beaten until the last whistle goes."

Prophetic words, indeed. Before the restart, O'Hehir was joined in his commentary position by O'Dwyer and O'Rourke.

O'Dwyer was an extraordinary man and when he spoke, his Mayo lilt still strong even at the age of 57 and having spent almost two-thirds of his life in New York, people listened.

He had left Bohola in 1910, having backed out of the priesthood, and arrived in New York harbour with a fistful of dollars in his pocket. His first job was as a labourer in the docks and in time he would earn a crust as a handyman, running errands, and as a deckhand, earning £15 a month. He travelled to South America on one trip – when a stoker died on the journey home, O'Dwyer took his job.

At the age of 27, he joined the NYPD where, on his first day on the beat, he disarmed a killer. He took to studying at night, qualifying as a lawyer six years later and setting up a practice.

He lived the American dream but his was a life touched by tragedy, too. His brother Jim had joined the fire brigade and was killed on a false alarm; his older brother, John, was shot dead while assisting a policeman make an arrest.

On his appointment as a magistrate in 1932, he devoted himself to the fight against organised crime and when he subsequently rose to become District Attorney, he was given the moniker 'The Gang Smasher' by the local press.

In 1941, he would run for the position of Mayor but after losing to Fiorello La Guardia, he enlisted in the US Army and fought in WW2, rising to the rank of Brigadier General.

On his discharge, he romped home in the Mayoral race in 1945. To the Irish-Americans, he was a living legend, the hopes and dreams of the old country made flesh.

So when he said, over the airwaves that since emigrating from Ireland he had "longed to see the All-Ireland final played in my adopted city of New York – both teams are a credit to Ireland", there was a weight of sincerity behind it.

O'Rourke reciprocated.

"It is a wonderful sight," he announced, "with spectators witnessing a wonderful game, one of the greatest ever in the history of the GAA."

*   *   *

The Magnet Cinema in Cavan town was packed. Projectionist Jimmy McCormack was listening to the match in his hut and, obviously unable to beam pictures from New York, was improvising. With every score, he made up a new slide and super-imposed it on the film. When the final whistle blew, hundreds would rush out to join the thousands dancing in the streets in the dusk.

*   *   *

There was hope for Cavan, and their thousands and thousands of supporters, thousands of miles from the action.

In deepest Roscommon, Joe McManus felt as far away from home as any of them.

"It came on to half-time and Cavan were leading by a point and I was hoping I wouldn't be caught out. Then when it was coming near full-time, O'Hehir started to say 'to anyone listening along the way, give us five minutes more, please give us five minutes more'.

"So I said I'd take my five minutes more and I left and went back to the station and thank God, everything was alright, the sergeant hadn't come back anyway. And then I was lonely thinking about home.

"My mother was in Lisdaran Hospital in Cavan and I was thinking, would she have heard it, and I was picturing the celebrations. I didn't get home for a good few months after that..."

*   *   *

In the dressing-room, Cavan were calm. Hughie and John Joe did the talking. Hughie later told The Anglo-Celt that his instructions had been simple: "You are in the lead and well fit to win it now".

The challengers showered and changed and took in as much water as possible before emerging first, Kerry, in their white baseball caps, leaving them waiting around in the heat for the game to throw in again.

And then they were off once more. A slick move at the start of the second half yielded a point from a free by Gega, but Donohoe cancelled it out with a sweet kick at the other end. In his time, he was renowned as the greatest striker of a dead ball the sport had seen, and Cavan needed him at his brilliant best.

Simon Deignan

Peter Donohoe was absolutely deadly with the frees and every point he was getting, it was being [tails off]... certainly the Americans loved it anyway. And I think he was so big in stature, he was such a gentleman and just played the game, that the American people and the Irish-Americans just took to him. And rightly so.

I don't know how many points he kicked from frees that day. Peter was a big bustling man, a grand footballer and a grand character. He fully deserved the adulation he subsequently got.

Peter Donohoe

Well, it was just something. I always fancied taking frees anyway, I practised it plenty. We decided that we'd take any chances came our way and that we wouldn't start looking for goals if they weren't there. Of course one by one we got into the game and then we got a couple of goals to even things out a bit. They came before half-time so that put us a point in the lead at half-time, so we were fairly confident at half-time that we were going to get there.

Joe Keohane
Peter Donohoe, the man I was marking, proceeded to give a fantastic display of accuracy with his kicking of the dead ball. On that day, he appeared to be a sort of Mikey Sheehy and Jimmy Keaveney rolled into one.

It was score for score. Back came Kerry and the Gega, back came Donohoe, back came Gega and again, back came Big Peter. With nine minutes remaining, Cavan led by 2-9 to 2-7.

In the commentary box, O'Hehir's navy tie danced a jig on his white shirt. After all the hassle, after all the worry over the broadcast, suddenly it dawned on him that the delay caused by the pre-match rituals might derail the whole thing.

Michael O'Hehir
As we approached five minutes to five I looked at my watch and I discovered that there was about 10 minutes left in the game and there was every possibility and every justification for somebody, somewhere along the line, with a piece of paper in front of him that said 'disconnect Polo Grounds at five o'clock', every indication that he might just pull out a plug and cut the broadcast off five minutes from the end.

And I began quite innocently saying: 'If there is anybody along the way there listening in, just give us five minutes more' and I kept begging for this five minutes more. There was a song at the time, "Give Me Five Minutes More", but I kept begging for this.

Whether it was that somebody along the way heard the appeal, I don't know, but the five minutes was left on and the entire All-Ireland final, from the Polo Grounds, was heard in Ireland.

The commentator would later joke that had the transmission been switched off, he would never have returned home – or if he did, it would have been in disguise.

Someone, somewhere, heard his plea. The broadcast stayed live until 5.06pm, or 10.06pm at home. By then, Kerry were bate, and the day was saved.

But not yet...

With Duke, John Joe and Deignan driving forward, the Gunner hurtling into tackles around the middle, and Higgins and Tighe dancing through, Cavan were creating chances but O'Keeffe, a veteran of seven All-Ireland wins, was equal to anything they threw at him.

Peter Donohoe
Danno O'Keeffe was brilliant, I mean he saved a few shots that day that nobody would have saved.

Patsy Lynch
But for the outstanding brilliance of Danno O'Keeffe in goal, we would surely have improved on our four-point victory.

Higgins, from 30 yards, curled in from play to open a four-point lead with five minutes remaining, but Kerry came in waves, hunting in packs, driving forward almost in a rolling maul in front of the Cavan goal. Teddy O'Sullivan tried to shoot the lights out from 14 yards but his shot smashed off the crossbar and rebounded to safety. Cavan, sweat stinging their eyes, clung on.

Seconds later, Kerry drove again, Tim Brosnan chipping a coat of paint from the butt of a goalpost as he watched a shot agonisingly scud wide. The champions would have to be carried off on their shields...

The Kerryman

Back came Kerry for that goal which meant everything. Have you ever seen the Atlantic breaking in its fury on your coast? Of course you have, and of course, too, you have wondered as you watched the thunderous breakers crash on the rocks, if those rocks could ever withstand the murderous assault. That's the way it was in the Polo Grounds when Kerry tried for that elusive goal.

With two minutes to go, Higgins, the coolest man in the city of his birth, sent over another from play. Kerry attacked again but Cavan cleared and Mick grabbed it at midfield.

And then O'Neill, standing just a couple of yards away, sounded the long whistle and signalled for the ball and it was over. Somehow, some way, Cavan had done enough.

*   *   *

The final whistle blew and, after the suffocating tension came an outpouring of ecstasy in Cavan. The county could breathe again. The streets and crossroads filled, people danced in the flickering light of bonfires. It could have been 1747, as someone wrote at the time. The unnamed Irish Press reporter who had been in Cavan town, filing his copy from Paddy Donohoe's work station, described the scenes.

"On the broadcaster's announcement that Cavan had won, every door was thrown open and the people hurried into the streets. Bonfires were lighted and children and their parents joined in singing local ballads and cheering."

There were joyous scenes in Oldcastle, hard on the Meath side of the Cavan border. The scenes in Bailieborough were, said The Celt, "beyond description".

Domiciled natives joined in the jubilation and there were loud cheers for the losers. An impromptu band was mobilised and paraded the town – the following night, there would be two.

Donohoe remembers the delight, dancing in the moonlight, men, drunk, embracing and crying with the novelty and brilliance of it all. And in the middle of it all, a panicked army reserve commander, trying to round up his men, like a scene from a silent comedy.

"One vivid memory I have is of a bus trying to get FCA men," he laughed, "who were there for a guard of honour during the day, on to the bus. But the commander forgot there was a second door on the bus! They went in one door and out the other. An awful caper."

*   *   *

In west Belfast, it was reported, thousands poured out of their homes on the Falls Rd when the match finished. Shouts of "Up Cavan, up Ulster!" rang in the air. The crowd was swollen by stragglers arriving from dance halls and cinemas and the streets were rocking until after midnight.

*   *   *

The pitch filled up and the players were chaired from the field. Higgins, Donohoe, Duke, Tighe and Doonan were the heroes, the men whose hands thousands wanted to shake, whose hair they wanted to tousle. It had been the most memorable game in football history, the end of a championship like no other. There was no presentation – the players struggled their way to the cool of the dressing-room and sat for a moment in exultation, the masses congregating outside.

Eventually, they made their way in to be with the new kings.

John Wilson
I never enjoyed a shower as much as the one afterwards. But when I came out my togs, socks and shoes had all

disappeared. I searched everywhere for them because in those days football boots were scarce. I must have been a victim of the American souvenir culture because they were nowhere to be found. Next day, however, a new pair arrived at the hotel for me. I still don't know if they were sent by the person who took my old ones.

Kerry accepted their defeat sportingly, but they were bitterly, bitterly disappointed. For the bluebloods of the game, second may as well be 32nd. In later years, they would blame the referee. For them, the final whistle, after all the razzmatazz, may have marked the biggest sporting anti-climax of all time.

Dinny Lyne
We were certain we'd win it after that [lead] of course, but when two are disallowed it's a big break... Heartbreak. Heartbreak altogether.

Peter Donohoe
And we just knew that we were fit enough and if we just got the breaks we had a good chance of staying in the game, and that's really what happened. We just took whatever chances came, we didn't panic and we didn't go looking for goals when there were points to be taken.

The goals that weren't would never be forgotten.

Dinny Lyne
I think they were very fair goals but we were leading so much by that stage that it was said that he wanted to make a match of it. I don't know if that's true or not. Made a match the wrong way for us anyway.

I'll tell you a story now. I live a half a mile outside Killarney and I got a phone call to come down to a pub. John Browne, he was a traveller for some place, and he was after moving to Wexford and he had a Wexford man with him who wanted to see me. So I came down to the pub to him and the one thing the Wexford man conveyed to me, he said that he was talking to Martin O'Neill and he told me if you ever meet Dinny Lyne or if you ever go to Killarney, tell him when they are counting up All-Irelands, add the Polo Grounds to it.

That's what the man from Wexford told me anyway.

Joe Keohane

It was a close and pulsating finish but in the final analysis, Cavan deserved to win. I only hope that Martin O'Neill, an outstanding player and referee and one of the GAA's greatest servants, regrets not giving Kerry those goals as much as we do.

The over-riding feeling differed, naturally, depending on which team was talking.

Joe Keohane

It was artificial in the sense that it wasn't Croke Park. We were 3,000 miles from home and there was an atmosphere completely different to what we were used to.

Simon Deignan

In my opinion it was the greatest showpiece that ever was for our game of football.

* * *

As the Cavan players filed out and made their way to the coach, signing autographs and soaking up the cheers of well-wishers, they might have thought of home. That night, they attended a banquet and partied like champions.

The players rose the next morning and got the papers. The New York press were lavish in their praise and one Cavan footballer, Peter

Donohoe, found himself earning a new nickname.

Arthur Daley, who would go on to win a Pulitzer prize during 47 years with the New York Times, christened Donohoe "the Babe Ruth of Gaelic football".

"He is Dead Eyed Dick with his accurate kicking," wrote Daley.

"Cavan were younger and fitter and able to carry their hand-passing game with speed and deadly accuracy while Kerry, with their more direct approach of catch and kick, played into the hands of the Cavan defence. It was amazing and uplifting to see two teams, after kicking the stuffing out of one another, go over and embrace one another at the end of a great final. If it was here they would surely each want to land another blow.

"Tighe of Cavan came in for dog's abuse; knocked out three times, he came back for more each time. Outside the stadium, an impromptu Fleadh Cheoil took place with musician singers and dancers displaying the custom and traditions of Ireland oblivious to the deafening roars of the nearby subway."

In the Herald Tribune, Harold Rosenthal concurred.

"The name Donohoe, a 23-year-old publican's assistant, rang out all over New York and throughout Ireland last night to acclaim the Cavan sharpshooter who was instrumental in landing Cavan's third senior All-Ireland title. It was a long afternoon of fierce battling in unrelenting heat where hard knocks were the order of the day and each embraced friend and foe at the end of the game."

The Daily News's Chris Kiernan chimed in, reporting that Cavan "completely out-played, out-kicked and out-manoeuvred their opposition after a very shaky start".

In the Daily Mirror, Wedger Meagher, brother of Kilkenny hurling legend Lory, noted that Cavan "played a brilliant type of football in an electric atmosphere, cheered on by an ecstatic crowd".

*　　*　　*

Confident predictions of a sell-out had been off the mark, with the early-morning rain and the admission prices – bleacher seats had been set at $2.40, almost five times the equivalent price for a final in Croke Park – blamed. John Kerry O'Donnell had his own conspiracy theory; some 'wise guys' had spread a rumour that the game was sold out, he reckoned.

In the end, the total attendance was 34,941, but the trip was still a roaring financial success. When O Caoimh later reported to Central Council on December 13, he stated that the profit had been £10,262, even after paying federal tax at 20 per cent, a fortune in the times that were in it.

Not the players, finally relaxing on the trip of a lifetime, would have been bothered. There were drinks to be drank, songs to be sung and toasts to be raised yet...

*　　*　　*

On the Monday night, the teams were guests of Commissioner Nolan at a reception in City Hall, and the following morning, many went to visit relatives or to Rockaway Beach. On Wednesday, they visited City Police Headquarters and then a handful headed out of town to the West point Military Academy, where army officers John Joe O'Reilly, Deignan and Keohane were given a huge welcome by the cadets.

Thursday saw the parties tour New York harbour by boat before a Cavan-Kerry selection played New York under lights at Gaelic Park on Friday night.

They were feted everywhere, the Cavan players each receiving a wallet of notes from the Cavan Association. And, suddenly, on Saturday morning, the bags were packed and it was time to go. Sam Maguire, who hadn't crossed the water, was waiting in Dublin. The champions set out for home...

The Homecoming

BY the time they hit the Queen Mary, the players were tired. It had been a month since many of them had left home and the training, the match and the celebrations took a toll. The craic was good, though, and was only starting.

Owen Roe McGovern had his head turned. On his return to the family farm, he would break his father's heart, telling him he was going back to New York. Owen was a hard worker, an outgoing personality who had been in the army and worked in a bar – he carried the swagger of the Big Apple in his head and he wanted more. In years to come, he would be a massive help to Irish emigrants arriving in the US and kept extremely close ties with home.

"The celebrations were great afterwards. We were wined and dined and never let buy a drink anywhere. There were a lot of people who wanted to celebrate with us and they all wanted us to come into their pub afterwards," he remembered.

The teams set off on September 26 on the Queen Mary, a liner much larger in size than the Mauretania which brought them out. There was a cinema, a swimming pool, bars, shops and restaurants – it was a floating city. "It was twice the size of Croke Park," noted Higgins, "it was a holiday in itself."

And while Cavan celebrated, the Kingdom players joined them. The two bunches knew each other well by this stage and socialised together. The men, as was the style at the time, wore suits and ties when going for a drink, many smoking cigarettes.

"It was a holiday atmosphere. A good time. We travelled home on the boat together, the Kerry lads were good losers. We had been twice in London on Easter Sunday playing Kerry," said Higgins.

That wasn't the only acquaintance from those Easter clashes which were renewed on the liner.

Travelling on the Queen Mary on the way back from Montreal was Cardinal Griffin, Archbishop of Westminster, who had met the teams in Mitcham Stadium the previous April and asked for them to be presented to him again by Dan O'Rourke, which they were.

They were feted by the captain on the second last night.

"The highlight of the journey home was a special meal for our party where the Captain entertained us with a banquet and where he issued special menus in Irish for the two teams with the names of all the players in Irish and decorated with Cavan and Kerry colours. I have my copy of the menu still," recalled Columba McDyer in 1992.

When they reached Southampton in the early hours of Friday morning, the team had hoped to slip quietly through England and on to Holyhead, and home. While the Cavan group had received 72 copies of the Anglo-Celt with a report on the consecration of the cathedral and the football final, and, almost miraculously, on the day after publication in Cavan, little did they realise the interest the Polo Grounds final had sparked. It was about to ignite.

"We hadn't a clue. We never dreamed of that," Higgins would say of the homecoming and the excitement Cavan and Kerry had generated.

Greeted off the boat by a delegation led by Mickey Walsh, chairman of the London county board, the players next boarded a train to the capital. Disembarking at Waterloo Station, porters were heard to refer to Higgins as "the Irish Tommy Lawton", then a dapper centre-forward with First Division Chelsea, who would score 235 goals in 383 appearances in a mesmeric career.

What may have caught the workers' eye was the match ball, safely tucked under Higgins' arm as he strode up the platform, emblazoned with 90 signatures of players, prominent Americans, Mayor O'Dwyer and even sentimental verses from exiles. Higgins had been the last man to handle the football before Martin O'Neill's long whistle sounded two weeks – which must have felt like two years by then – previously.

In London, they were treated to a meal at the Royal Hotel, sitting down just two hours before the train was due to leave Euston Station for Holyhead.

A dashing visitor, nipping in between functions was Irish High Commissioner JW Dulanty but the players hadn't time for much in the way of formalities – they had a train to catch and by 8pm, they were hurtling through the British countryside.

It was 8.30am on the following morning, Friday, when the Princess Maud boat, delayed for an hour due to fog, became visible through the mist. A small crowd had gathered on Carlisle Pier in Dun Laoghaire, where the teams were met by a few relatives and greeted by the local Dublin Corporation branch.

Next, they travelled by car to the Salthill Hotel in nearby Monkstown for breakfast. While they were eating, a crowd was beginning to assemble eight miles away in the city centre.

By 11am, the sun was shining and as the team arrived at the Mansion House, the streets were thronged by thousands of well-wishers. Hundreds of Gardaí, it was reported, were keeping a space clear at the front of the crowd for the teams. Street traders selling photographs, "hats, scarves, rosettes and headbands" did a brisk trade and, as the teams arrived in 13 cars, the crowd came to life.

John Joe O'Reilly finally emerged from one car with the gleaming cup in his hands, to an almighty roar.

As the dignitaries, led by Lord Mayor PJ Cahill and Taoiseach Eamon De Valera, welcomed the teams, the enormity of the occasion – and the fact that their lives had now changed – began to slowly dawn on the Cavan players.

"It was then," remembered Higgins, "we began to realise that there was a big difference between victory and defeat."

As Dinny Lyne, the magnificent Kerry forward, surveyed the heaving masses on Dawson St, he quickly came to the same conclusion.

"It was only then," rued Lyne, "that we were made to realise just how much we lost in the Polo Grounds."

Leaving the Mansion House, led by the Garda Band, the group proceeded through O'Connell St and on to Great Denmark St. From there, they were hosted at Áras an Úachtaráin by the President,

Sean T O'Kelly, and his wife, where they had lunch. It was the headiest of times.

And, at every step of the way, just as at the after-match banquet in New York, speakers took their chance to give their tuppence worth on the north – to a man, each called for an end to partition.

At the Mansion House, Pádraig Ó Caoimh, in a political statement which would be anathema to GAA leaders today, said that playing the game in the USA was not merely for the match but for the removal of the barrier that existed through the use of vile propaganda against Ireland.

"The conduct of the players and officials placed Ireland on the map as it never had been before," he said.

Their minds were at all times on the border, which they hoped would soon be removed and a "great and glorious Ireland" achieved.

That night, there was a huge reception in the Gresham Hotel on O'Connell St, attended by Canon Hamilton, and the following day, Saturday, was spent shopping, visiting friends and relatives and calling to a city-centre cinema to watch clips of the final before rocking back up to Barry's Hotel to meet callers and stay the night.

Before that, there was business to be tidied up with the officials. Ó Caoimh, for his part, made his way to a Central Council meeting on Saturday afternoon, reporting that despite the large expense, the American tour had been "a big success".

Although some accounts were still outstanding, he expected that the financial outcome would be satisfactory, noted the Irish Press.

*   *   *

On Sunday morning, as Kerry headed south on the train, Cavan's odyssey home began at last. The players waved goodbye to John Wilson, who returned to St Kieran's College in Kilkenny, and John Joe O'Reilly, who gave up the chance to lead home the winning team as captain in order to line out for the Curragh in a Kildare SFC match. Lieut Simon Deignan also returned to the Curragh while Colm McDyer headed for Donegal.

Wilson was taken aback on the Monday morning when approached by a head dean in the corridors of St Kieran's, who admonished him for returning so soon. "I didn't expect you back for a week," he was told. It was a mark of the man that he returned to his digs in John Street, near Nowlan Park, that Sunday evening, a common boarding house for teachers, commercial travellers and the like. As an aside, he wasn't in an exclusive club as the holder of a Celtic Cross on the St Kieran's staff, either – the soon to be Fr Ned Kavanagh from Urlingford, now hale and hearty in Sacramento, had won a hurling medal with the Cats the previous month.

* * *

Cavan boarded their yellow bus – driven by Patrick Donaghy from St Patrick's Terrace in the county town, a neighbour of Doonan's – and took off. The first stop on the 70-mile journey was in Navan, where the Cavan party received an address of welcome.

Down the road in Kells, the town band played the squad and officials through the streets. On reaching the Cavan border at Maghera, a banner draped across the road read: "Breifne welcomes home her heroes" and bonfires lined the road.

People were innocent, more genuine, perhaps, than today. At a huge reception in Virginia, too, the locals presented the team with scarves, not as a memento but as a precaution, even though the weather was reported as being more typical of June than early October.

"People were very thoughtful," noted Patsy Lynch of the gesture in Virginia, "feeling that we would feel the weather cold here after the torrid heat of New York."

Word was travelling ahead of the team as they made their way that they were coming and as cars, which were scarce, came out to greet them, the cavalcade grew to 300 motors.

When they reached Cavan town at 3.30pm, the party was greeted by 16 bands. In Emmet Place and Mitchell St, every house flew a blue and white flag.

Headed by the Cootehill Brass and Reed Band, a procession took off through Connolly St, Pearse St, McDermott St and Casement St en route to the Farnham Gardens, the site of the current county library. The crowd was estimated at 15,000, all jostling for a look at the heroes home with the spoils of war and kept in line by the local FCA, who formed an escort for the players and assisted in stewarding.

With John Joe on club duty in Kildare, vice-captain Joe Stafford was given the honour of carrying Sam on to the stage, where the team was received by a group headed by two clergymen, Bishop James Moynagh and Bishop Patrick Lyons.

Bishop Lyons, a white-haired man who would die in office 18 months later, was born in 1875 in Collon, Co Louth and had been the driving force behind the magnificent construction of the Cathedral, which, of course, had been re-consecrated on the day of the Polo Grounds final.

It is important to emphasise the social status of a bishop in 1947. Aside from the landed gentry, they were the closest thing to royalty in Irish society. Their houses were lavish and referred to, fittingly, as 'palaces'. Dr Lyons had his own chauffeur during the war years when petrol, let alone cars, was a precious commodity.

Bishop Moynagh, the then 44-year-old prefect of Calabar in Nigeria and titular bishop of Lambesis, had been instrumental in releasing Fr Jack Boylan, another Mullahoran footballer, from his studies to play in the 1945 All-Ireland final against Cork when Mick Higgins had suddenly fallen ill two days before the game.

Moynagh's impact in later life in spreading the gospel in Nigeria was remarkable. Today there is an avenue in Lagos named in his honour, an extraordinary tribute in an overwhelmingly Muslim country.

The pair shook hands with each member of the Cavan panel, who in turn kissed their rings.

After that, the Cootehill band played Faith of Our Fathers and then the national anthem.

Another official present was the chairman of the reception

committee and former county board chairman, Seamus Gilheaney, the headmaster at Drumcrave National School who numbered one W Doonan among his former pupils.

*   *   *

And then the speeches started, the tone growing, as they did at almost all the receptions, nearly jingoistic in tone.

"Anybody looking around at this vast assemblage of Gaels, old and young, would say that we are going to be here for a long time yet," remarked Lyons.

"The young men of Breffni O'Reilly give concrete evidence that all the blood of Ireland was not spilled on Vinegar Hill, that blood still courses freely in the veins of the O'Reillys and other great clans and septs of the territory and have not turned to whey after a thousand years' struggle on the hills and in the valleys of Breffni O'Reilly."

He added that they had with them that day a representative of Breffni-O Ruairc in the GAA President, Dan O'Rourke (O'Rourke, though a Roscommon man, was a native of Leitrim, which was part of the old barony of Breifne).

The President, addressing the fervent crowd, said:

"I want to tell you sincerely that there was no doubt whatever about the superiority of Cavan. As you know, in a matter of a few minutes, your team was eight points behind and it took a super team to catch up with Kerry and defeat them after that."

Cavan and Kerry were now on far better terms than ever before, he added.

"Cavan is a great Gaelic county, the one county in Ireland, to my knowledge, where foreign games are not played. And I hope that that state of affairs will long continue... Thank God the people of Cavan are not amongst those who wanted to be slavish imitators of John Bull's island," he said, whipping the crowd into a frenzy of nationalistic pride.

(It is interesting to note that O'Rourke's comments in general, and his reference to John Bull in particular, were toned down in the national press.)

Hughie O'Reilly was next to get in on the act, thanking "our exiled kit and kin to whose hospitality there was no limit during our stay in New York."

"Though forced to live in exile," he went on, warming to his subject, "their hearts were at home among the hills of Breffni and may God speed the day when the youth of the country will be able to get a decent living in the land that bore them, the land they love."

Coincidentally, with John Joe unable to attend the homecoming, it marked the second successive occasion on which Cavan's All-Ireland-winning senior captain didn't lead his team home. Hughie himself had worn the armband in 1935 and had been "unavoidably absent" when the team returned to Cavan the following day, September 23.

Also on the platform were surviving members of two teams which played in one of the first games in the county in 1888. Matt Mulvaney, Mick Fitzsimons, Paddy Neary (Maghera MacFinns) and Phil Morgan and John Gibson (Cross Independents).

The team retired at 8pm for yet another lavish banquet in the Farnham Arms Hotel, where they stayed that night, and the nationalistic fervour showed no signs of abating.

The first toast offered was just "Ireland" and in response, all sang the national anthem. The next was simply "the GAA", after which MJ 'Sonny' Magee, a blistering forward on the '33 and '35 teams, traced the history of the association in Cavan.

After yet more speeches, including one from The Anglo-Celt's Andy McEntee ("this victory compensates for half a dozen finals Cavan deserved to win"), a toast was raised to "our guests" by Andy O'Brien, the man who, over 50 years later, would write to The Celt explaining, at length, how he had traced Doonan's family tree and confirming that he was not from travelling stock.

Near the end of the banquet, John Joe arrived, fresh from battle with the Curragh. True to form, he immediately apologised for not being able to arrive with the other members of the team and expressed the hope that their victory in New York would be an incentive to the youth of the county to play the game and compensation to their thousands of loyal supporters for past defeats.

Those thousands would get a closer glimpse of their heroes sooner rather than later, too – the awards circuit was only just starting.

* * *

When Johnny Cusack won his All-Ireland medal with Cavan in 1952, the celebratory routine had changed little from '47. The team arrived, had a bash and then went on tour.

"We landed in Cavan and had a reception there and most of them stayed over night in the Farnham and the next day went to the college with the cup and around different places. We went to Paul McSeain's that night in Cornafean. Nearly every night there was a reception. There was one in Bailieborough, Kingscourt, Ballyconnell where we trained," said Cusack.

"It'd go on till the spring. There were presentations, we got wallets in places, we got travelling bags and different things."

That was how it was done. In '47, too, the team stayed in the Farnham on their first night back on home turf. Some stayed there for a couple of nights...

On Monday, the team took off. They visited the TB hospital on Monday morning and from there went to St Pat's, where they received a raucous welcome and watched an inter-class match.

On the Monday night, TP O'Reilly returned to Ballyconnell, flanked by his neighbour, Owen Roe McGovern.

Amid jubilant scenes, a banner bearing a slightly-cryptic message was placed on TP's car: "The March of Time, 1947".

Among those to greet the players were eight members of original Ballyconnell team, the first affiliated club in the province.

Francis O'Grady, the oldest surviving member, received an ovation.

"When the club was first formed, the members were playing on a field outside the town when the authorities arrived and every one of them was served with a summons for playing football on a Sunday. However, we banded ourselves together and defeated them," he announced to a huge cheer. The favour would be returned on Wednesday when a crowd of 300 turned out to greet TP and Owen Roe down the road in Swanlinbar.

On the same night as the Ballyconnell gig, what the Celt described as a "soul-stirring welcome" took place in Killadoon Hall for the four Mullahoran players, with 400 inside and the same number unable to gain admittance.

At the same time, Hughie O'Reilly was being mobbed in Cootehill. Escorted to his home, he returned to the Town Hall with his wife, receiving a "tumultuous reception" and a chiming clock.

In his acceptance speech, O'Reilly stressed the need for better conduct on the field and, in a reflection of the all-pervading 'Gaeldom' of proceedings, exhorted the young men and women to support Irish dancing.

Cornafean rolled out the red carpet the following night. John Joe and Big Tom were presented with silver trays.

"I'm glad to be back again among my clubmates and old neighbours, I will cherish their gift as a memento to treasured associations in old Cornafean," commented 'JJ', with his older brother, garrulous and funny as ever, chipping in to riotous applause: "Any man who learned to play football in Cornafean could not be beaten anywhere!"

The Eugene Leddy Céilí Band provided the soundtrack for the occasion.

(Leddy, a Butlersbridge native, was a keen GAA man as well as a nationally-renowned musician. His sons Ollie and the late Sean won All-Ireland club medals with UCD, with Sean winning a Hogan Cup medal with St Patrick's College in 1972. Eugene's grandson, Packie, won Ulster U21 medals with Cavan in 2011 and 2012.)

At the time of the '47 final, corner-back Paddy Smith was employed as a bank clerk in Granard. A fabulous actor, who had won a gold medal for best individual acting in the Cavan Drama Festival earlier that year, Smith was a Stradone native but was immensely popular in the Longford town. That, allied to Granard's proximity to strong GAA areas such as Mullahoran, resulted in a huge turn-out.

This Cavan team was new and confident and such a remarkable bunch that everyone wanted part of them.

"This is part of old Breffni and we don't care who knows," said one speaker in Granard, keen to include his town in Cavan's success.

Smith was feted on Thursday again, along with PJ Duke, in Stradone, while in west Cavan, the bonfires were still raging up until Sunday.

Sub Eunan Tiernan, from Corville in Templeport, had a *céilidhe* in his honour in Bawnboy Hall on that night. After a procession from Templeport Hall, carrying torches, headed by Templeport Band, a tar barrel was lit in the diamond in Bawnboy and at midnight, the first man to bring an All-Ireland medal to the parish was presented with a wallet of notes, a common token of appreciation at the time.

A noted Cavan player of old, Standish O'Grady, who had played with Eunan's father Jack, made the presentation.

And almost 50 miles away in Mullagh, Simon Deignan and Edwin Carolan were honoured, St Killian's Warpiper's Band and the Newcastle Brass and Reed Band playing and a nostalgic, and indignant, speaker claiming Ballyconnell stole Mullagh's thunder by naming their club the First Ulsters.

One of the largest functions in the county town was on the Thursday, when Doonan and McDyer, who wasn't present, were honoured.

There was applause at the mention of the name "Doonan", who was presented with a wallet of notes. Tommy Meehan, chairman of Cavan Slashers, accepted a similar gift for McDyer.

"Wilie Doonan is one of the plain people of the town, who came into prominence as a minor and since then filled many positions on club and county teams. Like most other good footballers, he shunned the limelight, in fact he is almost shy but once the game was on, the shyness disappeared and it was then he was seen at his best," stated Patrick Ruddy, a local schoolteacher, who pledged to "have a union of all the players in the town in one club in the coming season", something which wouldn't come to fruition for another decade.

There were more receptions, more wallets, more back-slapping and war whoops and riotous cheers, but it had to end some time.

Higgins, the most gifted and yet most modest of the lot, wasn't enamoured with the fuss.

"The villages were packed and the crossroads, you'd wonder what all the excitement was about. We passed no remarks," he remembered in his calm, humble way.

"We stayed in the Farnham, some of them stayed a couple of days in it, others went home. I went home. I was in the guards at the time and I was after getting six weeks off between the training and everything. It was time to do something."

And so it was.

*　　*　　*

The following Sunday, for some of the players at least, it was time to come back to earth. An inspired performance from goalkeeper Val Gannon helped Mullahoran beat Cornafean by 2-8 to 0-6 in the county semi-final, with the Gunner, Brian O'Reilly and Wilson featuring for the winners, Big Tom lining out for the Reds and Hughie O'Reilly's brother, Cavan selector Tommy, refereeing.

In the curtain-raiser, McDyer helped the Slashers see off Cross by three points, none other than TP himself reffing that one.

Time to relax for the rest? Not quite. Old pals Kerry were up next in a charity match in Croke Park, and with them came the chance to complete a rare treble in one season over the Kingdom. It was time to get back to work...

Glory Days

DAWN broke on 1948 and Cavan were still celebrating. Having won the most historic All-Ireland championship of all time, they were lauded like no team before them and the celebrations lasted well into the spring.

They had lost that third meeting with Kerry, but it made no odds. The make-up of the team changed little from the Polo Grounds, bar the emergence of Victor Sherlock at midfield. A native of Kingscourt, he came to prominence playing for Gypsum Rangers, a factory team, in Meath and had declared for the Royals, where his uncle in Navan was county secretary.

Sherlock was an outstanding left-footed midfielder-cum-half-forward who had won National League and Leinster medals with the Royals. He came into the Cavan side for the league clash against Monaghan and was still there by the time of the league final against Cork, when Peter Donohoe scored a last-minute 50-yard free to salvage a draw.

Cavan beat Down by five points in the Ulster opener, a game which featured a back-heeled goal from Willie Doonan, and easily saw off Monaghan by 1-9 to 0-7 in the semi-final.

The hype before the Ulster final against Antrim was through the roof and Hughie took his men to Ballyjamesduff to prepare again. Asked by a reporter how he felt his side would do, he thought for a second.

"Well," he replied. And at that the interview concluded.

They did, too. The momentum from the Polo Grounds had grown and Cavan were playing better than ever, goals from Edwin Carolan and Joe Stafford helping them to a 2-12 to 2-4 win before 32,200 supporters.

John Joe O'Reilly, marking the outstanding Kevin Armstrong that day, was a force of nature at No 6 all year. With Tony Tighe, the Gunner and Sherlock all on fire too, Cavan, it seemed, couldn't be beaten.

During camp, Higgins, who had been stationed in Drogheda, was asked to run through the Louth team. When he came to the corner-forward, he informed his teammates that the player was fast, skilful but, if it got rough, he wouldn't like it.

Doonan, picked at right corner-back, was listening and, when the game began, he beat the Louth man to the first two balls and half-volleyed them 40 yards down the field, as was his style.

The third time he tried it, the ball skewed off his boot and ended up in the stand. Supporters groaned, but Doonan was not the type to hang his head and made a virtue out of necessity.

"Now," he told his marker, pointing to the terraces, "do you see that ball? Well, that's where you'll be next time!"

They led Louth by 1-10 to 0-1 at half-time but were forced to withstand a late rally in the semi-final, with Mick Higgins, it was reported, "playing the game of his life, coming up smiling out of every ruck to smash through the Louth defence". They eventually won, 1-14 to 2-4.

The final against Mayo, who had beaten Galway in extra-time after two replays in Connacht and a tired Kerry team in the semi-final, was expected to be an epic, and it was, although it didn't play out as expected.

Before the match, a rabbit was released in Mayo colours and scuttled around in circles, nibbling the grass. In response, Cavan supporters released a hare clad in blue and white.

The hare's team got the start they wanted. With the wind, Cavan were awesome in the first half, Tighe burying two goals and helping a Cavan team which featured 11 starters from the Polo Grounds to a 3-2 to 0-0 half-time lead.

John Joe was forced off injured early in the second half and Cavan introduced Owen Roe McGovern, with Simon Deignan going to centre-back. Both men turned in incredible performances but Mayo would dominate and eventually drew level in a game which attracted an attendance of almost 75,000, with an estimated 25,000 locked outside.

With time almost up, and Cavan 4-5 to 4-4 ahead, the Connacht champions were awarded a straightforward free. As Padraig Carney, a doctor who had done his internship in Cavan General, prepared to take the kick, Higgins, who had retreated back to the full-back line to help out, slowly inched forward. He had studied Carney's kicking style and knew it followed a low trajectory. By the time boot hit leather, Mick, whose father had grown up a few miles away from Carney's home in Swinford, was in position and his fingertips blocked it. The ball was cleared and the whistle sounded.

The greatest footballing brain of them all had done it again. Oh, and they kicked five goals in hammering the Rebels in the league final replay a fortnight later, too. Cavan's star had never shone so brightly.

The team arrived back in Cavan on the Tuesday night, having taken an extra day in the capital. Four or five of the Cavan team, on the Monday, converged on a well-known GAA watering hole, Moore's on Cathedral St, and, by chance, found themselves sitting beside beaten Mayo captain Sean Flanagan.

Flanagan spent a while bemoaning his side's bad luck and eventually one man could take it no longer and snapped.

"All that's wrong with you," snapped the fiery Stafford, "is that Cavan were a match for you and you can't take it!"

*   *   *

The following year, the same spine was in place with a couple of new additions. Arva's Seamus Morris was in goal, after Des Benson and Val Gannon had shared the duties the previous year, playing a half each against Monaghan before Benson took over. Jim McCabe was a new face in the full-back line, after Doonan was dropped, allegedly, after a run-in with a priest. The story goes that Peter McDermott, the man in the cap, jumped for joy when he heard that Doonan wasn't to start.

Either way, after having beaten Armagh in the Ulster final by a point and Cork in the semi by three, the three-in-a-row eluded

Cavan when Meath won the final by 1-10 to 1-6.

Worse was to follow in 1950. Losing PJ Duke in May gutted the soul of the team. Armagh were coming on strong and they inflicted a rare Ulster final defeat in Clones, winning their first Ulster title in 47 years.

A week later, they were beaten in the 'home' National League final by a New York team which included Bill Carlos of Roscommon, who had marked Mick Higgins in the 1947 semi-final, and Sean Keane, a sub on the Kerry team in the Polo Grounds.

The greatest team of them all had started to decline and when they again lost the Ulster final, this time by a point to Antrim, the following summer, only five of the starting team from the 1947 final – Phil Brady, John Joe, Higgins, Donohoe and Tighe – were on board.

It looked as if the end had come sooner than expected.

* * *

By the time 1952 arrived, Hughie faced his greatest challenge yet – constructing a new team. For the Ulster final against Monaghan, only five – the Gunner, Higgins, Tighe, John Joe Cassidy and Edwin Carolan – of the entire Polo Grounds panel was on the starting team.

They got over Antrim in a rough semi-final and a late goal saw Monaghan beaten 1-8 to 0-8 in the Ulster final, but they were written off before playing Cork at the penultimate stage. The feeling in the camp in Ballyconnell, however, was positive, noted the Celt, who commented that "they were all in the best of spirits and seemed fit to tackle even an outpost in Korea.

However, the general consensus was that Cork would have too much but in a match which Higgins listed as his most memorable, Cavan came through by a solitary point, 0-10 to 2-3. They missed a penalty and trailed by four midway through the second-half but rallied to win. Brady, Higgins, who in the absence of Peter Donohoe had become a deadly freetaker, and Tighe, in particular, carried the team and the new players rose to the occasion.

An interesting sub-plot to the final was the tale of the three Maguire brothers. Des and Liam lined out in defence for Cavan while another brother, Brendan, was on board for Meath.

Cavan needed an impossible point from Edwin Carolan to salvage a draw the first day, a day of such poor weather that the minor final between Cavan, featuring a 16-year-old Jim McDonnell, and Galway was abandoned.

In the replay, Higgins kicked 0-7 as Cavan won by 0-9 to 0-5. By that stage, Higgins was captaining a Cavan side decimated by a death, emigration, retirements and withdrawals, and flanked at the back by the Gunner, he led them to the unlikeliest All-Ireland title of all.

In typically modest fashion, the best footballer in Ireland that year recalled his acceptance speech.

"Ah, you thanked this one and that one. My speech was very short, I can tell you," he laughed.

"It was a wet day and I didn't like keeping them out in the rain."

*   *   *

Johnny Cusack, who had watched the 1947 semi-final against Roscommon from the Hogan Stand, was corner-forward in '52. The shadow of the Polo Grounds, even then, hung over the Cavan team.

"Sure '47 was *the* thing, over to America and the celebrations when they came home, sure it was *the* match."

It miffed Cavan footballers who came after the Polo Grounds that they didn't get the credit they deserved. New York would tower over Cavan teams for generations. Years later, Cusack would ask Big Tom what was the best team he ever played on.

"I asked Big Tom, 'you were on the '33 and '35 teams and all those teams, what team would you say was the best?'" he explained.

"My brothers used to say that the '33 team was the best ever Cavan had.

"'Oh,' he says, 'the '47 team was the best.'

"How would you say that?

"'Well, in our time,' he says, 'there were great backs and centre-field but we were depending on MJ McGee from Killeshandra for scores. All the Cavan forwards in '47 could score. All six of them could score. They were the best ever...'"

The Decline

For some years past, Cavan's football exploits had slumped to such a low ebb that the team was treated as little more than a joke.
The Anglo-Celt on the eve of Cavan's 1962 Ulster final win over Down

TWENTY-TWO years had passed from his own greatest day, 17 from Cavan's last one, and TP had had enough. He'd been chairman of the Cavan county board for over a dozen years and despite the county being regularly ranked in the top five in the country, he saw his tenure as a failure.

Ignore the fact that Cavan won four Ulster titles and beat the All-Ireland champions in two of those finals; forget the Wembley tournament wins and the emergence of some of the best footballers in the country. TP O'Reilly was one of the men of '47 and, as such, traded in a different currency. Cavan were old money and didn't like the nouveau riche of Down rearing their heads. The aristocracy re-asserted itself on four occasions on their own estate but the age of dominance was over.

When TP stepped down in 1969, it was with an air of regret.

The end of the '60s was also the end of Cavan as a football superpower. The link was still strong in that decade with management, with county board, with players who had grown up watching it all happen. But when Mick Higgins' fabulous team failed to magic another All-Ireland, the flag fell to half-mast.

TP's son, Garrett, had played senior championship football for Ballyconnell at the age of 15 in 1963 and would win Ulster medals in '67 and '69. He remembers his father, high on victory, pounding on the steering wheel, "roaring and shouting", on the way home from big games.

"He wouldn't have been satisfied, the four [All-Ireland semi-final] defeats of the '60s probably prompted him to retire. I would imagine so. He took them very bad, he'd be very down. He was child-like nearly with excitement when we beat Down in '67 and '69.

"Cavan didn't think they did well in the '60s, that would have been the perception at the end of that decade."

Viewed by the standard of the subsequent decades, though, they did very well indeed.

*   *   *

TP was one of a string of professionals to play with Cavan. Originally from Drumlane, he qualified as a solicitor in the early 40s, set up practice in Ballyconnell and lived the life of a football-obsessed country solicitor until called to the bench in 1973.

To that point, successful Cavan teams had always been backboned by teachers, doctors, vets, solicitors, dentists. They were confident, successful and having played college football with the best in the country, knew they were as good.

"There were never that many farmers on the Cavan team. Maybe away back in the '30s but not in my time. They had too much work to do, I suppose, they hadn't much time to train. Fellas in college got a better chance, I think anyway. At home, fellas would maybe have to milk the cows when they got home, it wouldn't be out to the football field they go," recalled Jim McDonnell.

"When Cavan were going well, a lot of them were playing football at a high level in Dublin for example. You would have had four or five of the UCD team on the Cavan team and more fellas playing for clubs in Dublin, guards and so on, and more fellas playing at a high level in other counties. Looking back, I think Mick Higgins played in Louth and Kildare. The Gunner Brady won a championship medal in Cork with the guards. When we were in UCD, there was Charlie Gallagher, James Brady, James McCabe... Four or five of us on the team. You'd a good chance."

McDonnell had realised it as soon as he arrived in Belfield in 1954.

"The UCD team in my time, there were 15 county men and the subs were all county men as well, so I got to meet a lot of them, Jerome O'Shea, Sean Murphy, Paudie Sheehy, Jim Brosnan, all of those guys were there in UCD at the time so it helped us a lot. We saw that they weren't supermen. They were very ordinary fellas. I realised that."

Ten years previously, TP O'Reilly had graduated from the same college, having been a part of the UCD team that won the Dublin championship for the first time in 1943, beating Sean McDermotts in the final. The O'Reillys, from Drumlane, were well-off; Thomas Patrick was the eldest son and only became "TP" when he came on to the Cavan team, to distinguish himself from Big Tom O'Reilly of Cornafean. Years later, he would note that you could always tell how long someone knew him by their greeting – to his oldest friends, he was Tom. To his football comrades, it was TP.

He went on to play for Cavan until the end of 1949, a rangy corner-forward. By '57, he was in the chair and plotting a revival.

*   *   *

In terms of titles won, the '60s still stand as Cavan's most successful decade since the '40s and the fingerprints of the great team of that era were all over it.

At the time, selectors were elected by vote and, sometimes, men with little football knowledge politicked their way in. TP had other ideas.

He installed Higgins as manager in 1960 and Stafford, Simon Deignan and Tighe served at various times. Willie Doonan wasn't involved in the management but would attend training. The link was still strong.

It seemed like a dream set-up with the great schemer patrolling the sideline and moulding good young players into a winning shape. In '59, Cavan had won a rare Ulster minor title and reached an All-Ireland final, which they lost to Dublin, so there was talent coming through.

It took time, though – the revolution was not telegraphed and when the northern lights began to shine, Cavan found themselves mesmerised. The heaviest blows are the ones you don't see coming and the emergence of, first, Derry in 1958 and, then, Down in '59 left the county, who were already swaying, punch-drunk and on the ropes.

Hughie O'Reilly was still the boss but, by the late 50s, said McDonnell: "He was getting old, he had a lot of pains" and '59 would mark the last year of his tenure. Assisted by Joe Stafford and Higgins, he guided the team to the Ulster final, with The Anglo-Celt confidently predicting a Cavan win, noting that "if tradition counted for everything, then the match is as good as over".

Their correspondent PJ O'Neill, a Wexford native and brother of Polo Grounds referee Martin, spoke of the "deadly lethargy" that had plagued Cavan teams in the previous handful of championships.

"Cavan have had a lean time in the football world," he noted, "and the up and coming northern teams have gained in confidence with Cavan's downfall."

One had to go back to 1915, when Cavan won the title after a seven-year gap, for the last comparable famine, he said. But he expected Cavan to win and restore some pride.

The enthusiasm still comes through in TP O'Reilly's quote in the same article:

"The spirit is excellent and we are definitely out to take the title back to Cavan."

It didn't happen. The Celt's headline the following week – "Too bad to be true" – told its own tale as Down won their first Ulster title by an astonishing 2-16 to 0-7.

Peadar O'Brien in the Irish Press described Down's victory as "thoroughly deserved, utterly convincing and wonderfully popular". It was Down's first Ulster title and some of their supporters among the 30,000-strong crowd climbed the goalposts, O'Brien recorded, in celebration.

Cavan had never slipped so low and worse was to follow in the following two seasons. Hughie stepped aside and Higgins came in.

In his first year in charge, Mick led the team to the National League final, where they would meet, inevitably, upstarts Down.

Cavan had pushed the Ulster champions to two points in a

Wembley qualifier in Carrickmacross, a game which, in the build-up to the league final, TP described as "the best match we ever lost."

"It meant," he said, referring to the previous summer's Ulster final hiding, "that the book is closed on Clones now."

The match was preceded by a minor football challenge between the counties and the sparse official programme contained the bare essentials: the teams, the words to Slievenamon and The Soldier's Song and ads for three pubs — The Metro Bar and The Welcome Inn on Parnell St and Aherne's on Capel St, all of which claimed to serve "Dublin's best drinks" and two of which boasted of "freshly cut sandwiches".

How many of the 49,451 crowd put that to the test wasn't recorded but there was certainly no sense of revelry among the Cavan supporters afterwards. A young Down held on to win by 0-12 to 0-9, becoming the first team from Ulster besides Cavan to win a national football or hurling title. The old order had changed utterly, and for Cavan, a terrible beauty was born as they entered a new decade.

The promise of Carrickmacross and Croke Park was washed away that July when what the Celt described as the "crafty, cocky Down combination" broke through for two goals in the first two minutes of the Ulster final en route to a 3-7 to 1-8 win. They went on to win a first All-Ireland, 90,000 watching them bedazzle Offaly.

Cavan had set the bar, and Down had raised it again.

"The main barrier to a northern team winning a senior All-Ireland title in football was psychological," Maurice Hayes, Down official of the time, has written.

"One could only do one's best and put up a good show. And then there was Cavan, lying like a dragon in the path of any other Ulster county. The highest ambition any Ulster county could have was to beat Cavan once in a blue moon. That was their All-Ireland final. After that they had nothing left to achieve."

But the old order changeth and, for Higgins and Cavan. beating Down became an obsession. They were new and flashy, tracksuited (the first Gaelic team to bother) and slick. The emergence of intellectuals like Sean O'Neill and Joe Lennon saw them break new ground and while many of the players formed great friendships afterwards, it rankled Cavan at the time. Because they weren't just winning, they were doing it in style.

In '61, Cavan never even made it as far as a crack at them as Armagh inflicted the county's first opening round defeat in 56 years. The mood was despondent.

"We had taken hammerings from Down in '59 and '60," recalled McDonnell.

"There was one particular game I remember in Newry in the McKenna Cup around about that time. Down didn't put out their full team. That time you could put on as many subs as you wanted and by the time it was nearly over, they had their full team on. We went Down-mad to get at them of course. We beat them anyway and it was a great boost, at the time we thought we couldn't beat them. It was around '61."

It was actually in April of the following year that that game took place. Down were understrength but Cavan shocked them in Newry, winning by five points. The following month, a junior team featuring Gallagher, Tom Lynch and a pair of schoolboys, Ray Carolan and Jimmy Stafford, beat the same opposition to win a first Ulster junior title in six seasons. Suddenly, Cavan and Higgins were on the march again.

Meanwhile, something was afoot in St Pat's. St Patrick's College's contribution to Cavan football at the time was similar to that of the fee-paying schools such as Blackrock College and Clongowes Wood to Leinster rugby. It churned out players, hard lads honed in the house style. And they regularly slotted in to county teams, little clusters of big-boned schoolboys emerging almost fully-finished.

"I'm not saying that all the footballers came out of St Pat's but there was always a backbone," remembers McDonnell.

"Most years you would get two or three players from St Pat's who would get on the county team."

*   *   *

McDonnell's own association with the school goes back to when he entered in 1943, the year Cavan lost the All-Ireland senior final to Roscommon. He played on the first ever Corn na nOg-winning side and went on to enjoy a magnificent senior career, captaining Cavan to the Anglo-Celt Cup twice in the '60s, having been an Ulster medallist alongside the likes of Peter Donohoe and Phil the Gunner as far back as 1955.

He taught in St Pat's for four decades, training the MacRory-winning team of '61 on which Ray Carolan and Peter Pritchard (midfielder and corner-forward for the seniors a year later alongside their teacher) made their names. He would even run for the national GAA presidency in 1991, when vice principal of the school. Had he won and worn the Celtic Cross, he still wouldn't have been top dog in the St Pat's staff-room (or "priest's ref" as it was at the time); principal there was Fr Dan Gallogly, Ulster GAA President.

McDonnell had begun training teams in 1960 and the first two he took charge of won the MacRory Cup in 1960 and 1961, losing to St Jarlath's of Tuam in the semi-final both years. Those sides produced Carolan, Stafford, Pat Gaffney, Paddy Lyons and Peter Pritchard, all of whom would go on to win Ulster senior medals.

By May of '62, Carolan, who turned 19 that April, and Stafford, whose 19th birthday wasn't until October, had won their second MacRory, the Ulster junior title and were preparing with their teammates for a tilt at the All-Ireland champions in the Ulster senior decider. They were the young guns and the missing link.

Stafford, who made his name as a full-back at colleges level, showed his uncle Joe's instincts as he pounced for two first-half goals, Gallagher kicked four points and Cavan beat the three-in-a-row seeking All-Ireland champions by 10 points.

"Down were the team then," says Tony Morris, wing-back in '62 and '64.

"If they had beat us, they'd have won the All-Ireland. But it was a mighty day, a real hot day in Belfast and we tore into them."

Supporters had real reason for optimism by 5pm on that Sunday evening, not least over the emergence of Carolan. Under the searing Belfast sun, Down tried five different markers on the teenager that afternoon; nothing worked.

"Down were heroes at the time," Carolan recalled.

"I was playing in the middle of the field in the final and caught the first ball and came down with it and I never saw anybody. And I got such a fright I nearly dropped the ball.

"And the second ball came out and I went up and caught it and I sort of looked around to see where the hell were these fellas. And then you start to think, 'Jesus, I'm better than these fellas'."

Cavan were better, all over the field than the All-Ireland champions and The Anglo-Celt's headline reflected the mood of the county: "Resurgent Cavan crush All-Ireland champions — Golden prospects of sixth All-Ireland".

For Cavan, you see, an Ulster title was no good. It had to be the big one and the feeling was that the time had come again.

* * *

Roscommon, surprise winners in Connacht, were up next in mid-August but the semi-final was a disaster as Cavan spurned chance after chance and Roscommon advanced. The famine continued.

"We were too naive. We couldn't adapt," remembered Carolan. McDonnell concurred.

"We went out against a mediocre enough Roscommon team in the semi-final and got beaten by two points, having missed 12 frees. That was one we should have won really," he said.

On the way home, TP called into Higgins' home in Virginia for the post-mortem.

"It was a poor Roscommon team. I remember there was terrible depression that night," said Garrett, then a 14-year-old engrossed in football.

"We were at Higgins' for a while. Mick mightn't show it as much as my father would show it. He would be totally gutted. Life wasn't worth living. Because it'd be almost a child-like excitement beforehand."

Morris summed it up.

"We should've beat Roscommon, Roscommon were no good of a team."

*   *   *

For TP, Higgins and Cavan, it was back to work. Down won again in '63 but Cavan were back for more the following year. Wins over Derry (3-9 to 2-3) and Donegal (1-9 to 0-7) saw them through to the Ulster final, where two goals from sub Peter Pritchard, he of the '62 MacRory team, helped turn a five-point deficit into a three-point win. The county was delirious with excitement once more, evidenced by the fact that a chartered plane was arranged to fly a group of 130 "Breffni exiles", members of the Cavanmen's Association in New York, home for the game, with a committee hastily convened to greet them at the airport.

The Celt's headline was almost pleading in its tone: NO SLIP UP THIS TIME.

It didn't work out that way.

*   *   *

In his preview, Mick Dunne pointed out that Cavan's forwards had kicked 32 wides in their previous two trips to Croke Park, 18 against Roscommon in '62 and four less in the NFL semi-final against Down that spring. The performance of that set of forwards (and Dunne named them in his opening paragraph – "O'Reilly, O'Donnell, Pritchard, Cahill, Gallagher and McDonnell") would decide whether Cavan would beat Kerry in Croke Park for the first time, having lost semi-finals in 1923, '26 and '37.

What wasn't mentioned in Dunne's report was that the team had booked themselves into a two-week training camp in Kilnacrott College, outside Ballyjamesduff, before the Kerry match. Cavan had pioneered collective training when they were winning All-Irelands and, stung by the Roscommon defeat two summers before, relied again on the tried and trusted. If it was good enough in '47, '48 and '52...

"I took two weeks off work without pay and went down to Kilnacrott for full-time training," remembered Morris.

"At that time in the guards if you were playing football they'd look after you. We used to be up at six o'clock in the morning out walking on the roads. Back in, make the bed, go down and get the breakfast, hang around for a while and out to the field, no balls. You'd be running around the field. Back in and lie around, then a big lunch and back out in the evening with footballs, seven-a-side, ten-a-side, backs and forwards.

"You'd go out the road again at night and you'd be in bed at half ten.

"I was fairly young and it didn't do me any harm but some of them that were older, they were stuck to the ground when they went into Croke Park."

Collective training was a thorny issue. It had been banned by Croke Park a decade before after a grumble at Ard Comhairle level that it was getting too professional. It had been debated at a Cavan county convention back then, when it was revealed that the county board had spent "close on £2,000" on the camp in 1952.

Hughie O'Reilly was quoted as saying that he believed the practice "raised the standard of the game" while a Mr Gilheaney spoke up to say that "the public expected teams turn out fit and the only way to do that was collective training".

Collective training had served Cavan well on the field but after the revolution, things had changed. Cavan's famine years from '55 to '62 allowed an unprecedented three counties to win a first Ulster title and when the county finally tasted the drink again, it went to their heads.

"It [collective training] was a bit illegal too and any time we did it, I think we got beaten. We stayed in Bailieborough in '59, we were all brought into the hotel there and we trained in Kilnacrott in '64

I think. You were all kept together and trained a couple of times a day," said McDonnell.

In Croke Park, against a Kingdom team boasting Mick O'Connell, Tom Long and fit-again Mick O'Dwyer, Cavan collapsed.

Kerry led by four points at half-time and ran out 2-12 to 0-6 winners.

The reaction in the county can be gauged from the writing of PJ O'Neill, who spared no-one in the Celt. Under a piece headed "Fans humiliated", he castigated the players as non-triers and described Kerry as "a moderate team". Cavan players, he said, allowed themselves to be "tossed about like snuff at a wake".

*   *   *

By 1967, Cavan had an injection of fresh blood. They lost to Down in the '65 Ulster final, with Phil the Gunner as a selector alongside Higgins, but by '67, new names were popping up to supplement the spine of the side. Jim McDonnell and Tom Maguire retired in '66 but Carolan, Gabriel Kelly and Gallagher were still there. The emergence of the likes of Andy McCabe, Pat Tinnelly, Garret O'Reilly and Steve Duggan saw Higgins put together what would be remembered as the best Cavan team not to win an All-Ireland.

Higgins' team could live with the best and regularly proved it in Ulster, beating the All-Ireland champions in two finals, and in tournaments, taking down three-in-a-row All-Ireland winners Galway in Wembley in '66 and beating Meath in a Grounds Tournament final when they were champions the following year.

Those four-team tournaments were played on the eve of championship, with the previous year's semi-final pairings reversed, and it was serious business.

"We could take on and beat every team at the time, no matter who they were, but we just didn't beat the right teams at the right time," said Carolan.

Of all the years, 1967 was the one that got away. Cavan were outstanding in beating Down by 10 points in the Ulster final in

Casement Park. With Maguire having hung them up, Carolan manned the centre of the half-back line.

"I knew we couldn't get beaten, everybody was up for the match. Leaving the Farnham, if I had £1,000 in my pocket I'd have put it on Cavan to win. We got on the bus and it was so calm, it was unreal. There was so much confidence there."

*   *   *

Slotting him in at number six, however, robbed Cavan of their main ball-winner at midfield and while they got through Ulster alright, they came unstuck in the semi-final against Cork, somehow losing by 2-7 to 0-12.

Garrett O'Reilly, then aged 19, came on at corner-forward that day and still remembers just how close they came.

"There was a penalty we definitely should have got. We had a last minute free to equalise it but we lost by a point.

"There was a guy Mick Burke played midfield for Cork that day and he was brilliant. We were told don't worry about Burke, Mick O'Loughlin was the man to watch at midfield. But Burke had a storming game.

"We conceded two terribly soft goals. John Joe [O'Reilly, from Crosserlough] was pulled down on the square, it was clearly in the square but we got no penalty."

Steve Duggan was one of the younger brigade and had come into the team the previous year, bringing electrifying pace to the half-forward line.

"We reckoned that day we should have got a penalty that we never got," remembers Duggan, now a bar manager and music promoter in New York.

"Cork got a penalty that they shouldn't have got. Someone pushed Peter Pritchard and he fell on the ball and they gave a penalty, it should've been a free out. Cork beat us."

Years later, when asked what his greatest disappointment in football was, Charlie Gallagher didn't hesitate in nominating the 67 semi-final. "This was one game," he said, "that Cavan should have won."

To make things worse at the time, Meath's Red Collier tangled with Burke 10 minutes into the final. The Corkman put out his collar-bone, the Royals won and headed off on what Duggan described as "the best trip ever – to Australia".

When the Royals returned, Cavan played them in the Grounds Tournament final and won. The right team, the wrong time...

*   *   *

The men of '47-52 were still there. Tony Tighe attended training and would act as selector for a time, while Joe Stafford stayed involved. By this time, he owned a guesthouse in Dublin, The Antrim Arms in Drumcondra, and he would chauffeur the capital-based players to training and matches. There was a bond there between the men of '47 anyway.

"My father was an awful man for asking people to do things," remembers Garrett O'Reilly.

"Joe would be coming down from Dublin with a desk on top of his car or something because TP saw it in some ad. He was a fierce open-hearted, generous sort of guy anyway, Joe. They were all close."

And the players loved Higgins, who is routinely described as "a great man".

Higgins had a way of instilling calm in players. He was universally respected. In 1967, Eugene McGee's brother Fr Phil arrived at his home and cajoled him into helping Longford out. He combined this with his duties in Cavan and helped Longford win a National League and their only Leinster title. His roles clashed on one occasion and it was the only time his players saw him lose his temper.

"The only time I ever heard him roaring, well, it wasn't roaring, just a little more animated than other times was one time he was helping out Longford at the same time that he was managing Cavan. We played them in Croke Park in a qualifying match to go to Wembley, it was in '67," recalled O'Reilly.

"In the first half we were dreadful, very poor and he tore into us at half-time and kind of said 'people will be laughing at me'. Something like that. I remember we won the game through sheer willpower, I don't think we played an awful lot better. But we had to win it then."

A conflict of interests, not that there'd have been a choice to make, was avoided in '68 in any case. Down ran out five-point winners in the Ulster final and Cavan could only watch frustrated as O'Neill and Co ("a great Croke Park team" as McDonnell described them) high-fived their way through their next two matches, beating Galway and then Kerry to pick up their third All-Ireland in eight years.

*   *   *

By the dawn of 1969, the Cavan team was getting old.

Gallagher was still in place and was playing as well as ever. The previous year, his cumulative tally of scores in the National League amounted to more than hurling's top scorer, Eddie Keher, managed.

Charlie, born across the road from Hughie O'Reilly's house in Cootehill, was the real deal. He had the looks, he had the skills and he had the swagger to go with it.

Asked once in an interview who he would most like to meet, he thought for a minute and replied: "Sophia Loren".

GAA journalist Kevin Carney was born across the road from Gallagher's home in Cootehill. When Carney was selected on the Cavan team for the Centenary Cup semi-final in 1984, the first person to ring and congratulate him was Charlie.

"Charlie was the embodiment of what young Gaelic footballers in Cootehill aspired to as we watched him practice for hours in Celtic Park and then practice some more," Carney has written.

"He was suffused with ambition, laced with talent, brim-full of bravado, pace and precision. He got bums off their seats before there were seats. Charlie fired over balls over the bar with all the accuracy of a nuclear clock and all of Cavan loved him for it. He was cheeky Charlie and sprinkled stardust onto every team he ever played with."

In '64, he had been one of only seven footballers in the country selected to travel to the US for the JF Kennedy Memorial Games and he would win four Railway Cup titles. Gallagher was a dentist based in Derry, where he was employed by Barney Cully, the full-back who was done out of his place on the Polo Grounds team in the committee room for having played a soccer match.

He drove a Singer sports car and crowds would gather on the corner in Cootehill on Friday evenings when Charlie was due home, waiting for a glimpse and a wink.

"I remember in 1967 in Breffni Park, we were training for the All-Ireland semi-final against Cork and Mick Dunne, who was working with RTE at the time, came down to Breffni Park to get some shots," recalled Duggan.

"I remember him getting shots of Micheál Greenan and myself and he wanted to get one of Charlie, just running up along the 45 and kicking the ball. Just to see him in action soloing.

"Charlie went up along the sideline anyway, down towards the Royal School, and he took a shot from about 60 yards with his left foot and put it over the black spot. And says he, is that good enough for you? And your man didn't care if he kicked it 10 yards wide, it was just to see him in action."

Supporters loved him for just that; he was brilliant and, in the swinging '60s, he was cool.

The bigger the match, the cooler Charlie was. Carolan remembers him scoring "one of those spectacular points of his", trotting back to his position and grinning aloud "what'd you think of that one, Carolan?"

"But he didn't say it in a selfish or smart way, it was just the character that was in the individual. He was a sheer opportunist. He was one of those characters. He was flamboyant."

After matches, men would swarm around him in the pub. One supporter remembers a scene from a Sunday in Navan in the mid-60s on the way home from a Railway Cup final win in Croke

Park. Gallagher was holding court in a pub full of Meathmen and one approached him.

"Your man says: "Are you Charlie Gallagher?' and Charlie says 'I am'.

"'Jaysus, I have to shake your hand', he said. 'You killed us in Pairc Tailteann in one game ya hoor ya, you scored a point from the left-hand line, 50 yards out in the first half and you did the same in the second. Do you remember it?'"

"'Oh I do', says Charlie, glancing around, 'but say it a bit louder'."

That was the type of him, witty, engaging but, on the field, dynamite.

By the end of 1969, however, he was done, his career over in inglorious circumstances. And with him went Cavan's hopes.

*   *   *

The campaign started poorly, with chairman TP and veteran Gabriel Kelly "lacerating" the players in the dressing-room after a lacklustre two-point opening round win over Fermanagh.

Attendance at training had been poor, the Celt reported, and Cavan showed "every semblance of a team ill-prepared, ill-conceived and, most certainly, ill-equipped".

Higgins wielded the axe for the semi-final, dropping PJ Smith, Larry McCormack and, of all men, Gallagher, with a young seminary student from Mountnugent, Declan Coyle, taking Charlie's spot at full-forward.

A first-half goal from teenage sensation Gene Cusack helped Cavan win the replay by five points with an improved performance but they still entered the Ulster final as underdogs against a Down side who were the reigning Ulster, All-Ireland and National League champions.

It was a day that Higgins and his seven-man selection committee, reported the Celt, had been planning towards for 10 months. With Carolan and Hughie Newman dominating against a magnificent Down midfield of Colm McAlarney and Jim Milligan, Cavan raced into the lead with the deadly Cusack burying a goal from a tight angle in the first half. Brendan Donohoe snuffed out Sean O'Neill and Cavan ran out seven-point winners in front of 45,000 supporters in Casement Park.

Offaly were waiting in the semi-final and the feeling was that this, at last, would be Cavan's year.

Offaly were appearing in their first semi-final in eight years and had just three survivors, Paddy McCormack, Greg Hughes and Johnny Egan from that team. However, an All-Ireland minor win in '64 had yielded Martin Furlong, Eugene Mulligan, Mick Ryan, Tony McTeague, Willie Bryan and Sean Evans and, in GAA parlance, they were a coming team.

Unfortunately for Cavan, for Higgins, for Gallagher, they arrived too early.

*　　*　　*

The Celt's preview was prescient.

"Many supporters," wrote Eamonn Gaffney, "believe that if Cavan don't win an All-Ireland title this year, they never will as players like Charlie Gallagher, Gabriel Kelly, John Joe O'Reilly and Tom Lynch are not likely to remain on the team for many more years to come."

The first day out produced a draw, 1-9 to 0-12, with McTeague kicking 10 of the Faithful's points, seven of them from frees. Cavan played the better football but Offaly hung tough and took the lead with 10 minutes on the clock. Cavan laid siege to their goal for the final 10 minutes but kicked three successive wides.

Someone made the decision to substitute Gallagher and his replacement, Greenan, somehow missed a 21-yard free.

It took an impossible late point from the youngest man on the team, Cusack, to snatch the draw but Cavan still thought they'd finish the job the next time out.

Carolan: "Even coming off the first day, I was glad we drew because I was fully sure we'd win the replay. I said to myself, 'we'll bloody beat these fellas the next day'. But it was another fierce wet day and we got beaten again.

"They were two really wet old days. They took Charlie off and we got a 21-yard free in front of the goals. Micheál Greenan took it and he didn't rise it, it went wide. That was it."

Higgins explained the decision after the game, stating that Charlie was wandering out to the middle and his marker, Paddy McCormack, was coming with him and doing damage.

Intriguingly, he added that when Gallagher was brought back on with two minutes to go, he was "down near the Offaly goals urging the boys on and I don't know whose decision it was". This was bizarre because it had been confirmed at a county board meeting that the manager had the final say.

"Someone took Charlie Gallagher off in '69 and nobody knew what happened," says Enda McGowan, wing-back that day and a mainstay for another decade.

"Cavan got a free afterwards and they didn't score it. They probably should've won the drawn match. Micheál Greenan had only just come on and wasn't really into the game. It wasn't his fault, nobody was to blame."

To this day, there are those who will swear that had Gallagher been on the field during that furious late rampage, he'd have taken a couple of chances, not least Greenan's free. But he wasn't, he didn't and it was Offaly who learned their lessons in time for the replay.

Ambrose Hickey was fit for the replay, while Sean Kilroy had recovered from a fractured jaw and was able to come on. Offaly led by two goals at half-time and while Cavan battled hard, a third green flag ended the dream.

"I don't blame them in the sense, they were all trying to do their best but there wasn't enough foresight or thinking. Carolan should've been midfield and Tom Lynch centre half. Maybe Fergus McCauley and JJ Reilly should have been on the team," says one player.

A crestfallen John Joe O'Reilly cut a frustrated figure when interviewed after the game.

"We were fighting all the time to get back into the game and we simply could not fight back hard enough. Everything we threw at them was taken."

"Since Sunday's game, the post-mortems have been many," noted the following Friday's Anglo-Celt.

"Should Cavan have gone for points, which were there for the taking on a few occasions, instead of being so goal-hungry? Should they have...? And so the chat will go on. The result is now history: Offaly 3-8; Cavan 1-10."

*　　*　　*

The fall-out was seismic. TP O'Reilly stepped down at the county convention the following January. He'd had enough. Higgins did likewise.

Maybe the old magic had faded a little. One former player said that Cavan "prepared in the '60s the same way as we did in the '40s. With a bit more planning we'd have won that All-Ireland."

In 1960, when Patsy Lynch was Central Council delegate, Cavan and Meath brought a motion to Congress asking for the re-introduction of collective training. It was defeated heavily. Cavan were looking back instead of forward.

And still, they weren't far away. Hughie Smyth, secretary since 1938 and all the way through the golden days, and always insisted that had Cavan got a break in 1967 against Cork, they had the potential to win three All-Irelands of their own.

Regardless, the chance was missed and things moved on. Two former players took on the chairman and manager's jobs, Jim McDonnell and Gabriel Kelly respectively.

Charlie Gallagher turned 32 the following Christmas Day, but that Offaly replay would be his last match for the county. Exactly 20 years later, he was gone, drowned in a tragic accident outside Cootehill. Carolan was still only 26 and had won the lot, bar the Celtic Cross, but he wouldn't win another inter-county medal before he packed it in aged 31. It still lingers.

"I was thinking about it there recently. Ah, we should've won an All-Ireland. No doubt."

Cavan's ship sailed away with an unheralded team from the midlands on a couple of rainy September Sundays; never again would the county start the season towards the forefront of the betting for Sam Maguire.

The '60s were over and Charlie was gone, as was Mick and TP and the other links to the greatest team Cavan had ever seen. Little did anyone know that the county would waste their next 28 summers, as someone sang, praying in vain for a saviour to rise from these streets.

*   *   *

Not long afterwards, Bundoran hotelier Brian McEniff – left half-back on a brilliant Railway Cup team managed by Higgins to six successes – and Mick's old teammate, Columba McDyer, arrived at his door as asked him to help out with Donegal.

The county were desperate for success and the men had seen what Higgins had done for Cavan and for Longford. Mick couldn't say no.

Within months, they were Ulster champions. Mick's amazing Midas touch had done the trick again.

An interesting little sub-plot regarding Higgins playing out on the pages of the Celt, too. It was noted that Higgins assisted McEniff, who was player-manager, as they beat Down in the first game but by the following week's Anglo-Celt, Higgins was being listed as Donegal team manager.

That was quickly clarified before the semi-final replay when it was pointed out that Donegal were managed by Brian McEniff, who had "some tactical assistance earlier in the season by former Cavan manager Mick Higgins".

Mick had been in touch, clearly, and let readers know where his allegiances lay. Cavan came first, always.

Hopes were high after St Pat's won a Hogan Cup that year and a core of those players, and their manager Fr Bennie Maguire, graduated to senior ranks, that not winning an All-Ireland in the 60s was a blip and that normal order would be restored.

But a combination of injuries, friction with the county board and pure dumb luck saw Cavan fail to break through, losing an Ulster final in extra time after a replay in 1976 and another two years later.

The St Pat's breeding ground became fallow, the Hogan Cup team hadn't delivered the Anglo-Celt Cups Cavan expected and there was a backlash. Fr Bennie, they said, was too easy on his former pupils. They partied like it was 1972, or so the logic went, and it caught up with them. When he stepped aside, the team broke up and the worst two decades of Cavan's history followed.

Speaking at the county convention in St Pat's in January 1980, county board chairman Paddy Donohoe, the man who had observed the drunken FCA men in Cavan town all those years before, summed it up.

"Sustained defeat is hard on us all," he noted.

"It is harder still in Cavan where we are haunted by the ghosts of past glory. We all feel it hard and grow discouraged by times."

Thirty-three years and a single Ulster title later and Cavan are still going, still discouraged, by times, but still hoping.

Still haunted.

Missing Medals

WILSON kept his medals in a Sweet Afton box, a battered little gold tin that sat in a drawer at his writing desk. Occasionally, his wife would see him with the box out, thumbing the little pieces of metal, his Railway Cup medals, his Celtic Crosses, his county medals. Ordinarily, though, they were in the drawer, the tin clasped shut. There they lay for decades at his home in Churchtown, before they went missing.

John took it badly. He wasn't the type to show emotion but tears would well up in his eyes when the subject of the medals came up. They were his link to a previous life, a connection to a band of brothers, many of whom long since departed.

The family frantically searched their home and, eventually, conceded that perhaps the box was burgled while they were out of the country. For 25 years, the medals were gone.

And then Wilson died, in July 2005. He turned 84 on a Sunday and passed away the following day. With family members delayed returning from France, it was Friday before he was buried.

On the Sunday, the Ulster final between Armagh and Tyrone was on television and, watching at home, John's son and daughter-in-law became emotional at an unexpected minute's silence.

They called John's wife who, lonesome and still mourning her loss, was sifting through files and drawers, a lifetime of achievement stored away in holdalls, presses, bags and filing cabinets.

Ita's eye was drawn to one particular briefcase, one she had searched before again and again. She tried to open it but found it fastened shut and put it down.

A few moments later, she felt compelled to try it again, with the same result. The third time, the buckle snapped open. Reaching in, her hand felt the cold, tattered metal.

The medals were inside. Nothing, Ita recalled later, upset her husband, but that did. To find them again was poetic – fitting for a man reared on the Classics.

*   *   *

There was a sting in the tail for Caughoo, too. The horse would never again scale the heights of the wondrous win at Aintree in the spring of 1947.

The horse ran over the National fences again but its best days were gone and it was retired. Eddie Dempsey went back to his old life as a journeyman jockey but in 1955, he must have wished he'd never heard the name 'Caughoo'.

Returning from sales in Ballsbridge with Danny McCann, his neighbour and the jockey who had ridden second-placed Lough Conn, drink was taken and an argument arose. McCann asserted that Dempsey hadn't completed the whole course and had cost him £2,000.

The pair had been friendly all their lives but as time passed, McCann grew bitter about the National. On a cold November night, it came to a head and McCann and his brother battered him at the side of the road, leaving his face "like pulp".

The men were later convicted for the assault, and sentenced to four months with hard labour. The story of Caughoo mirrored that of the Cavan team of 1947. By 1956, Cavan's downfall had begun in earnest, too. The men of '47 were all gone and the glory of that magical year felt like a lifetime away.

Three decades later, there was yet another morbid twist when Caughoo, or at least his head, returned to Aintree. A colourful former mayor of Drogheda called Frank Godfrey had bought the horse's head from an apprentice taxidermist in Dublin, with whom it had been left in 1961 and never collected. The man who sold it, for £50, used to dust off the head each year, open two bottles of stout and watch the Grand National.

In 1987, Godfrey and some friends brought the head with them to Aintree, where some policemen had to be convinced it wasn't a bomb. The head is buried in Dublin, but the amazing story, with its sad denouement, lives on.

* * *

The feast of St Philip and St James falls on May 1. In 1950, the feast brought with it a terrible irony when Philip James 'PJ' Duke died, aged 25, in St Vincent's Hospital, Dublin. The first of the men of '47 had fallen.

The death of one of its number shook the Cavan team, who had lost just one championship match in the previous 16 to its core. They were mortal, after all. Horribly so.

And to lose a man like PJ made it doubly hard. He had made his name, like so many Cavan footballers of the era, in St Pat's and first came on to the county team in 1945, playing wing-back in that year's All-Ireland final against Cork. He was hugely-popular with teammates, a boyish bundle of energy, modest and unassuming yet brilliant on the field. When death stole in during the night and took Duke, it rattled Cavan – they wouldn't win an Ulster final for another two years, having won 12 of the previous 15.

The team were seasoned by now and living their lives away from football. Paddy Smith, a neighbour of Duke's from Pullamore and a clubmate with Stradone, had been married the week before, the third member of the team to do so in a matter of weeks after Simon Deignan and Tony Tighe. Suddenly, they were halted in their tracks and confronted with the harshest truth of all – nothing lasts forever.

He was a dentistry student in UCD and had been due to sit his final exams the following month. He was a hero in the college, having won Sigerson Cup medals in 1945, '47 (as captain) and '49 and he was at the absolute peak of his powers on the field before he died.

In early 1950, he had represented the Combined Universities against the Rest of Ireland, famously marking his Cavan teammate Victor Sherlock, and that St Patrick's Day he won a Railway Cup medal with Ulster at Croke Park. He was an integral part of one of the greatest half-back lines in history alongside John Joe O'Reilly and Simon Deignan. It was generally presumed that his best years were ahead of him and he would be the successor to John Joe, seven years his senior, in the centre-half's shirt.

He hadn't been ill long; he was named earlier in the week as a starter for Cavan in a National League semi-final against Kerry in Croke Park which Cavan won, on the day before he passed away, but the end came quickly.

When he was laid out in the mortuary at St Vincent's, a short walk from his student digs, the reality struck for his teammates, who wept as they filed past the coffin.

Phil Brady took it hard. He and PJ were the same age and had roomed together on away trips, including in New York. They got on well, the young garda from Mullahoran, the trainee dentist from 20 miles up the road in Stradone. Gunner was tall, strong, dark, and hard on the field while Duke was light, cheery, with reddish hair and a beaming smile.

On one occasion, Cavan were playing a league semi-final in Croker and the Gunner went up to Dublin the night before to stay with Duke, whose younger brother Tommy was also playing for the Cavan juniors at the time. They went for a drink or two and next morning, slept in.

When they stirred, they were running late and pulled their gear together and tore off in the direction of the north side.

The only problem was, this was a match day, and the trams were full. Somewhere around Donnybrook, after a long wait, they grew impatient. The tram stopped and the pair were told, no, you can't get on.

Duke was more streetwise than Brady and pleaded their case, pointing out to the conductor that he had just let a half a dozen passengers off. No, said the official, it's too full. They shouldn't have been on in the first place.

The men looked at each other and to the conductor and eventually PJ explained the situation. "We have to get to Croke Park," he said. "I'm PJ Duke and this is Phil the Gunner."

"Right," said the man on the tram, closing the door, "and I'm Michael O'Hehir!"

How they made it to Dublin 3 that day isn't recorded, but PJ's last journey is.

When the cortege passed through O'Connell St, it brought they city centre to a standstill.

"Gardaí," noted The Celt, "said they had never seen anything like it. One said: 'it was like a state funeral'."

He was buried on the Wednesday in Laragh after one of the largest funerals the diocese had ever witnessed, his coffin draped in UCD and Cavan colours. Perched on top were his football boots.

Slowly, though they didn't know it at the time, the Cavan team of 1947 was breaking up. Old players were retiring, younger players, with plenty more to give were dropping off and PJ was gone.

Glorious 1947 must have seemed further away than ever.

*　　*　　*

The news broke on the morning of Saturday, November 22, 1952. It led the bulletin on Radio Éireann at 8am – Cavan football had lost its leader.

The GAA world had spun off its axis. At 34 years of age, the greatest captain football had known was gone. How it happened has been the subject of speculation for six decades. What is known is that he took a blow playing in a Kildare championship match for The Curragh against Ardclough.

For the majority of John Joe's senior career, he was based in Kildare, where he and his wife Olive lived with their four children. After he married, his younger brother, Frank, came to visit and ended up staying in Naas, training as a chemist and establishing his own practice. The O'Reilly's Kildare links are strong to this day.

In the early 1950s, he decided to build a home away from the Curragh camp. He chose Kilcullen, whose local GAA team he had helped to win an Intermediate Championship.

He or his family would never move into the house. By the time it was ready, John Joe had departed.

There was bad blood between the Ardclough and the Cavanman. John Joe had refereed a quarter-final in 1950 between Ardclough and Sarsfields, a game which attracted a record non-final attendance of 7,730. It broke another record, too – the Leinster Leader described it as "the worst exhibition of dangerous play seen in the county for many years".

Three players were injured and O'Reilly reported that Ardclough "adopted a very threatening attitude towards myself and questioned all my decisions".

Some refused to give their names and the match ended, he said, with one player throwing the ball at him and another threatening to "cut the side of the head off me".

The entire Ardclough team was handed a three-year suspension, although many were reduced on appeal.

Fast forward two years and John Joe was lining out in the colours of the Curragh. At some stage in the game, or so the story goes, he fell to the ground and received a kick.

The following day, he called to his brother's pharmacy in Naas, complaining of pain. His kidney was damaged, catastrophically so as it turned out. By that stage, he was reaching the end of his playing days, with 16 years of service at senior inter-county level behind him, and the kidney, and an ankle injury, were ailing him.

He didn't play in the early rounds of the Ulster Championship, although in June he did travel to Cavan to play in the official opening of Breffni Park against Kerry. Cavan lost the match but the local reporter described his return to action as an "auspicious" one. It wasn't. Slotted in at corner-back, John Joe struggled with the speed of the game. He was old in footballing terms at the time but the truth was, he wasn't well.

That morning, he had travelled down from Dublin in the company of teammates Simon Deignan and Aidan Corrigan from Drumlane, a sub on the Cavan team at the time. On the way, he stopped half a dozen times to go to the toilet. Something wasn't right.

Before reaching Cavan, he had a job to do. John Joe had been instrumental in having a memorial to PJ Duke erected at Laragh ceremony, and he officially unveiled it on the morning of the match, before heading to Breffni Park. Poignantly, it would be his final match in the blue jersey.

A new-look Cavan team won the Ulster title anyway and on the Monday before they played Cork in the All-Ireland semi-final, he arrived at the team's training camp to lend a hand.

Cavan unexpectedly beat the Rebels and went into collective training again for the final, a week before which he and Peter Donohoe were surprise recalls to the playing panel. They went through their paces with the squad and Big Peter took his place on the match-day panel, but John Joe didn't.

A month later, he was gone.

John Joe needed an operation and as an army officer, undertook it in the Curragh Hospital. Something went wrong.

By the time he was moved to the Meath Hospital in Dublin, the Gallant John Joe could stand no more. He breathed his last on the way.

The news prompted absolute devastation among the people of Cavan and beyond.

"It was the end of a week's long watching and waiting for news from the Curragh hospital, shared with the anxious parents, brothers and sisters living here, on the progress he was making after a serious abdominal operation," reported the Celt.

"Men and women going to their work in the mornings, farmers going to the creamery, business people and customers alike asked each other each morning, 'How is John Joe?'

"The homes of his parents at the Derries and of his sister, Mrs E O'Dowd, Main St, were besieged daily for the latest news. Then when hopes had risen for his recovery, the announcement came..."

Word came through to the family in Killeshandra quickly.

An army officer and John Joe's wife, Olive, and family arrived and stayed the night, before taking his parents and brother Vincent to the Curragh to see him. His younger sister Annie stayed at home to mind the farm and deal with the business of looking after the floods of callers. She was sick with worry and unable to eat.

At the funeral, teammates, some of whom shouldered the coffin on its final journey, visibly wept. The story led the national newspapers.

His old pal John Wilson put pen to paper days after his burial.

"The leonine head, the honesty and goodness that suffused his countenance, the upright elastic step, the step of a dignified officer when leading his soldiers down O'Connell Street in an Easter Week parade, the step of a true athlete when leading his team to victory in Dublin, London or New York, all these we had seen and had come to think of him as an essential part of our small world," wrote Wilson.

"Death has robbed his loyal and devoted wife and tender family of his companionship and solicitude. The country sympathises with and prays for them. Death has robbed thousands of a football idol, and many of an intimate friend. But the memory of lion-hearted displays on many fields, of lively discussions in various training camps, of titanic laughter at his own hearth, of the joy that emanated from his great and limber frame – the memory of those remains, the Joy of Life.

"Death has taken him away. These memories it cannot take, and we are grateful for the memories.

"The shadows lengthened and the evening came. His busy world is hushed. For him, the fever of life is over and his work is done. May God grant his soul eternal rest, and peace at the last."

The tributes flowed for weeks in print. Tony Myles, writing in the Irish Press, spoke of the pain of being present at the funeral.

"This was Cavan sorrowfully bringing back one of its finest sons. But it was Ireland, too, for John Joe O'Reilly belonged, not to Cavan only, but to all of us no matter what county we come from, who appreciate a gentleman, a soldier and a Gael. He had played the game of life to its finish and he played it as he played the game of football he loved – a sportsman and a gentleman."

The Anglo-Celt echoed those sentiments.

"It is not given to many mortals to attain heroic stature or legendary reputation, even in a long lifetime, yet, John Joe O'Reilly, soldier and athlete, was both a hero and a legend before he was 30 years old... Above all, a sportsman without peer."

And the Gaelic Sportsman, on December 6, 1952, followed up:

"All Ireland knew him as John Joe. All Ireland knew him too as a great footballer, a born leader of men, a genial, warm-hearted, quiet-spoken Gael, as generous in victory as he was glorious in defeat."

John Joe has never been replaced. He is, as Fr Dan Gallogly referred to him in Cavan's Football Story, Breffni's lost leader. Had he never played football, his would have been a life less ordinary. That he did, that he led his men to the greatest victory in the history of the sport, ensured his memory will never fade.

"He was a representative of the new nation, which was only a couple of years old," GAA historian Eoghan Corry has said.

"He was a member of the army during the Emergency and captained the winning team in New York in 1947 and again in 1948. Four years later, he was dead. All the aspects of the legend came together."

Needless to say, his death was a gigantic blow to his family. The 13 siblings had only been together once, the previous summer, as the older ones had left before the younger ones were born. That, in itself, maybe provided some comfort.

He lives on, more than anything, through stories and song. Ian Corrigan, a star of the showband era and nephew of Aidan, who travelled with John Joe for that match with Kerry in '52, made the Gallant John Joe, written by Swanlinbar man Albert McGovern, famous.

"I remember having my breakfast and getting ready to go to school," recalled Corrigan, a self-confessed football fanatic.

"The news came on and the first thing was that this morning, Commandant John Joe O'Reilly died. Nobody could believe it."

Corrigan's pedigree is strong – he attended John Joe's final game.

"I went with my father and a couple of local people. John Joe went off about 10 or 15 minutes into the second half. I remember there was a man beside me, who was TP O'Reilly's father, we had got a lift with him to the game.

"And I remember him saying, that's the end of John Joe. Little did anybody know..."

Twenty years later, the connection grew.

"I was playing in London in 1966 or 67, in the Gresham in the Holloway Rd and a fella from Corlough came up and said: 'Did you ever learn that song The Gallant John Joe?' And I said no, but I will when I go home, because I had been asked a couple of times.

"I went down to Albert McGovern in Swanlinbar and got the song and recorded it. I released it on a Monday and I launched it out in Donnybrook, that was around April 1971."

The song entered the top 10 at number nine and the following week, Corrigan and his band were gigging in Donegal. On the way, they tuned into Gay Byrne reading out the top 10 and when their song wasn't in the first couple listed, they presumed it had dropped out. But when Byrne reached number two, and realised The Beatles' Penny Lane had been knocked off top spot, the butterflies began to flutter. They had made it.

"You wouldn't believe how popular the song is," says Corrigan. "I could go to any county in Ireland and it's requested, it's one of the best selling Irish songs there has been."

Tom MacIntyre, the former Cavan goalkeeper and playwright, wrote a one-man play called the Gallant John Joe, which starred Tom Hickey and told the story of a bewildered widower whose only solace is telling stories about John Joe.

"Commandant John Joe O'Reilly," recounted the mesmeric Hickey, "was an army man through and through and playing football for the army, took a belt in the kidneys that went wrong. He was removed to the army hospital, from there to the coffin.... The coffin only goes one place."

*   *   *

The GAA connection with the Polo Grounds grew stronger after '47. With vast immigration to the US and, overwhelmingly, to New York, from Ireland, the NY board sought entry into the football and hurling National Leagues in 1950, which was granted by Central Council.

In July of that year, New York were down to play the winners of the football league on the prompting of Croke Park. By coincidence, Cavan, not league specialists, had come through the home final.

As it happened, the Gunner's sister, Rose, was living in the city at the time and doing a line with a strapping Mayo full-back called Tom Gallagher. She knew Phil's form and, keen that big brother wouldn't scupper the romance, took out her pen.

"Whatever you do," she wrote to her mother in Mullahoran, "don't let Phil start fighting with Tom."

The rest of the story writes itself. Twenty-five minutes in and Tony Tighe is upended. There is sorting out to be done and Phil does it; ref points to the line. No quarter asked, none given.

Phil would laugh about it afterwards. Presumably, Rose did as well. A few years later, she ended up marrying a man by the name of Pat White. And New York won the match, too, producing the GAA shock of the century to win by 2-8 to 0-12, with Roscommon's Bill Carlos lining out at centre half-back against a Cavan team which featured 10 – Deignan, Smith, John Joe, Cassidy, Gunner, Tighe, Higgins, Carolan, Donohoe and sub Stafford – of the men who had travelled overseas three years earlier.

Later that year, on September 24, Tipperary beat New York by two points, 1-12 to 3-4, in the hurling decider.

The ties became even closer in 1951 when league champions Meath and Galway both travelled to New York to play the 'away' finals in the Polo Grounds, both winning before 26,000 fans, the hosts featuring none other than Gega O'Connor in the forward line.

But John 'Kerry' O'Donnell's crankiness didn't endear him to the authorities at home the following year and after some acrimony, the link to the National Leagues was dissolved, with the home winners now playing New York in the St Brendan's Cup.

Dublin and Kerry footballers were brought over for an exhibition in 1956, drawing 25,000 paying punters, and Galway (footballers and hurlers), Wexford and Cork hurlers and Tyrone footballers, who had just won The Anglo-Celt Cup for the first time, all travelled in the following years.

The final exhibitions were in '58, New York beating both Louth and Kilkenny, but by then changes were afoot in New York that not even John Kerry could halt.

The Dodgers franchise vacated Brooklyn, heading for Los Angeles, and the Giants, whose attendances had fallen off a cliff and reached a low of 1,604 at one game, followed, dropping their bombshell on August 19, 1957. The Polo Grounds was crumbling and the team's status had plummeted. The neighbourhood around the stadium had never been the safest but was becoming downright dangerous, and the fans were staying away. It had to happen.

They had toyed with the idea of upping sticks to the Metropolitan Stadium in Minneapolis-St Paul but after lobbying from the San Francisco mayor George Christopher and urged on by Dodgers owner Walter O'Malley, who needed another team to move to California to seal that LA deal, majority owner Horace Stoneham took the plunge.

The Giants' final game was the following month, when they were trounced by the Pittsburgh Pirates. Even their last-ever match could only draw just over a fifth of the capacity, fans shouting insults at Stoneham's office and tearing up the fixtures as souvenirs.

Soon, they were gone. By the following year, a midget car track had been installed, making the pitch unplayable for Gaelic games. The Polo Grounds had witness the last thwock of a sliotar, the final thud of an O'Neill's size five. For a time, the Yankees were the only baseball show in town before the Mets franchise arrived on the scene in 1962 and while they re-located to the Polo Grounds for a few months, paying out of their own pocket for extra police on match-days, it was never going to be a long-term deal.

The city had guaranteed a new stadium at Flushing – without it, the Mets would have been stillborn. By late 1963, they, too, were gone. The area around the stadium had become almost a no-go zone, with muggings and car break-ins rife, the problem quickly escalating after the construction of nearby housing projects in 1951. The city itself was struggling, ghettos were springing up and the Polo Grounds was just another victim.

In April, 1964, the Mets moved into their new home. The same month, the wrecking balls arrived at the Polo Grounds. When it was tossed, four 30-storey high-rise towers – projects, with all of the delinquency and social problems that term suggests – were constructed and named Polo Grounds Towers, consisting of 1,612 apartments.

In 2010, it was reported that pizza delivery chains insist that residents of the towers meet the courier a block away, at 155th St Subway Station, for fear of attacks. Two years later, at a public meeting, a tenant asked: "If the cops are afraid to come in here with guns, how am I supposed to feel?"

Today, they are among the worst projects in the five boroughs, immortalised in hip-hop tracks, with crime rates among the highest in the city. A park in the shadow of the towers houses six compact basketball courts, named for Willie Mays, and a small plaque is all that remains to show the history of the place.

Asked for a 2013 documentary, one resident summed it up.

"I thought it was just a forest and they turned it into a housing development. I didn't know it was a baseball field, back in the day," he said.

Fans of the Giants never got over their sense of mourning.

"There's nothing there, it's a housing project. So we don't have anywhere really," says Bill Kent, who runs the New York Baseball Giants Nostalgia Society.

The novelist and journalist Pete Hamill said it best when he spoke of the grief that still hangs over the stadium, the team and the city all these years later.

"I don't think the nostalgia is sentimentality," Hamill has said. "It was based on a memory of something that did exist, that was not a Norman Rockwell painting."

Kent's words could be about the '47 final, the fresh-faced men of Kerry and Cavan, almost all gone, like the ground they played in.

"When we live it," he says, looking back, "it didn't die."

* * *

Slowly, one by one, the players started fading away. The dazzling light of the the 1940s and early '50s dimmed over time. PJ and John Joe were the first to go, Mick and Owen Roe the last.

In between, the Gunner slipped away in 1980. Of all the men of '47, none were more famous. It was the nickname but it was more – he embodied the spirit of the group who departed for the greatest GAA showpiece of them all; young, fearless, good-natured and courageous.

He was 55 when he died, on duty in his squad car when his huge heart gave up. It was completely unexpected, although, looking back, there had been a sign or two.

At the time, Phil's son Martin was building his house and had to bury an ESB cable three feet in the ground. His father was at the site helping out one Saturday and Martin was struggling with the shovel in the rock-hard ground.

Above the garden, he had planted apple trees, and when he looked up, exasperated and with the sweat stinging his eyes, he saw the old fella above, picking the buds from the trees.

"For feck's sake, Daddy," he said, "I brought you out here to give me a hand."

"No," said his father, uncharacteristically, "I wouldn't be fit for that."

Early in the growth of an apple tree, the buds are picked off so they can grow stronger. The thought didn't strike Martin for a couple of months afterwards, of the day his father helped him in the garden.

By then, the great oak had fallen.

The Men of Cavan 1947

Val Gannon

Had been born in Ballina, Co Mayo but moved to Kilcogy aged four when his father was made station master of Drumhownagh Station in 1923. Won six SFC medals with Mullahoran between 1942 and 1950.

Called into the Cavan panel in 1947 aged 28 after an injury to Brendan Kelly. The All-Ireland semi-final against Roscommon was his first time in Croke Park.

Made a name as an outstanding shot-stopper and tremendously brave player. Lost an eye to an old football injury in later years, when he served the Dreadnoughts with distinction as team trainer.

Sons Gerry and Val played for Mullahoran and Cavan. Died in 1986, aged 67.

Willie Doonan

Made his name at right corner-back on the All-Ireland winning Cavan minor team in 1938. Fought in World War II, seeing action in Italy in Anzio, before being honourably discharged after catching a bullet in the ankle, an injury which he would carry his whole career.

A soccer player of international class, he played for British Army representative teams and for a while lined out for St Mirren. A folk hero among supporters, he was famed for his long clearances and swaggering demeanour and was hugely popular with teammates. Retired from county football at the end of 1949 with two All-Ireland senior medals and a National League medal. Worked as a labourer in England for 15 years and never married. Returned to Cavan and managed Cavan Gaels to a league title in 1971 before he died in August 1976, aged 56.

Brian O'Reilly

A native of Carnaross, moved to Ballinagh as a teenager to work as a shop assistant and captained the club to successive minor championships in 1940 and 1941. Known as "White's Brian", after the family in Killydoon who owned the shop in which he later worked. Transferred to Mullahoran, winning six SFC medals. Made history in 1946 when he lined out on the winning side in a Railway Cup semi-final before he had played championship football for Cavan.

Made a name as a player who could kick equally well with either foot. Kept the famous Jack McQuillan of Roscommon scoreless in 1947 semi-final and won a second All-Ireland medal and a National League in 1948. Very private man.Emigrated to Melbourne in the early 1950s, throwing his lot in with the St Kevin's club. Became successful in construction and died in Australia in May 1997, aged 72.

Paddy Smith

Began a long career with Bank of Ireland in 1937, serving in various locations including Rathfriland, Co Down, Ardee, Armagh, Drogheda, Wicklow and Oldcastle. Managed branches in Bailieborough and Trim, where he retired in 1982.

A member of the St Vincent de Paul Society for 53 years, he won championship medals in Louth and Armagh and a Dr McKenna Cup medal with Down in 1944, and later trained St Patrick's of Wicklow to a hat-trick of SFC successes. As a player, he was fast, fiercely-committed and dependable, and gained representative honours with Ulster.

A true gentleman who also had a love of amateur dramatics, in which he excelled. His wife, Mary, was a sister of Louth 1957 All-Ireland winner Kevin Behan. Died in 1993, aged 74.

PJ Duke

One of the best defenders ever to play for Cavan, fast and comfortable on the ball. Operated generally at wing-back but sometimes midfield. His switch to mark Batt Garvey in the 1947 final was credited with turning the match in Cavan's favour. Enjoyed a stellar career with St Pat's before attending UCD, where he won three Sigerson Cups, one as captain.

From Stradone. Played in four All-Ireland senior finals, winning two, and picked up a National League medal, a Railway Cup medal and represented the Combined Universities against the Rest of Ireland.

The Railway Cup win on St Patrick's Day, 1947 was the last time he wore a pair of football boots. His funeral was one of the largest ever seen in the county and his death was front-page news in the national newspapers.

Said The Anglo-Celt in his obituary: "PJ Duke is enshrined in the sporting heart of the nation and will be cherished in Breffni as long as football is played."

Laragh United's home grounds in Stradone are named PJ Duke Memorial Park in his honour.

Died of tuberculosis in April, 1950, aged 25.

John Joe O'Reilly

Described by historian Fr Dan Gallogly as "the lost leader of Cavan football" and by Mick Higgins as "the greatest leader of men I ever saw, on or off the field", he was ear-marked as a future Chief of Staff of the Irish Army and had risen to the rank of commandant by the age of 27. A native of Killeshandra who played his club football with Cornafean and later The Curragh in Kildare.

An outstanding athlete, he won three MacRory Cups with St Pat's and would win eight Ulster SFC medals and captain Cavan to two All-Irelands.

Married with four children when he died after a failed kidney operation, his death prompted an outpouring of grief nationally. Was the face of the Cavan team, a uniquely gifted leader and an incredible sportsman, as exemplified when he refused to kick a penalty over the bar to beat Monaghan in the first round of the Ulster Championship in 1947. Remembered in song by the ballad The Gallant John Joe, arguably the most famous GAA song ever written.

In 1984, John Joe was chosen on the GAA Team of the Century at centre half-back, and he was also named on the Team of the Millennium 15 years later.

His son Brian played minor football with Cavan and a grand-nephew, Kevin McLaughlin, currently plays in the back row with the Leinster and Irish rugby teams.

Died in November, 1952, aged 34.

Simon Deignan

One of an elite group who have won All-Ireland medals and also refereed senior finals. Won a minor All-Ireland in 1938 and was on board for all three senior wins under Hughie O'Reilly. In all, he featured in 12 All-Ireland finals and played for the Cavan senior team from 1940 until 1953, generally at wing-back or midfield and finishing up at full-forward.

Amazingly, he reffed the 1947 Munster final between Cork and Kerry. Acted as a selector for Cavan for a number of seasons, having also been physical trainer during his playing days on occasion. Originally a lieutenant in the army, he settled in Finglas and became a successful auctioneer and a driving force behind the Erin's Isle GAA club. Grand-nephew Johnny Cooper is an All-Ireland U21 medallist with Dublin.

Died aged 84 in 2006.

John Wilson

Gifted classical scholar. Strong, physical footballer who starred for Mullahoran throughout the 1940s and played for Cavan for six years. Taught in Donegal, Kilkenny and Dublin and was president of the ASTI before going into politics, where he held a seat for Fianna Fáil in Cavan-Monaghan from 1973 to 1992, when he retired. Lost the race to become the party's presidential candidate in 1990 at a time when he was considered a live bet for the Park.

Served variously as Minister for Education, Minister for Posts and Telegraphs, Minister for Tourism and Transport and Tánaiste. Noted as an extraordinary orator, a linguist and a man who retained the common touch – he would spend his spare time at a holiday home in Finea, a couple of miles from his old homestead in Callinagh.

He was described in Jim Farrelly's 1989 November edition of

Who's Who in Irish Politics as an "urbane, witty orator and classics scholar who can also be a stubborn countryman, and a non-violent Republican".

His grandson, also John, is currently a member of the Meath U-16 team. Died in July 2007, the day after his 84th birthday.

Phil 'The Gunner' Brady

A folk hero in Cavan football circles, and a household name nationally. A fearsome competitor who was a ferociously strong and played on the edge. Came into the Cavan team as a teenager in 1945 and his strength and athleticism were crucial at midfield.

When the team had problems at the back, he was converted into a full-back and he played there with distinction in 1952 when winning his third All-Ireland medal. A committed family man who served as a Garda, notably in Castleblayney, where he settled and won the Scott Medal for valour after disarming a man. Married teammate Victor Sherlock's sister and his sons were hugely involved with the local Faughs club.

Nephew Paul is a four-time world handball champion and commonly regarded as the greatest player ever to play the game.

Died while on duty in his patrol car in May 1980, aged 56.

Columba McDyer

A native of Kilraine, outside Glenties in Donegal. Won Railway Cup medals in 1942 and 1943. His father Alec had been joint-secretary of the first Donegal county board. Played for the Donegal senior team in a challenge game at the age of 16 in 1937.

Worked as a carpenter and travelled to various counties, playing for Sligo, Cavan, Donegal and Dublin. In later years he formed a close friendship with a young Jim McGuinness and, spotting his coaching potential, gifted him a whistle, which McGuinness used in Croke Park to oversee the warm-up in the 2012 All-Ireland final.

Father of 12 children. Was a selector with the first Donegal team to win the Ulster Championship, trained by Mick Higgins, in 1972.

Died in September 2001 in Donegal at the age of 80. His funeral was attended by Higgins and Peter Donohoe.

Mick Higgins

The Polo Grounds was famously a homecoming for Higgins, who was born in the city in 1922, on the day Michael Collins was killed. Regarded as one of the greatest forwards to ever play the game, he was an extremely clever player with pace, vision and wicked ball skills. A big game player, he didn't suffer from nerves.

Retired from playing at the age of 31 in 1953, after 10 years on the Cavan and Ulster teams, during which he became one of the GAA's first superstars.

A shy, extremely modest man, he was also a champion greyhound trainer and was an outstanding team manager with Cavan in the 1960s, leading them to four Ulster titles. Also trained Longford to a Leinster title and Donegal to their first Ulster title.

Finished with three All-Ireland medals, one as captain. Asked what game stood out for him, he named the 1952 semi-final win over Cork, which a new-look Cavan won by a point.

Died in January 2010, aged 87.

Tony Tighe

One of the greatest forwards ever to play the game. A flamboyant, gifted, hard-working attacker who saved his best performances for the big day and was the fastest ball-carrier in the sport. Netted twice in the 1948 final against Mayo and twice more in the 1952 drawn final against Meath, while his goal in the 1947 semi-final against Roscommon was rated, to that point, as the best ever scored in Croke Park.

In the final, the 20-year-old played without fear in turning the match. After swerving past a Kerry defender, he was clattered by another, which drew prolonged booing from the crowd. Unnerved, the Kerry defence stood off a little on the next attack and Cavan made them pay, Joe Stafford hitting the net.

He was a native of Ballyjamesduff, where his father was bank manager. In 1945, he played for both the minor and senior teams in the same day against Monaghan.

Forced to retire at the age of 26 in 1953 due to a back injury, he resided in Clones, where he worked as an insurance broker. He took up golf, getting down to a handicap of seven and serving as captain and president of Clones Golf Club.

A prolific finisher, he scored a total of 10-25 in nine championship campaigns and won three All-Ireland medals.

"The team celebrations [in '52], I believe, were fervent and prolonged," the playwright Tom MacIntyre has written.

"The story, fact or fiction, is told that when Cavan's right wing three-quarter saw daylight again, he discovered himself to be a watching a cock-fight in a farmyard near the town of Mullagh, and it was Tuesday!"

In 1948, he had turned in a Man of the Match performance against Mayo. In 1953, he played his last match for Cavan, a league game, against the same county. And in 2005, when the teams met again in championship for the first time in 57 years, Tony attended.

Tony died that August day, aged 77, while attending the Cavan v Mayo All-Ireland qualifier match in Hyde Park, Roscommon.

Joe Stafford

An aggressive, rambunctious corner-forward who, in 1943, became the first man ever to be sent off in an All-Ireland senior final, his greatest gift was his ability to poach goals. Fearless in the tackle, he had the knack of hitting the net from even a half-chance, as he did in the Polo Grounds, and he would score 12 championship goals in all for Cavan.

Native of Killinkere, he won a minor All-Ireland in 1937 and, as a teenager, won a "long kick" competition with a kick of 56 yards. At the time of the 1947 win, he was working for Cully's Bakery in Arva, and lining out for the local team. He later re-located to Dublin, where he had a fruit and veg business before purchasing the Antrim Arms guesthouse in Drumcondra in 1960. Kept close links to Cavan football, serving as a selector for a time.

His nephew Jimmy Stafford was an outstanding player for Cavan in the 1960s, winning two Ulster medals. In 1999, he was named as corner-forward on the Cavan Team of the Millennium.

Joe died in Dublin in June 2000, aged 82.

Peter Donohoe

The man famously christened "The Babe Ruth of Gaelic football" shot Cavan to another All-Ireland title in 1948 and kicked 0-6 in the 1949 final defeat to Meath, after which he hung up his boots. Renowned as one of the greatest place-kickers in the history of the sport.

Was called back into the panel a fortnight before the 1952 final and took his place in the team photo at Croke Park but saw no action. Ran as a candidate for the fledgling Clann na Poblachta in the late 40s, missing out on the Dáil by just 109 votes. Continued to play with Banba and later Westerns in Dublin before returning to the Cavan colours in 1955, winning a last Ulster medal.

Helped Crosserlough to their first Cavan SFC in 1958, before emigrating to London, where he married Kingscourt lady Brigid Yorke, an old teenage flame, in 1967 at the age of 42.

His new wife helped him give up drinking and he built up a successful off-sales business before returning to Kingscourt in 1989, where the pair ran a pub for five years before retiring.

Died in April 2004 aged 78.

TP O'Reilly

A native of Uragh, outside Milltown, he played in the Cavan forward line from 1938 to 1949.

On the field, his was a career of firsts – he was a member of the first Ulster team to win the Railway Cup (in 1942, alongside such notables as John Joe O'Reilly, Columba McDyer and future GAA President Alf Murray), the first St Pat's team to win the MacRory, the first Cavan team to All-Ireland minor championship, the first UCD team to win a Dublin county title and, of course, the only team to win an All-Ireland outside of Ireland.

He sat as chairman of the Cavan county board from 1956 to 1970, a period during which the county reached an All-Ireland minor final and won four Ulster senior championships, and later Central Council delegate. After 29 years running his own legal practice in Ballyconnell, he was appointed District Justice in July 1973. In 1976, he ran for the presidency of the GAA. He had earlier run for Fine Gael in the 1948 General Election.

Asked for an article in 1983 what his greatest ever Cavan 15 was, he would name seven; Paddy Smith, PJ Duke, John Joe O'Reilly, Tony Tighe, Mick Higgins, Joe Stafford and Peter Donohoe, of his teammates from the Polo Grounds.

TP's son Garrett played senior football for Cavan for over 10 years and won Ulster medals in 1967 and 1969.

He died in November 1989, aged 71.

Edwin Carolan

A native of Mullagh who played for the county from 1947 to 1955. A great character off the field and a magnificent, elusive forward on it. A noted pianist and singer and a warm, friendly person, he played on the successful 1948 and 1952 teams as well as '47. Won a Sigerson Cup medal with UCD, from where he qualified as a vet. Represented the Combined Universities and the Ireland team.

While working as a veterinary inspector in McCarren's in Cavan town, helped to establish the Cavan Gaels club. Later relocated to Tipperary, where he had a successful professional career. Narrowly missed out on the starting team for the final in 1947 due to illness in New York, having started the Ulster final and All-Ireland semi-final.

In 1952 he scored an impossible point, via the upright, to salvage a draw for Cavan in the All-Ireland final against Meath.

His brother Paddy was also a key player on the 1952 team and nephew Ronan won Ulster U21 and senior medals with the county in 1988 and 1997 respectively. Cuchulainns GFC named their new grounds in his honour in 1985.

Tragically drowned in Carrick-on-Suir in January 1982, aged 55.

John Joe Cassidy

A native of Fair Green, Arva. Christened John James, he was known as John Joe all his life. Was honorary president of Cavan GFC in New York for many years before his death. His wife was a sister of star Kilkenny hurler Terry Leahy, who turned in a Man of the Match performance in the 1947 final against Cork. They had six sons and one daughter.

In 1946, he had helped Arva's neighbours Dromard with a Longford junior title.

Returned to New York shortly after winning his third All-Ireland medal in 1952 and worked in the bar trade, running establishments in Queens and the Bronx and working in Moran's Killarney Rose bar in Manhattan for a number of years.

A reliable free-taker with an eye for goal, he lined out with Banba in Dublin, alongside Peter Donohoe, for a couple of seasons.

The gallant John Joe was played on the violin at his funeral before he was laid to rest at the Gates of Heaven cemetery, Valhalla, New York. John Joe died in February 1995 in Calvary Hospital, New York aged 70.

Owen Roe McGovern

Came into the Cavan team at the age of 27 in 1945. Versatile defender who was strong and tough, he came on at half-time in the 1948 All-Ireland final against Meath for the injured John Joe O'Reilly and turned in a brilliant performance.

Picked up a National League medal at right half-back in 1949.

A member of the Irish army from 1940 to 1945, he was fit and committed, a friendly character and extremely popular with teammates. Came from a large family in Swanlinbar but never lost touch with home after moving to New York in 1957, and spoke with a strong Cavan accent all his life.

Settled in Elizabeth, New Jersey, where he founded the Elizabeth Gaels club and ran a successful pub called Morley and McGovern's in Roselle.

His son Brian was a stand-out American footballer and his

granddaughter is an up and coming soccer player. A leader of the Irish community in his area, Owen Roe was a great help to young emigrants.

The last of the 1947 team to pass away, Owen died in May 2011 in his 93rd year.

Eunan Tiernan

A tall, rangy player who enjoyed a short career with Cavan. One of the youngest players on the 1947 team, he was a forward who came to prominence when playing an outstanding match against Kerry in London at Easter of the Polo Grounds year.

Father Jack had been a star defender for Cavan in the 1920s and his uncle, Fr Tom Maguire, was county board chairman from 1937 to 1942. Won a MacRory Cup with St Pat's in 1943 and an Ulster junior medal with Cavan the following year, before enrolling in UCD. Was a member of the Cavan panel in '48 but a serious injury sustained on club duty with Civil Service in Dublin ruled him out of football for a number of years. Returned to play with Templeport in 1954 and 1955, having won a Junior Championship with them in 1942 as a 16-year-old.

Worked for the Department of Labour and resided in Clonskeagh, although he returned frequently to Cavan, where he kept in touch with the football scene. Was one of only three west Cavanmen on the 1947 team, TP and Owen Roe McGovern being the others.

Died aged 60 in March 1986. His coffin was draped in the Cavan colours and teammates from 1947 and members of the Templeport club formed a guard of honour.

Big Tom O'Reilly

A household name from the time he came on to the Cavan team, winning an All-Ireland medal at midfield in 1933 and again two years later. A genial giant of a man who was known, even in family circles, simply as "Big Tom", he was a barrel-chested man who could play in any position on the field. Winner of nine Cavan championships and captain on seven occasions. The year 1947 was his last on the county team; by that stage he was already a serving TD, having won a seat in the old Cavan constituency in 1944 as an independent. He was beaten in the 1948 election, running for Fine Gael, and didn't stand again.

In later years he moved to Dublin, where he was very successful in business and as a property developer. He retained his love for Cavan football throughout his life.

Michael O'Hehir once famously described John Joe as Tom's "little brother" with the immortal line: "Under the Cusack Stand I see a little glimmer of blue and white and here come Cavan led by their captain, the only and only Big Tom O'Reilly, the pride of Gaeldom and the idol of Ulster, followed by his little brother, John Joe."

In 1990, he was elected as honorary chieftain of the O'Reilly clan.

Big Tom died at his home in Rathgar in February 1995, aged 80.

Brendan Kelly

A thoroughly reliable goalkeeper who lost his place due to injury before the 1947 championship threw in. Was on holidays in Bundoran when word came through that he was needed for the trip to America as Jim Deignan was unable to travel. Was regarded as the top goalkeeper in the county for close to 10 years in the 1940s.

In all, won four Ulster senior medals and was also between the posts in 1945, when Cavan lost the All-Ireland final to Cork. Was one of seven Cavanmen on the successful Ulster Railway Cup team in 1942.

Died in January 2002, aged 83.

Fr Jim Deignan

A strong, powerful footballer who was a sub on the Cavan team in 1947 but was prevented from travelling due to regulations – he was studying for the priesthood, and would be ordained the following summer, one of 53 in his class.

Played minor football with Cavan for three years. A brother of

Simon's, he joined the teaching staff in St Finian's College, Mullingar in 1951 and became president in 1970, holding the position for 10 years.

During his time, he coached football in the school and helped re-establish his alma mater, with whom he had won a Leinster Colleges SFC medal in 1939, among the leading lights in the province.

Later, he was parish priest in Clara, Co Offaly. Died in April 1998, aged 76.

Fr Dan Danaher

A tall, skilful player who won six Senior Championship medals with Mullahoran. Was studying for the priesthood in 1947 in St Patrick's College, Carlow and was refused leave to travel to New York. Ordained in June 1949.

As a child, had been given a 50-50 chance of survival after a burst appendix but he recovered and enjoyed an illustrious career with the Dreadnoughts. After a spell teaching in Knockbeg College, Carlow, he ministered in Brixham, England until 2003. Kept close contact with home and returned for a month each year. Died in Plymouth, England in May 2009 aged 84.

Patsy Lynch

A legend among Cavan footballers. Was the youngest player ever to win an adult All-Ireland medal when he played full-back on the successful Cavan junior team at the age of 16 in 1927. Wore the number three shirt six years later in Cavan's first senior success but his career was cut short when he received a bad leg injury following a tangle with Galway's John Donnellan in the 1935 All-Ireland semi-final. Made a brief return as a forward later in his career but excelled as an administrator, holding the position of chairman from 1945 till 1949, during which Cavan contested four All-Ireland finals out of five.

A butcher by trade, first in his native Bailieborough and, from 1948, in Irishtown in Dublin.

Had toured America with Cavan in the 1930s but the '47 trip was the most memorable, and not just for the football as he met his future wife Lila on the Mauretania on the way over.

Died in Dublin in November 1994, aged 81.

Hughie O'Reilly

No other individual ever played as great a role in as many Ulster All-Ireland successes. An outstanding midfielder who won All-Irelands as a player in 1933 and 1935, he trained the Cavan team – effectively manager before the term was coined – from 1937 and was still involved in 1959.

Hughie also led Cootehill to a three-in-a-row of senior championships from 1952-54 inclusive. A noted hurler who, in later years, represented Cavan on Central Council, he was a stern man, a disciplinarian who shunned the limelight, but also possessed a dry sense of humour.

On one occasion, he bumped into Willie Doonan and the pair bought some cans of beer and sausages for an impromptu mini-party. When Doonan dropped one of the beers, breaking it open, Hughie snorted: "Good man Willie, at least you didn't break the sausages!"

Held strong nationalist views and was interned for a period in The Curragh in 1922. He produced a list of 28 tips for footballers which are still relevant today. A groundbreaking tactician who was a born winner and had the priceless ability to breed confidence into his teams. Played an integral role in each of Cavan's five All-Ireland wins.

Died in November 1976, aged 72.

Hughie Smyth

Appointed secretary of the Cavan county board at the age of 23 in 1937, he held the position unbroken until 1974, serving under eight chairmen. A noted handballer who partnered John Molloy to Cavan's first adult All-Ireland, the 1930 Junior Softball Doubles, he also served as a selector to the county team, a position he held in 1947. Delegates were astounded when he was beaten by

Crosserlough's Jimmy Smith for the position of treasurer by 107 votes to 98, at the county convention in January 1974.

His father Joe had been the first treasurer when the GAA was revitalised in the county in 1903. Travelled with the Cavan team to America in 1938. An eccentric man in some ways, he never married and although a plasterer in his younger days, worked as keeper of Cavan courthouse, where county board meetings were generally held at the time.

At Cavan matches, he would stand beside the goals, invariably carrying an umbrella, and move behind it, pointing the umbrella skywards as a directional aid for forwards when Cavan were on the attack.

He attended mass in the Cathedral in Cavan every morning.

Died in February 1984, aged 70.

Index

INDEX

CAVAN'S PATH TO THE FINAL
ULSTER SFC QUARTER-FINAL
JUNE 15, BREFFNI PARK: CAVAN 0–9 MONAGHAN 1–6
Scorers: M Higgins 0-4, T Tighe 0-2, JJ Cassidy 0-2, E Carolan 0-1

ULSTER SFC QUARTER-FINAL REPLAY
JUNE 22, CLONES: CAVAN 1–11 MONAGHAN 1–9
Scorers: P Donohoe 0-3, T Tighe 0-3, J Stafford 1-2, TP O'Reilly 0-1, E Carolan 0-1, M Higgins 0-1

ULSTER SFC SEMI-FINAL
JULY 6, DUNGANNON: CAVAN 4–5 TYRONE 0–2
Scorers: P Donohoe 1-2, J Stafford 1-1, E Carolan 1-0, J Deignan 0-1, JJ Cassidy 0-2

ULSTER FINAL
JULY 20, CLONES: CAVAN 3–4 ANTRIM 1–6
Scorers: P Donohoe 1-2, J Stafford 1-2, TP O'Reilly 1-0

ALL-IRELAND SEMI-FINAL
AUGUST 3, CROKE PARK: CAVAN 2–4 ROSCOMMON 0–6
Scorers: P Donohoe 1-4, T Tighe 1-0

ALL-IRELAND FINAL
SEPTEMBER 14, POLO GROUNDS: CAVAN 2–11 KERRY 2–7

CAVAN TEAM
VAL GANNON
Mullahoran

WILLIE DOONAN   BRIAN O'REILLY   PADDY SMITH
Cavan Harps   *Mullahoran*   *Stradone*

JOHN WILSON   JOHN JOE O'REILLY   SIMON DEIGNAN
Mullahoran   *Curragh*   *Curragh*

PJ DUKE   PHIL BRADY
Stradone   *Mullahoran*

TONY TIGHE   MICK HIGGINS   COLM McDYER
Mountnugent   *Mountnugent*   *Cavan Slashers*

JOE STAFFORD   PETER DONOHOE   TP O'REILLY
Arva   *Mountnugent*   *Ballyconnell*

Subs: Edwin Carolan (Mullagh), Terry Sheridan (Killinkere),
Owen Roe McGovern (Swanlinbar), John Joe Cassidy (Arva), Tom O'Reilly (Cornafean),
Eunan Tiernan (Templeport), Brendan Kelly (Bailieborough)
Scorers: P Donohoe 0-8, M Higgins 1-2, J Stafford 1-0, C McDyer 0-1

KERRY TEAM
Dan O'Keeffe (Kerins O'Rahilly's);
Dinny Lyne (Killarney Legion), Joe Keohane (John Mitchels), Paddy Bawn Brosnan (Dingle);
Jackie Lyne (Killarney Legion), Bill Casey (Lispole), Eddie Walsh (Knocknagoshel);
Eddie Dowling (Ballydonoghue, 1-0), Teddy O'Connor (Dr Crokes);
Teddy O'Sullivan (Killarney Legion), Dan Kavanagh (Dr Crokes), Batt Garvey (Dingle, 1-0);
Frank O'Keeffe (John Mitchels), Tom 'Gega' O'Connor (Dingle, 0-6), Paddy Kennedy (Kerins O'Rahilly's, 0-1)
Subs used: Willie O'Donnell, Mick Finucane, Tim Brosnan, Ger Teahan

---

Cavan Trainer: Hughie O'Reilly   **Masseur:** John McGeough
Secretary: Hugh L Smyth   **Chairman:** Patsy Lynch